NICKY BARR

AN AUSTRALIAN AIR ACE

Dear Pa,
Happy father's day 2005
We love
Ya.
Rebecca
Xavier
Solomon.

Peter Dornan was educated at Brisbane Boys College. For 35 years he has been a physiotherapist in the fields of sporting injuries and manipulative therapy, working with many international sporting teams, including the Queensland rugby team, the Wallabies and the Kangaroos. He has also been an Olympic Games Advisor and Commonwealth Games physiotherapist.

He is a Fellow of Sports Medicine Australia, and has written two successful books on sporting injuries, as well as designing and marketing a video exercise program. In 2000 Peter was awarded the Duncan Travelling Fellowship to study aspects of cancer, and was also awarded the Commemorative 2000 Australian Sports Medal for achievement in sport.

Peter has studied classical sculpture for more than 20 years and has works displayed in many prominent Queensland and national institutions. Peter has also been freelance writing for some years and his first factional book, *The Silent Men,* is an account of the Kokoda Trail Campaign and is being made into a movie.

In 2002 Peter was appointed as a Member of the General Division of the Order of Australia (AM).

Peter has been married to Dimity, a speech pathologist, for more than 30 years. They have two adult children, Melissa and Roderick.

NICKY BARR

AN AUSTRALIAN AIR ACE

*a story of courage
and adventure*

PETER DORNAN

ALLEN&UNWIN

Allen & Unwin
83 Alexander Street
Crows Nest NSW 2065
Australia
Phone: (61 2) 8425 0100
Fax: (61 2) 9906 2218
Email: info@allenandunwin.com
Web: www.allenandunwin.com

National Library of Australia
Cataloguing-in-Publication entry:

Dornan, Peter, 1943- .
  Nicky Barr, an Australian air ace : a story of courage and
  adventure.

  Bibliography.
  ISBN 1 74114 529 5.

  1. Barr, Andrew W., 1915- . 2. Australia. Royal Australian
  Air Force - Biography. 3. Fighter pilots - Australia -
  Biography. 4. World War, 1939-1945 - Africa, North -
  Aerial operations, Australian. I. Title.

940.544994

Set in 11pt/13.5pt Minion by Asset Typesetting, Bergalia
Printed by McPherson's Printing Group, Maryborough

10 9 8 7 6 5 4 3 2 1

I dedicate this book to my grandson Oliver Bruijn, and to the memory of QX6275: Ollie's 'Pop-Pop'—his great-grandfather—Captain Dick Crist, 2/2nd Machine-Gun Battalion, Ninth Division AIF, a member of Monty's Desert Eighth Army, both of whom have played a major influence on my life.

HIGH FLIGHT, a war poem

O, I have slipped the surly bonds of earth
And danced the skies on laughter-silvered wings;
Sunward I've climbed and joined the tumbling mirth,
Of sun-split clouds—and done a hundred things
You have not dreamed of—wheeled and soared and swung
High in the sunlit silence. Hov'ring there
I've chased the shouting wind along and flung
My eager craft through footless halls of air.
Up, up the long delirious, burning blue
I've topped the wind-swept heights with easy grace
Where never lark, or even eagles flew;
And, while with silent, lifting mind I've trod
The high untrespassed sanctity of space,
Put out my hand, and touched the face of God.

John Gillespie Magee
(killed in action with the Royal Canadian Air Force)

Contents

Acknowledgements

I wish to express my gratitude to a number of special people whose assistance in the preparation of this book was indispensable. I have relied heavily on the oral histories given to me by those who lived through the events described. I am extremely grateful to the many fighter pilots, ground staff and RAAF personnel who have entrusted me with precious memories of their experiences.

I would also like to give special thanks to Nicky Barr's wife, Dot, for her substantial contribution to the book and also for her role as a gracious hostess during my many months of interviewing Nicky.

I owe much to the help and ready encouragement given by Bobby Gibbes and have made consistent use of his autobiography, especially when referring to the Desert Campaign. Lex McAulay's book *Four Aces* was also useful.

I am also indebted to the War Memorial in Canberra, the RSL and the librarians at the Royal United Services Institute in Brisbane.

I am obliged to my brother-in-law, David Ryan, who filled in as an enthusiastic, knowledgeable and competent research assistant. A special accolade goes to my patient typist, Carol Jackson, whose comments were always welcome. Also to my

Acknowledgements

fellow choralist Werner Kroll for his invaluable assistance with aviation matters. I must also thank my two editors, Jude McGee and Louise Thurtell.

I am particularly grateful to my wife, Dimity, who was my on-the-spot editor and a critical reviewer of the drafts as they emerged, as well as being my support system and cheer squad when I felt the problems were getting too large.

Even though this story emerges from my pen, I have to thank Nicky Barr for his patience, openness and willingness to share his unique experiences, to relive all which has passed, and allow them to finally take their place beside some of the proudest stories which make up Australia's military heritage.

Peter Dornan, Brisbane 2001

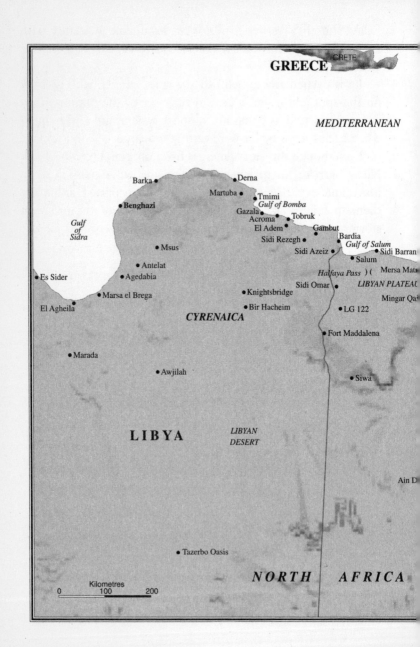

North Africa, circa World War Two

Italy, circa World War Two

Close-up of the Abruzzi region, Italy, circa World War Two

Introduction

Nicky Barr knew he was grinning; he couldn't help it. His exhilaration and freedom felt complete as the Tiger Moth responded to his every touch on the joystick. He could feel his throat pulse with excitement as the earth fell away beneath him, joyfully fulfilling youthful fantasies.

His breathing settled as he steadily moved the joystick forward, levelling the plane at 1000 feet. With his left hand, he reduced the throttle to cruising speed. Methodically, he rechecked the instruments, then flew towards the training area.

It was March 1940, and Nicky was undergoing *ab initio* training—the 'weeding out' process—at Essendon Airport in Melbourne as part of his entrance into the Royal Australian Air Force Academy at Point Cook. It was only his third solo flight, and it was still exciting. Green fields and sleepy outer Melbourne suburbs went by down below, although he hardly noticed this incidental scenery, being completely absorbed in his own reverie.

Then, out of the corner of his eye, he caught sight of another Tiger Moth closing in on him. Curious, and just a little concerned, he recognised his instructor, Lou Lohse, leaning out the front cockpit of the approaching plane laughing. In his hand, he was holding a wheel. With a shock, and after some pantomime, Nicky realised it was his wheel—the right one.

Nicky's impish grin faded. The fantasy transformed to gritty reality as he realised he was going to have to land the plane with only the left wheel. He was very aware that aircraft were considered to be precious. Damage had to be averted at all costs, otherwise —out! Banking off, he directed his aircraft towards home, his mind racing as he tried to recall the 'forced landing' procedure.

He would have to make a short field landing, banking his plane to the left while simultaneously keeping the tail low, hopefully allowing him to land on the left wheel and skid at the same time. It was going to be risky, and he was relieved to see a stiff breeze was holding the windsock horizontal and beautifully steady; a fact to his advantage, as Tiger Moths are not equipped with brakes.

As he positioned himself downwind, he glanced briefly at the tarmac in front of the Ansett hangar, and noticed his classmates and other ground personnel lining up to witness the spectacle. He was to be the main event. Damn! As he turned to base to land into the wind, he checked his harness, pulling it tight, reminding himself to turn off the fuel and switches just before touchdown.

Throttling back now, he worked to maintain a constant landing speed of 50 knots, feeling the plane drop steadily out of the sky ... 200 feet ... 100 feet. He was committed now. His heart seemed to be pounding louder than the motor as the little machine flew over the aerodrome boundary. When he could identify the blades of grass on the field below, he cut the fuel, killed the switches and quickly banked the plane to the left. Nicky braced as she touched, the plane rocked a few seconds, then the right wing dropped, forcing the axle into the ground.

The aircraft swung violently, metal screeching in protest at the sudden rotation. The frame shuddered, and the plane came to rest the right way up. Then silence.

Unscathed, but shaky, Nicky emerged from the cockpit to the

cheers of his classmates and onlookers. A few minutes later his instructor landed behind him, slightly damaging his own plane —the humorous aspect evoking more cheers from his classmates.

Thus began the remarkable fortunes of Andrew 'Nicky' Barr, Australian Air Ace. If, with twinkling deep blue eyes and an infectious smile, he had set out to court adventure, he could not have orchestrated a more exciting and interesting full-blooded narrative than that which was to befall him, firstly as a fighter pilot in the Middle East during World War Two, and thereafter.

To represent his country at rugby—as Nicky had—would have satisfied most young men. However, Nicky was to far surpass this, shooting down twelve-and-a-half enemy aircraft confirmed and at least three more probables in combat. He was also to be shot down three times, once in flames, and to force land in enemy territory and escape, then to be captured and escape at least three times—once from a moving German train—and then, while behind enemy lines, take part in clandestine activities while helping Allied prisoners of war to escape. Who could ask for more?

As well as becoming one of Australia's most decorated and legendary fighter pilots of World War Two, Nicky's exploits earned him the right to claim membership in several select air force 'clubs'. He qualified for the 'Caterpillar Club' (that is, he 'hit the silk' and had his life saved by the use of a parachute—his caterpillar had red ruby eyes because his plane had caught fire), three times for the 'Flying Boot' or 'Late Arrivals' club (earned by those who reach their home bases after forced landings behind enemy lines and then return to operational flying), and three times for 'the Escaper' (awarded to flying men who were prisoners of war and succeeded in escaping).

It would be easy to dismiss Nicky Barr's adventures as classic 'Boys' Own' tales. However, his full story deserves far more attention than a superficial telling of heroic achievements.

Certainly Barr represents a particular heroic image, although this Homeric mantle sits uneasily on his shoulders. His modesty and reluctance to accept this role fully are as much a part of his character as are his blond hair and blue eyes. He is insistent on acknowledging he did little by himself, and is quick to credit other factors for most of his achievements. These revelations inherently provide an insight into the dedication and selfless teamwork of the many individuals and institutions committed to a common goal of ridding the world of a sinister regime.

The story of Nicky Barr provides an insight into human limitations and into the power of the human spirit in its determination to survive. It also explores how this resolve could be utilised for the collective good. When he was called upon, Nicky demonstrated a gift for command. He exhibited a level of personal force and psychological savvy that allowed him to inspire the men in his squadron, and behind the lines, the commandos and escaped prisoners for whom he assumed responsibility through difficult circumstances.

Classically, through strong example, he was a man defined by his actions rather than his words. He could be an action hero with presence, intelligence and lucidity in high pressure situations.

At another level, the story of Nicky Barr also explores some of the deepest concerns of mankind: the relationships of individuals, love, honour, war, the universal pity of death, the terror of mortality and the concept of an afterlife.

To those fortunate people, untouched by war—the carnage, the enslaving fear, the inhumanity—it may be difficult to accept that the impact of a lengthy conflict is shattering. Adjustment requires a re-evaluation of values, beliefs, one's faith and the very purpose of being.

Like so many service personnel in World War Two, Nicky was directly involved in fighting the enemy. He was one of the people called upon to do the killing or be killed themselves—the bottom line for any war!

Most individuals operational in opposing the enemy in the front-line of war regularly experience periods of abject fear and depression, needing to call upon all their reserves of body and spirit in order to survive. Often the impact on their lives is devastating.

Cumulative and continual exposure to the possibility of a slow and painful death affects even the most hardened of warriors. Situations arise when it seems the option of 'allowing it to happen' —to die—merits some consideration when matched up against a continued involvement in the mayhem of a stupid, futile-seeming conflict where you could easily end up dying anyway. Many times, Nicky Barr was placed in circumstances where it would have been easier to choose to die.

Courage emerges at these times, in all its forms and gradations. To have the fortitude, the will and the spirit to persevere, to fight on when the outlook is seemingly desperate, when the perceived odds of surviving are slim, surely requires a special quality.

When no place exists for self-pity, recriminations and hatreds, the complexity of returning successfully to a world of peace is greatly simplified. A lasting detestation of war often comes most forcibly from these veterans who have experienced the ugliness of war and from those called upon to do the killing. As history shows, it seems that with the passing of each generation, the new world has to learn the lessons all over again.

Nicky's story is timeless, back to the Homeric days and the Heroic Age. Yet there does seem a paradox when you meet the man, knowing the adventures he has been through. He has been able to come to terms with the emotional, physical, spiritual and political events he has withstood, and he appears largely content with life. He carries many scars, emotional as well as physical, yet with a marked degree of humility, humour and wit he demonstrates that he is comfortable with the past. When there is the courage to choose to live there are no regrets, just the reward of contentment and the comfort that you have survived.

Indeed, many such survivors enjoy a quiet, inner calm, a warmth provided by the knowledge they fought as best as they could to restore the world to peace. Yet as Nicky himself observes, anything that establishes a loss of dignity leaves a scar—there is no way you can forget it, it is there forever. It is how you handle it that is important.

Nicky was aware that many factors contributed to his good fortune, enabling him to survive. Initially, he was grateful for the thorough training process he undertook before he encountered an enemy in combat—almost 600 hours logged in all possible situations. Further, his natural athletic ability, honed by gymnastics, springboard diving and rugby assisted him to develop his flying and combative skills to a high level. However, once in combat his fate was often largely reliant on the team of skilled, dedicated support staff, both the air crews who flew with him and the ground crews, who kept him and his planes in the air. The latter were on call day and night, working as long as it took to make the aircraft serviceable, and to ensure a squadron was mobile and ready to move, advance or retreat, and fight at a minute's notice. This dedication reached its peak on 16 June 1942, when his ground crew, with 12 planes to keep operational while retreating, created a record of 69 sorties in a day. Because of his reliance and respect for his ground crew, Nicky bonded strongly with his personal armourer, Felix Sainsbury, engineer, Ernie 'Kaiser' Wehrman, and air frame mechanic, Ray Dunning.

As well, behind the lines, there were whole legions of selfless people, both individually and in underground networks, who assisted him, often anonymously and at great risk to themselves and families.

To stay alive he developed many coping mechanisms, particularly in relation to how he handled fear. Nicky confronted fear many times and knew it as intimately as he knew helplessness, despair, anger, frustration, loneliness, sadness and degradation. However, the thought that motivated him most strongly to persevere, the one which triggered a strong incentive and compelling purpose to survive, was the constant objective to be reunited with his wife, Dot. She was the light and magnet in his soul, his thoughts of her providing him with the spirit and energy to stay alive, particularly while he was languishing in prisoner-of-war hospitals, and later while operating in snow-covered enemy-held territory. His memories of her were with him all the time, during each plane flight and while under enemy attack. She provided the resolve for Nicky to discover hidden reserves in every challenge he encountered. She was—and still is—an integral part of Nicky Barr's achievements.

Ultimately, theirs is a story of enduring love. Now, some 60 years after exchanging their marriage vows, Nicky and Dot have been brought closer together than ever. Relishing the time they have for joint projects, they are settled in retirement in a beautiful villa on Queensland's Gold Coast. They have their extended family around them, including six grandchildren and one great-granddaughter. In Nicky's words: 'It is a wondrous thing to be part of an everlasting love story.'

Time now to experience the real Nicky Barr story.

The Morning Before

I n the half light of the dawn, the austere beauty of the desert helped soothe the senses of the lone airman. Squadron Leader Nicky Barr would regularly stroll in these cool, early hours, appreciating the gentle wind playing around the sand-filled wadis. Today, as much as any, he needed the solitude of the surrounding ancient wilderness. It was 26 June 1942, and Nicky was tired—very tired. He had been in action in the Middle East for nine months rising quickly through the ranks to become, at 26, squadron leader of No. 3 Squadron RAAF.

The entire Allied Forces in the North African Desert—the British Eighth Army—had been in desperate withdrawal for some months, sorely feeling the pressure from Rommel's heel as he unleashed his consistent *blitzkrieg* offensive. The Battle of the Cauldron was behind them, leaving the Eighth Army reeling and now set up in defence at Mersa Matruh.

Nicky's handsome, boyish features were drawn, his face lined and etched from long hours squinting into the unforgiving Sahara sun and from coping with unrelenting battle tension. Any youthful exuberance or misdirected enthusiasm for war had long been snuffed out by the desert *khamsins*.

On the tarmac behind him, a dozen or more Kittyhawks of the squadron were nestling in the early morning haze. Ground crew were working frantically to improve the serviceability numbers for the day's operations. Highlighting the squadron's nomadic existence, tents of all sizes were spread within the camp's perimeter.

As the shimmering sun, magnified by the haze, reflected its first rays of light from the planes, Nicky knew it would be another hot day—and eventful. As surely as the ancient Egyptians knew the sun god Ra would bring life, Nicky knew that today would bring glimpses of terror and sudden death. The war was no longer a rousing adventure, but a reality that challenged and forced a man to seek, then exploit, opportunities for deadly advantage, a situation to confront mortality and to test principles of altruism and gallantry, even to the supreme sacrifice.

Today, although he did not know it, he would be tested like never before.

Nicky continued to meander around the perimeter, breaking his meditation now and then to encourage any ground crew he came across. The planes had been mauled considerably after yesterday's strafing mission west of Mersa Matruh. Repairs to the ailerons of one plane were being completed, while on another an airframe rigger polished the leading edge of the fin with beeswax to cut air friction. Nicky moved back to his two-man tent, refocusing his thoughts on the day's coming operations.

After breakfast, he briefed the remnants of his squadron. Nicky stood at the front of a circle of faces, many of them bronzed by the sun, deep lines etched on most of their features. They were the faces of fighters; visages which could relax into grins or hearty laughter, or just as suddenly become stony masks above guns which flamed death. Eight planes could still fly. Their first mission of the day, he informed them, would be to take off at 9.00 a.m. and to seek, then strafe and bomb, Rommel's Spearhead. There were much easier missions.

The temperature was already climbing to sticky hot, and Nicky was grateful to be wearing khaki shorts and shirt.

Incongruously, he wore regulation flying boots with fur fringing the opening. He rolled his sleeves up, then climbed onto the wing of his Kittyhawk, smiling wryly to himself as he glanced at his personal insignia painted onto the nose of the fuselage—a cheeky black devil holding a trident. It was somehow comforting. His ground crew assisted him into his parachute, then he moved into the cockpit.

With the Sutton harness, he strapped himself into the seat, stabilising his body very firmly into his fighting position. He plugged the radio transmitter and oxygen outlets into their sockets and switched the radio on. He carried out the routine cockpit drill, leaning out to check on movements of ailerons, rudder and elevators, then he looked around to await signals from his squadron that all was ready.

Almost as one, along the line, the big 12-cylinder Allison engines coughed and burst into a healthy staccato roar. Within seconds, they were humming like hornets, ready to sting. He counted the two groups of four planes, neatly lined up in straight formation, gave a quick wave to the ground crew for 'chocks away', pushed the throttle firmly to full 'revs', steadied the aircraft with the rudder, and then, with a throaty barrage heralding a blast of dust, the eight planes moved forward as one. Pebbles sprayed under the fuselage, there was a strong smell of dust and fuel intermingled with an adrenalin buzzing sensation of speed. Then, suddenly, the squadron was airborne.

As usual, soon after he began flying, Nicky gave a customary burst of the six .5-mm machine-guns to ensure they were firing; it was too late to find they were not working during combat. Nicky glanced quickly outside his cockpit. With height, the desert seemed on fire with the early morning sun.

The responsibility of leading a squadron in the air always weighed heavily on Nicky, as he was well aware that poor leadership could easily result in disaster. However, to Nicky, the situation never completely distracted from that moment of pure existence that flying generates—no past or future, just the pulse-pounding present. There is a rapture of freedom, motion and speed that is intoxicating and for a compelling few moments the collective spirit of the squadron is charged with primitive tribal bonding, emotions which must have emanated long before the days of chivalry, knighthood and charging cavalries.

However, the desert landscape quickly tarnished the romance as, down below, it displayed the folly of war, a harvest of burnt-out tanks, trucks and smoking vehicles. Crumpled, distorted steel and iron fragments were all that remained—and there was one of their crashed Kittyhawks, a funeral pyre of black smoke curling from it as a sentinel. There was still some distance before they would reach the front elements of Rommel's army and, after some minutes, Nicky's tiredness, the sighting of the downed Kittyhawk, and the steady throbbing of the planes' engines caused him to meditate over the fate of many of his squadron friends. The faces of the dead danced before him now as he matched characters, names and events to them. To his despair, the list had been growing almost daily. He knew some had perished with their planes in flames, and he knew some had also parachuted to relative safety and were most likely prisoners of war—some small consolation.

The constant drone now rolled his reveries further back to Dot, his family and a more peaceful life in Melbourne. It seemed a millennium away.

ONE

The Early Years

Nicky Barr remembers very little of his first six years of life in New Zealand, where he was born in 1915. But he has warm memories of growing up in Melbourne after his family moved to Australia.

Nicky and his twin brother John were extremely close, and, as is often the case with twins, their sensitivity to each other could be disarming. They were somehow innately aware of the other's situation, regularly registering similar reactions without the stimulus of contact. Eventually, Jack, as his twin was known, became an engineer and secured a job with Beaurepair Tyres, while Nicky attended Swinburne Technical College to study building construction. But this didn't last and he remembers the excitement of his first real job as a Bradford Mills wool buyer, particularly when he was selected to do a wool-classing course.

His cadetship at Bradford Mills involved part-time university study, working towards an economics and accounting qualification. However, he soon realised there were more wool classers than sheep, and he reflected how fortunate it was that the study he'd been doing was enough to gain selection with Australian Estates Limited. He eventually earned a diploma in accountancy attending a Hemingway and Robinson course part-time.

Nicky had always revelled in the competition of sport, winning the Victorian Schoolboys' 100 yards championship three years in a row—in 1926, 1927 and 1928—while attending Kew Public School. There were other events and certain institutions which also influenced him, such as the Kew Methodist Church, where he enjoyed the gymnasium, fellowship classes and other non-religious activities. He also became a member of the YMCA where he gained assistance with his athletic training.

However, the most impressionable event in Nicky's young life was an invitation to join the Lord Somers Camp and Power House organisation. This was founded by the Governor of Victoria, Lord Somers, in 1929. When Nicky joined in 1931 as a 15-year-old 'runner' to the camp chief Dr C. G. McAdam, he became the youngest member. The camp system was modelled on a movement begun in 1921 by Prince Albert, the Duke of York, in England, in an attempt to bring together boys from the workforce with public school boys in the hope that they would develop a common understanding and a sense of mutual appreciation and loyalty.

The Somers camp, situated at Victoria's Western Port Bay, was only part of the process. Probably the more important function of the movement found expression in the institution known as Power House. It was here that a boy began to fully learn the spirit of service and duty and to understand that he had responsibilities, both to himself and others.

To Nicky's delight, the Power House institution possessed many thriving sporting and social clubs, a number of which he joined, including the rugby club. Nicky believes that most of the challenges of this time shaped the pattern of his life for the immediate years ahead.

Nicky possessed and capitalised on a strong desire to win, and even though he excelled at diving, swimming and gymnastics, it was football that really fired him. He had played all his early football under the Australian Rules code, and actually gained first grade representation with the Hawthorn club.

However, towards the end of 1935, he took part in a fateful rugby union game to oblige a friend from Power House club, whose team was a man short. He found he enjoyed the all-out contact, the fulltime involvement, and the discipline of the game, to the extent that he changed codes.

As he could sprint in football boots over the 100 yards in 10.4 seconds, he remembered with satisfaction how he forced his way into the Victorian team the next year. Although thought to be too light for the position, he played hooker, a position in which, remarkably, he continued to represent Victoria up to 1939, playing against the Springboks, New Zealand, New South Wales and Queensland.

Towards the end of 1938, Nicky's life changed irrevocably when he was introduced to Dorothy Gore on a blind date at the theatre. He was immediately entranced by her pretty face, good figure and lively conversation. For Nicky, the evening moved as if in a dream. After the show, he offered to take her home. He was determined to see her again.

'Where do you live?' he asked her.

'At Malvern.'

'That's funny. So do I.' Nicky winced. It sounded like a line.

'Really?' Dot smiled, raising her eyebrows in mock disbelief.

Nevertheless, he convinced her it was the truth. He did take her home. He was so pleased to be with her, he had to make sure he could see her again.

'Would you like to go to the dance at Power House, next Saturday?' he asked.

'I've never heard of Power House.'

Nicky wasn't deterred, and eventually won her over.

This was to be the beginning of a long romance. Nicky found that Dot danced delightfully, she mixed with his friends, and easily became one of the group. There was no turning back for him.

Overall, Nicky admired Dot's straight talk and appreciated knowing exactly where he stood with her. She warmed to Nicky and encouraged and supported him in all aspects of his life, including his rugby, which had become increasingly important to Nicky.

Nudging 6 feet and weighing in at 80 kilograms, Nicky worked at improving his rugby game with the incentive of being given the chance of touring with the Wallabies—Australia's national rugby team—in 1939.

This extended tour was to be for ten months—one of the great prizes of the sporting world—playing a large number of matches with tests against England, Scotland, Wales and Ireland. The team was also to play games in several other countries, including Canada, the United States, France and New Zealand.

When the team was announced, Nicky was thrilled that his name was on the list. In fact, the selection of Nicky, Stan Bisset and Max Carpenter symbolised the pinnacle of achievement for Power House, as only a handful of Victorians had ever played rugby for Australia.

In late July, amid cheers and sad farewells from friends, the Wallabies boarded the P&O Liner *Mooltan*. To assist team bonding over the six-week sea voyage, Nicky, who played the piano accordion, and Stan Bisset, an outstanding baritone, were commissioned by the team captain to write a team song. As well as training and socialising on board, these extra activities kept Stan and Nicky busy and they led many concerts during the voyage.

All members of the team were aware that war clouds had been settling over Europe for some time, and there was a certain unease as the ship approached European waters. Hitler had recently invaded Poland and the world was watching as he stalked France. After docking at the French Mediterranean seaport of Marseille, the ship was required to be blacked out.

Though no more than a nuisance to the boys, the experience was nonetheless a niggling, sinister shadow.

They crossed the English Channel, disembarked in Southampton and were driven to the seaside town of Torquay in Devon, where they stayed at the Grand Hotel facing the ocean.

They had been there only a few hours when Prime Minister Chamberlain informed the nation that Britain was officially at war with Germany. It was 11.15 a.m., on Sunday 3 September, and everything was about to change. The shadow became a reality. Within minutes of Chamberlain's speech, Londoners experienced their first wartime air-raid alert. In Paris and Berlin, sirens sounded later the same day, and the citizens of all three cities took to their shelters.

To the boys the news was shattering, not least because the authorities decided to abandon the tour. To Nicky, the announcement rankled his sense of fair play. The team spent two weeks at Torquay filling sandbags to place around the hotel, preparing for an expected Nazi invasion. They then travelled to London, where anti-aircraft balloons floated over the city and sandbags bolstered walls and stairways. The city was blacked out and everyone was carrying a gasmask, as it was expected poison gases would be released over target territories.

Nicky and Stan Bisset were so incensed they made enquiries about joining the air force and army respectively. Nicky had always considered that if war was declared, he'd like to be a pilot and preferably a fighter pilot. With this in mind, he volunteered for the Royal Air Force (RAF), hoping for an arrangement whereby he could fly with an Australian squadron. However, to his frustration, he was told it would be a long time before he saw an aircraft, as a lot of Englishmen were also volunteering, but he could have a commission as a pay officer in administration.

Nicky certainly didn't intend that to be his fate, so he sought out Lord Somers, who was now living back in England. With

Somers' help he was able to withdraw his application for the RAF in preparation for returning to Australia where he intended volunteering.

The day before their return to Australia, the team was received at Buckingham Palace by King George VI and the Queen. This was rather precious to Nicky and the other members of Power House as in 1921 the King (then Prince Albert, the Duke of York) had founded the movement on which Lord Somers had modelled his Somers Camp Organisation.

The team left England on the ship *Strathaird* facing a hazardous trip back to Australia, zigzagging to avoid possible submarine attack.

Back in Australia, the Minister for Air was developing a flying training program which was to become known as the Empire Air Training Scheme. On his return, Nicky volunteered for the Royal Australian Air Force (RAAF) and was accepted into the final cadet course before the Empire Air Training Scheme commenced.

When he was advised of his selection to the scheme, Nicky immediately bought a book entitled *How to Fly in Five Easy Lessons*. He read it eagerly, and became very excited at the prospect of putting his new-found knowledge into practice—he couldn't wait! In March 1940, Nicky commenced his *ab initio* training in Tiger Moths at Essendon Airport, and by the time he went up for his first dual flight with an instructor, his excitement had reached its peak. His greatest thrill was to be told he could go solo after the first ten hours of learning the basics.

His first solo flight was supposed to last 15 minutes but Nicky was so entranced he stayed up for over 30 minutes. It felt so natural and thrilling to be behind the controls—touching the joystick, pushing the rudder, banking, rolls off the top, trying sideslip left and right—he became oblivious to time and lost awareness of those waiting for him. This wasn't the last time he would get into hot water.

Nicky's independent streak often rebelled in the RAAF's environment of conformity. He was a determined young spirit who sought the freedom of the air, but often found himself in front of command for minor misdemeanours. Accumulatively, his instructors tagged him as displaying elements of devilry. Among other punishments, he particularly resented being made to do unreasonable numbers of push-ups by drill sergeants.

After some time, and many misadventures, Nicky's fellow cadets attributed his independent and unconventional nature to some Machiavellian spirit related to the devil. His given name 'Andrew' was forever lost to be replaced by 'Nicky', as in 'Old Nick', the name given by the Puritans to the devil. (The Puritans believed that Saint Nicholas—Santa Claus—and Christmas were Pagan notions.)

In the meantime, Nicky's twin brother Jack had become frustrated with his lot. He had tried to join the army, but was restricted from enlisting by his work at Beaurepairs. The Australian Government had requested Beaurepairs make cables, and Jack's expertise was considered vital for this project. As the work was designated an 'essential service', Jack was effectively rendered ineligible for military service.

While at Essendon, Nicky interceded on Jack's behalf and rang Frank (later Sir Frank) Beaurepair. Nicky knew him quite well, as he had earlier taught Nicky and Jack how to swim. However Beaurepair could not be swayed, saying, 'He'll be all right here.'

Nicky was pleased to be graded 'above average' when he graduated in August, then he moved to the RAAF Base Point Cook, the Air Force Academy not far from Melbourne, for completion of the course. To the 40 cadets, Point Cook was a challenge from all aspects. It possessed no airstrip, only a paddock that wasn't well maintained. The ground was often under repair with boggy patches delineated with sticks, forming an extra obstacle for the cadets.

Point Cook trained both bomber and fighter pilots, and even though Nicky had every respect for the Anson bombers and the teamwork and discipline that was necessary to form an efficient crew, he tried desperately to be selected to fly the fighter planes. He believed even at this stage he was something of a loner, a characteristic which apparently suited the make-up of a fighter pilot. He deliberately slew the bombs away from the target while on the Ansons and was not unhappy to record a below average rating.

On the other hand, he loved the Hawker Demons with their open cockpit. These were marvellous, albeit obsolete, biplane fighters. Nicky revelled in aerobatics and tested the powerful Rolls Royce Kestrel engines through all essential skills. Night flying was particularly challenging. The exhaust stubs on either side of the motor would glow red to white hot. It was difficult to land at night as, looking forward, there was not much vision of the landing strip, so Nicky learned the trick of looking sideways, unlike day flying. Some of the men couldn't cope with this part of flying and had to drop out of the course.

The cadets crammed a great deal into those few months, normally a one-year course. The intensity of training, however, didn't stop the normal high jinks of young men. Nicky had become engaged to Dot by now after courting her at the Saturday night Power House dances that he had helped organise and run. On one occasion, desperate to see her, he hid in the boot of a friend's car and was caught, which resulted in him being confined to barracks.

His closest friend at Point Cook was Freddy Eggleston, whom he shared quarters with. At 28, Freddy was some years older than the rest of the recruits, and was something of a daredevil. Like Nicky, he also played the piano accordion. A brilliant student and pilot, he actually topped the course but on the final day he and five other spirited cadets took a joy flight in an Anson piloted by one of the other cadets, and buzzed every paddock between Wonthaggi and Point Cook. It created a major uproar, cows bolting through fences and some calving out of fright, causing the local farmers to complain. The young men were bawled out in front of the Commanding Officer in a military court appearance and, instead of graduating as pilot officers with wings, they became sergeant pilots. Nicky, who was second on the course, had to reluctantly accept first place. Nicky graduated to 'wings' standard in September 1940, rating above average as a pilot and in air-gunnery, average-plus as a pilot navigator and, unashamedly, below average for bombing.

Proud of his new commission, Nicky was posted to the City of Brisbane No. 23 Squadron based at Archerfield in Brisbane. The squadron's prime purpose was the defence of Brisbane, but its main activity was the training of its pilots in war-type operations. The squadron was the supply source for replacement pilots to operational units, and consisted of two Wirraway and one Lockhead Hudson Flight.

The Wirraway was Australian built, and was a single-engined training aircraft. It had a reliable radial engine and was pressed into service as a fighter, reconnaissance and dive bomber, carrying an air gunner (or observer) perched in a seat behind the pilot. Nicky began his conversion flights in December 1940 and, even with 222 hours of previous experience, found the machine a handful.

One of its real problems, he found, was that it could lose its lift characteristics very quickly, stall, then degenerate into a spin. The experience, although challenging, served to rapidly hone Nicky's flying skills and to sharpen his survival instincts.

Such was Nicky's desire to be a proficient pilot, he regularly pushed himself and his plane to the limits. His air observer, 21-year-old Peter White, sitting in the rear seat, often blacked out as Nicky threw the plane around the sky. Multiple G-forces drained the blood from his brain as the Wirraway was forced into tight turns, loops and savage pullouts during dive bombing practice.

On one occasion, during a meteorological flight while breeching at 12 000 feet, Nicky told White he was going to find out the terminal velocity of the plane. With that, he rolled the Wirraway over into an almost vertical dive, put the throttle to full power and set the propellers at fully fine—that is, he adjusted the propeller pitch to give it maximum revs.

The plane screeched downward at an ever-increasing speed until the motor could take no more and seized. With some strength and skill, Nicky fought with the controls for some time, then manoeuvred the plane into a perfect 'dead stick' landing, coming to rest right in the middle of the aerodrome.

When the two young men examined the plane later, still somewhat shakily, they noticed that the fairings—the aluminium coverings on the undercarriage—were either stripped off or severely bent. All the fabric surfaces on the fuselage were ripped and torn, and the aluminium-covered wings had actually rippled.

Although the action displayed elements of youthful exuber-ance, even bordering on recklessness, the exercise did help to define both the plane and the pilots' limits, something a fighter pilot has to know.

Meanwhile, overseas, the war was developing. The pilots of No. 23 Squadron had followed Hitler's occupation of most of Europe with some frustration and were incensed when Italy, after conquering Ethiopia, sided with Nazi Germany in June 1940. Germany's thirst for oil to keep her tanks, aircraft and submarines fighting increased the strategic importance of the Middle East. The North African desert was developing into a major battle-ground. Italy had advanced towards Cairo, as Egypt and Libya were the south-western gateways to the Middle East's oil supplies.

To counter this, the Australian Sixth Division entered the war at Bardia in January 1941 as part of the 'Desert Army' and soundly defeated Mussolini's Italians, pushing them westward to Cyrenaica (Western Libya) beating them in successive actions at Tobruk, Derna and Benghazi. By March, however, the Italians were being reinforced by a small German force under the command of General Erwin Rommel, and were regrouping for what everyone knew would be a major offensive by the Axis armies in the desert.

Further, the air force graduates had witnessed the young pilots of Britain engage in an heroic stand over the skies of England in late 1940, as the Battle of Britain raged. As stories of the epic dogfights between the English Spitfires and the German Messerschmitts reached the ears of the young men of the RAAF squadrons in Australia, the shortcomings of the Wirraway as a modern air combat aircraft became quickly obvious.

However, Nicky patiently continued his training and settled into Brisbane life, utilising the time as efficiently as possible. He quickly became accepted into the establishment, particularly after his commanding officer found out he was an accountant. Group Captain Walters explained that No. 23 Squadron supplied other squadrons in the field with replacements, and when the pilots left for overseas service, they threw a monumental party. As a result, the squadron owed money all over Brisbane. He appointed Nicky to take over the duties of Mess Secretary 'to look at the finances, sort them out and tell me where we're going'. Juniors can never refuse.

Nicky instituted a plan which, over some months, slowly refilled the coffers. Levies were imposed on all officers, parties were paid for in advance, and he negotiated with suppliers for extended credit. Often this personal communication and enlightenment was all suppliers needed to waive the bill.

The CO was impressed. Later, he asked Nicky if he would act as honorary aide-de-camp (air force) for the Queensland Governor, Sir Lesley Wilson. This entitled Nicky to the temporary rank of flight lieutenant for official occasions—but with no extra pay—a new uniform and duties which included picking up and taking the governor to RAAF functions in the government car. There were other duties around Government House that Nicky enjoyed as he learned to move in different levels of society, making contacts and many new friends.

He was also aware of the honour carried with the position, although he was becoming concerned this might be the extent of his war—'standing one pace to the side and two steps to the rear', carrying an umbrella instead of a gun.

While these duties and his flying schedule filled his official hours, there were plenty of other activities to fill his leisure time.

His love and talent for sport was highlighted as, during the year, he won the high diving championships for the RAAF in Service sports, and also captained the RAAF rugby team. He still has strong memories of the final moments of a championship game between RAAF and an Army XV, captained by Bill McLean, a friend and one of his fellow Wallaby teammates from 1939.

A free kick had been awarded to the air force on their own goal line. The finish bell rang and RAAF were leading by a point. All Nicky had to do was kick the ball into touch and the game was over. By rugby standards he was entitled to do that, but Nicky elected to keep the ball in play, giving Army a sporting chance to win. They failed.

The press made a great deal of Nicky's chivalrous decision and praised his sportsmanship. However, at the time, Nicky realised his character and his decision-making processes had been mainly influenced and imbued with the philosophies espoused at Power House through its club motto: 'It's only the game that counts.'

During his time with No. 23 Squadron, the stability of Nicky's position at Government House induced him to phone his fiancée Dot in Melbourne, to talk about convincing her parents it would be all right to get married—'now that I am working for the Governor'. The situation worked in his favour. With some insight he realised Dot's parents weren't about to let their daughter marry someone who was probably going to leave for war, and it could be construed that as an 'aide-de-camp' of the governor he might have to stay in Australia.

As fate would have it, his call up for overseas duty came soon after completing these negotiations. In August he was accepted as a reinforcement for No. 3 Fighter RAAF Squadron serving in Northern Africa.

The situation in the Middle East had changed dramatically. In March 1941, Rommel and his elite Afrika Korps had recaptured most of the positions lost by the Italians. By early April, Germany had the Australian Ninth Division and part of the Seventh Division bottled up in the Tobruk fortress in Libya, along with elements of the British Army. The Sixth Division was in trouble in Greece, fighting a heroic withdrawal in the face of a furious German onslaught.

For five weeks in June and July, the Seventh Division fought a bitter and costly campaign in Syria and Lebanon as Hitler tried to approach the Suez Canal and Cairo from the north. They were now dug in, holding a watchdog situation on the Turkish border.

By August, all that stood between the enemy and Cairo was Tobruk. The defenders were withstanding a stifling and lengthy siege in order to give the Allies time to prevent Rommel's run towards Cairo and to reorganise a counterattack. Reinforcements were needed urgently.

Nicky's last flight in Brisbane was on 8 August. It was an aerobatic routine he enjoyed and to which he had conditioned himself to a high degree of precision. By now he'd gained a valuable 598 hours flying time and been graded 'above average'. He wrote in his logbook: 'How fortunate to have all these hours before going to war.' (Some Battle of Britain pilots had had less than ten hours.)

Nicky and Dot were married on 12 August 1941 in the pretty bluestone Church of England at Malvern, Victoria. As they stood before the altar and pledged their love and loyalty to each other, the image of Dot's face and her smile became etched forever in Nicky's heart. The vision would comfort and motivate him throughout his wartime service and beyond.

After the wedding, Nicky and Dot honeymooned at Lorne and the Wye River in Victoria for three weeks. They had just returned when Nicky had to report to Bradfield Park Barracks in Sydney prior to embarkation.

While preparations were underway, the newlyweds stayed with Nicky's cousin, Guy Crick, whose brother Stan was then Lord Mayor of Sydney. They savoured their last few precious days together before sailing.

To Nicky, the farewell was devastating and he told Dot, 'I'll get this rotten war over as fast as I can. I'll make certain I'll come back.'

There was no need to tell her. She believed he would come back.

There was supposed to be strict secrecy for the voyage, but on the day of boarding Sydney Harbour was ablaze with colour and movement. Hundreds of launches and boats of all sizes laden with well-wishers created a cacophony of sound with their horns, hooters and whistles. So much for hush-hush!

Nicky boarded the grand liner, the *Queen Mary*, which had been converted to a troop ship. In convoy with the *Queen Elizabeth* the two ships made their way out to Sydney Heads. There were about 12 000 troops on each ship, mainly soldiers, and there was much fun and excitement as they left the harbour, the men waving and throwing trinkets to the armada of supporters in the ships below.

Meanwhile, Nicky had already met up with the 11 airmen who were the reinforcements for the No. 3 Squadron. His close friend Freddy Eggleston was among them, as well as Don Knight and Les Bradbury, all friends who received their 'wings' together from Point Cook days. As well, he met up with Geoff Chinchen, Lou Spence and Graham Pace and five others from other squadrons around Australia.

On issue, the servicemen were given four condoms each. Nicky was amused when some of his friends wrote a letter, then poked it with a tuppenny stamp into a blown-up condom, knotted it, and dropped it down to the milling craft below. There was music somewhere, and much laughter—spirits were high.

Soon the ships passed through Sydney Heads and moved out to the open sea. As the Australian coastline faded in the evening light, there was some brief sadness tinged with impending trepidation. Most on board had never been outside their home town, let alone their country. To them this was pure adventure.

Nicky stood with his friends on the bow and was quickly caught up in the energy and intent of the massed body of men. He too, prepared for the adventure ahead.

Never, at any time, did he think he might not return.

T W O

Khartoum

As the ships passed Aden, heading for the Red Sea, Nicky was struck by how only two years had passed since he'd travelled this way as a member of the touring Wallabies. He had a flashback to an incident in which he and Stan Bisset, both wearing fez caps, had skylarked at the Pyramids in Cairo during their brief stopover on the way to England. It was so disappointing that the tour had been irrefutably halted; to Nicky, the Nazis already had a lot to answer for. Would he ever know whether he could match it on the rugby field with the best that Europe had to offer?

The convoy stopped at Port Tewfik, at the southern end of the Suez Canal, where Nicky and his fellow airmen disembarked. From here, they boarded a train and headed north-west to Alexandria in Egypt, then penetrated deeper west into the North African Desert. From his train window Nicky contemplated the Sahara as it stretched dry and desolate before him. Even though he could appreciate its beauty and the sensuous allure in the curving architecture of the dunes, he also sensed a deeper, eerie menace masked in its shadow—one he knew he might have to contend with in the coming months.

The train moved methodically past the siding of El Alamein towards Mersa Matruh, the legendry Mediterranean playground of Cleopatra and Antony. To his right, along the coast, the waters of the Mediterranean took on myriad hues of green, blue and turquoise and palms reared from the white sands. Here, the railway line hugged the coast and was accompanied by the ever-present telephone poles snaking alongside it. From Mersa Matruh, they were taken to their final destination of Sidi Heneish, some 500 kilometres west of the Suez Canal.

On arrival at Sidi Heneish, Nicky could not contain his deep sense of excitement. With his friends, there was a feeling and expectancy that they were at the beginning of a great adventure. They were prepared for anything.

Sidi Heneish was simply a dot on the map and was represented by a small cairn of stones to honour a long-gone prophet. It was perched on an escarpment just in from the battle frontier and commanded superb views of the Mediterranean. Graders had levelled the terrain to provide aircraft landing areas. Further west was Halfaya Pass, where the extension of the road out of Egypt climbed the escarpment and ran on to Bardia and then to Tobruk in Libya. The Pass caused huge bottlenecks as traffic banked up on both sides, presenting a prime target. At this stage, Tobruk was besieged, but the Pass was in Allied hands, and was in No. 3 Squadron's protective territory.

No. 3 Squadron RAAF was raised in 1925 during peacetime, tracing its lineage to the Australian Flying Corps of World War One. When it arrived in the Middle East to begin operations in August 1940, it was to be under the command of the Sixth Australian Division. When No. 450 Squadron RAAF arrived as a fighter-bomber unit, both squadrons came under the command of the Desert Air Force, along with some 18 other Allied squadrons. They began their war against the Italians, supporting the British Western Desert Force in the ebb and flow of the desert campaign, equipped with Gladiator aircraft.

By January 1941, No. 3 Squadron was allocated modern aircraft in the form of Hurricanes and by the beginning of the

Syrian campaign, in June, they had been re-equipped with Curtiss P40 Tomahawks.

By October 1941, the squadron had met and matched Italian, French and German fighters, and their score against enemy aircraft had continued to mount despite the fact that the German Messerschmitt Me-109s were superior to the Tomahawks in air-to-air combat at rated altitude.

Since September, the Desert Air Force was officially known as part of the British Eighth Army, and No. 3 Squadron had established itself as the Desert Air Force's pre-eminent fighter squadron. Nicky and the other newly arrived reinforcements were well aware of this formidable reputation and, when lined up to be introduced to the commanding officer, Squadron Leader Peter Jeffrey, they caught some characteristically direct but unexpected flak. Jeffrey had joined the RAAF before the outbreak of war, and the air force was his career. He had been in the desert with No. 3 Squadron since 1940, and had been in command since February 1941. He was an ace already (a pilot is recognised as an ace after being credited with shooting down five or more enemy aircraft), and was known to be forthright. He asked the new pilots bluntly whether any of them were married.

It was an off-the-cuff question, but was nevertheless confronting to the new recruits. Jeffrey needed to quickly evaluate whether a man could give 100 per cent effort. He considered a married man, and a volunteer at that, might be preoccupied.

Four men, including Nicky, stepped forward. In a loud voice, for all and sundry to hear, Jeffrey proclaimed that they would be of little use to him. Surprised, Nicky took issue with this statement and retorted, 'I believe you're wrong, Sir. Those of us who are married have much more to fight for.'

Nicky's comments were not well received. Jeffrey wasn't used to having his statements debated, inflammatory as they were. For Nicky's sake, it was probably opportune that the replacements had arrived when there was a pause in proceedings as, virtually straight away, they were transferred to Operational Training Unit (OTU) No. 71 near Khartoum for conversion onto Tomahawks.

The capital of Sudan, Khartoum, is about 1600 kilometres south of Cairo, at the junction of the Blue Nile and White Nile Rivers. It was under Anglo-Egyptian rule and was renowned for the infamous year-long siege of 1885, during which the city was defended by General Gordon. Gordon was killed by rebellious Muslim dervishes two days before help arrived.

En route to Khartoum, the pilots enjoyed a pleasurable Nile journey on a houseboat, visiting such historic sites as Karnak Temple, Luxor and the Valley of the Kings, all an unexpected bonus. The aerodrome was at a place called Gordon's Tree, a little distance from Khartoum and quite civilised as it had been an established RAF base in peacetime. It boasted a fine officers' mess, terraced swimming pool and highly trained Sudanese mess staff and servants.

With the benefit of this comfortable existence, a long way from the war, training began immediately and with some enthusiasm.

Nicky's checkout flights were in Harvards and Hurricanes. However, a few days later, towards the end of October, he began conversion onto Mohawks and Tomahawks.

Both the Mohawk and Tomahawk were designed and built in the US Curtiss factory, and were originally ordered by the French. With the defeat of France, the RAF took the orders and shipped them to the Middle East. The Mohawk was a radial-engined fighter and, although tough, it was slow and almost obsolete by 1941. It was plagued with problems, which caused a great deal of them to literally fall out of the sky.

In only his fourth flight in a Mohawk, during a routine air-to-ground firing practice session in the deep south of Sudan, Nicky's Mohawk engine simply cut out.

Suppressing his initial shock, and following his now well-learned forced landing procedures, Nicky radioed his position and situation to base, then searched for a suitable landing site. Selecting a cleared area, he steadily glided his plane to a clean landing, rejoicing in the philosophy espoused by his teachers that 'any landing you walk away from is a good one'.

Some hours later, he and his plane were retrieved by the squadron, where it was found that oil had not been replaced in the engine after servicing, causing shutdown. (He was intrigued to learn some months later that the metallurgy of the piston rings of many of the Mohawks had been sabotaged at the Allison plant in the US.)

The plane that pleased Nicky the most was the Tomahawk. It was equipped with a powerful Allison engine that gave it great manoeuvrability, allowing it to perform smartly at low altitude. It was a rugged plane, ideally suited for desert fighting and well armed, boasting two .50 machine guns in the cockpit that were calibrated to fire through the propeller and two .30 guns projecting from each wing.

Nicky would delight to sit in the cockpit when the guns were being reloaded—the central guns were loaded from inside the cockpit. There was a closeness to combat that seemed to relate well to Nicky's make-up. After firing, there was always a strong smell of cordite in the cockpit that stimulated his adrenalin, not unlike the smell of lineament before a football game. He really felt he was at war; serious stuff.

And he was ready for it.

Once in the air, he relished the freedom of the vast desert landscape. He threw the plane around the sky, practising gunnery, deflection attacks, dogfights against Hurricanes and testing himself under G-forces and with aerobatics and spins performed at speed and height. In rare flashes, between adrenalin bursts, the desert seemed to signal to him, revealing tantalising glimpses of often transcendent beauty. But he remained mindful that it was a cruel, harsh environment that he should never underestimate.

After 40 hours of intensive training, Nicky was graded above average. His final preparation involved receiving his 'goolie chit', which was to be carried at all times. This was a parchment document designed to protect troops should they one day find themselves in Arab hands. When the Italians had earlier occupied these lands they had generally treated the Arabs poorly, so when an Italian pilot was forced down the Arabs would often capture then torture him, sometimes castrating him with a curved sharp knife before killing him. The Ethiopians had initiated this treatment during the Italian invasion of their country.

As the Arabs could not quickly distinguish between Allied pilots and Italians, the British High Command in the East supplied all Allied pilots with a chit which ostensibly said in Arabic—'don't kill the bearer, feed him and protect him, take him to the English and you will be rewarded. Peace be upon you.'

Nicky left Khartoum on 17 November 1941, as well equipped as any would-be knight of the air could be, ready to rejoin No. 3 Squadron in the desert and do battle.

THREE

Landing Ground 122

While Nicky had been completing his course at Khartoum, No. 3 Squadron had been engaged in an intensive, vicious and costly campaign as part of the newly launched Operation Crusader.

The commander of the Middle East forces, General Sir Claude Auchinleck, sponsored the offensive in a concerted effort to relieve pressure on besieged Tobruk. This involved throwing the might of the Axis and Allied armies directly against each other, an element of which incorporated the Desert Air Force attacking the Axis' formidable artillery and tank units surrounding Tobruk. The 20 squadrons of Desert Air Force had a total of about 200 aircraft and they were more than matched by the Axis fighter force, which also totalled about 200 fighters, but included some 40 Messerschmitt Me-109s, a superior plane.

The Me-109 was known as BF109 up until July 1938, the BF standing for Bayerische Flugzeugwerke, when it was renamed. It was powered by an efficient 1150 horsepower Daimler-Benz engine, and its early armament were two 7.9 mm MG-17 machine guns through the propeller arc and two 20 mm cannon mounted in the wings outside the propeller arc. It was designed as a lethal, modern fighter plane, and performed superbly in all types of air battle, particularly at its rated height.

As well, some of the German pilots were highly experienced,

having been continually in battle since the Spanish Civil War in 1937, where the planes were first combat tested.

For this offensive, the No. 3 Squadron had moved forward from Sidi Heneish to an area with the utility title of Landing Ground 122 (LG 122). These landing strips were set out by Wing Commander Fred Rosier of Advanced RAF Headquarters, whose staff would plan the synchronisation of squadron operations. He would take off in his clapped-out Battle of Britain Hurricane, search for the most strategic landing sites, then mark out the area for the strip. Graders and engineers and their equipment would move forward and prepare the site, complete with fuel, tents and supplies, ready for the squadrons to fly in. From the air, the main thing that distinguished a desert landing ground from the rest of the empty sandy area was the white 'L' marking at the corners of the runway.

On the day Nicky arrived back at Sidi Heneish he learned his squadron had recently suffered its most devastating losses. They had lost nine aircraft on 22 November, reducing its pilot strength by 50 per cent in one blow. In a disastrous series of morning dogfights with Me-109s, they lost three pilots, all killed, and in the continuing afternoon battles, hammering away at Rommel's armoured columns, lost a further four, two killed and two taken prisoner.

By the time Nicky and three of the new pilots—Lou Spence, Geoff Chinchen and Don Knight—had flown forward to LG 122, where the commander welcomed them warmly, there were only four serviceable aircraft available that day to the squadron.

Nicky's first impression of LG 122 was one of desolation: beautiful in its way, but barren. However, he also realised it was probably an ideal place to stage a war; nobody should be hurt except the belligerents.

There had been a change of leadership also, as Alan Rawlinson had replaced Peter Jeffrey. Jeffrey had been promoted to Wing Commander Flying, and was still in the squadron. Even though he had queried Nicky earlier, the matter was quickly put behind them. Jeffrey was well known as a popular and efficient commander, introducing a 'family' and team attitude to the squadron, which helped to raise and maintain morale. He directed all pilots to drink and eat together instead of in their separate officers' and sergeants' messes. He believed it was senseless sharing one's life with fellow pilots during operations, then retiring separately after the event when they should be recounting and learning from their experiences as a team. He established a pilots' mess and progressively the RAF and South African squadrons followed.

Rawlinson was an ace pilot too and was one of the originals of No. 3 Squadron. He was also well liked, and known as an articulate and good leader, and a tough and courageous pilot.

The four new pilots were informed of the situation, and of the last few days of battle. The stories, often unsettling, were of sudden, horrific deaths, of planes disintegrating into the stony hard desert, of other planes bursting into flames and of shocking midair collisions as the dominant Messerschmitts clashed with the aggressive Tomahawks.

They were also told of the heroism of the men of No. 3 Squadron who, on 22 November, had flown and fought the Me-109s to a standstill, long after the sun had sunk and dusk had tinged the sky dark blue. And of the reverses three days later when Wing Commander Peter Jeffrey led 20 planes from the combined No. 3 Squadron and the RAF's No. 112 Squadron against 70 enemy aircraft over Sidi Rezegh near Tobruk. In full view of the wildly enthusiastic British and Australian soldiers, besieged on the ground below, they destroyed ten enemy aircraft for the loss of a single Tomahawk.

The losses and the reality of the battle close up did not depress Nicky. The news was disturbing, but in himself, Nicky felt confident. He appreciated that he was as well trained for battle as anybody, and he was ready for it. He looked forward to the challenge.

Nicky and the new pilots were informed they were to prepare for a patrol in the afternoon. Nicky was restless to go, then abruptly his stomach turned. A natural sudden fear reaction gripped him as he realised the implications of the bold bottom line of the command. Like others, he was about to put his life on the line after years of training. He knew, however, that he was strongly motivated to do well, and he was confident of his own abilities. Even though he understood the randomness of the unknown when facing any foe or contesting any event, and he appreciated the role luck and the bounce of the ball could play, he knew he was well prepared psychologically and physically to embrace the challenges he faced. His heart rate settled and his lips moistened again as he walked towards his plane. By the time he had stepped onto the wing of the Tomahawk and begun the routine check procedures, his fear had been replaced by a strong resolve and a sense of excitement.

The squadron was to escort a Free French Squadron flying Blenheim Bombers. They carried the Cross of Lorraine emblem on their fuselages, evoking images of Joan of Arc. Their mission was to bomb the Bir el Arid Aerodrome, situated some distance behind enemy lines.

As Nicky lifted his Tomahawk into the afternoon sky, his heart thumped, his senses quickly attained maximum alertness, and his hands automatically controlled the plane while his eyes searched the sky with intense acuity.

As the flight penetrated deeper into enemy territory, he felt the tension build as he wondered when and how the enemy might appear, and how he would react to first contact. He felt unusually vulnerable, not really knowing what to expect, stimulating him to tighten his right hand over the gun button.

The words of his instructors kept coming back 'beware the Hun in the sun', intensifying his need to swivel his head in every possible direction, eyes scanning the heavens. He realised now that the silk cravat that pilots wore was not just an affectation; it actually protected the skin from the rough edges of air force issue collars as the head moved relentlessly in all directions.

Dot had bought him a beautiful white silk scarf before he left Australia. It was decorated with mosaic patterns around the border, and he decided he would need to wear it every time he went aloft in future.

Increasing his tension, Nicky noted that the Frenchmen were flying in shockingly poor formation, which would be difficult for the Tomahawks to adequately defend if they were attacked. Perhaps they were deliberately making it difficult for the Luftwaffe to shoot them down?

As the formation neared the aerodrome, the situation was defused a little as heavy low cloud cover prevented a clear sighting of the target area. With some frustration, the leader signalled a return to base. Some 30 minutes later, as Nicky's Tomahawk touched down back at LG 122, he realised he wasn't completely unhappy at not having sighted an enemy aircraft. The first-time experience gave him some security and comfort which he knew he could build on.

The next day he was shot at—not by aircraft, but by enemy flak. The patrol began with some drama as, on take-off, one of the new pilots, Geoff Chinchen, was accidentally forced into a sand-filled 44-gallon petrol drum marking the intersection of the crossed runways. Chinchen's plane received a gaping hole in the leading edge of his port wing, but he skilfully and courageously stayed with the squadron.

The squadron carried out a fighter sweep over the Tobruk area and allowed Nicky a chance to view the extent of Rommel's army, particularly noting tanks and anti-aircraft guns pointing skywards around Tobruk. As they approached Tobruk, Nicky was a little disconcerted as bursts of black ack-ack smoke appeared and exploded around him, but luckily, they didn't exact any damage.

Nicky also had a chance to examine Fortress Tobruk from the air and he marvelled at the resilience of the men down below who had defied the Axis troops for so long in their effort to deny Rommel a clear run to Cairo. No. 3 Squadron's mission that day was to cover the exit, and to give safe passage out of Tobruk to a high ranking officer who was leaving in a Blenheim Bomber.

As they circled, waiting for the plane to take off from the scarred aerodrome below, Nicky was full of admiration for the men who had dug and manned what looked like, from the air, rabbit warrens of slit trenches and had also built massive earthworks around the battered town. He also noted the appalling sight of wrecked and sunken ships glutting the harbour —testimony to the desperation and intensity of the German air force trying to prevent Allied ships from supplying the Rats of Tobruk.

The next day, 30 November, was also programmed as a fighter sweep over the Tobruk area. No. 3 Squadron and No. 112 RAF Squadron took off in the morning, but after ten minutes out, Nicky's plane lost power and the engine started to splutter. Reluctantly he turned for home and, on landing, passed his Tomahawk over to his mechanic. It was to be another day of high drama in the air as the story was relayed to Nicky that night.

The two squadrons had encountered a Balbo of enemy aircraft over Bir el Gobi some time after crossing into enemy territory. (Balbo was the name of an Italian air commander who never ventured into battle without 50 or more planes in the flight. He was a famous pre-war aviator and was Italy's first Air Marshal. The name Balbo was given to any large number of enemy planes flying en masse.) There were at least 50 planes in this lot, composed of German Ju87s and Me-109s and Italian Macchi 200s and G50s. The two squadrons from the Desert Air Force had the morning sun behind them and, largely unobserved by the enemy planes, quickly climbed above them and closed to within attacking range.

Jabbering Italian and German voices were heard over the Allied squadron radios, indicating they had been seen. Almost immediately, the sky became a madhouse of whirling planes and stuttering machine-guns as the two groups locked into deadly battle. The fierce mêlée lasted only a few minutes but resulted in No. 3 Squadron claiming a further eight enemy destroyed and 12 damaged.

Once again, stories of heroism and drama were related back at the base, such as that of Wilf 'Woof' Arthur who, although flying a damaged plane himself, became the first Allied pilot to shoot down four enemy aircraft in a combat. There was also Peter Jeffrey, who was awarded an immediate (that is, awarded in the field) Distinguished Flying Cross (DFC) for his leadership and for landing behind enemy lines to pick up one of his downed sergeant pilots, 'Tiny' Cameron. Cameron, a 6-foot, 6-inch sheep station owner from western Queensland, and one of the characters of the squadron, had crash-landed below the battle as it was still going on overhead. His downed plane had been strafed by two Me-109s, but he had just managed to jump out in time. Jeffrey landed beside his burning aircraft, discarded his parachute and squeezed Cameron into the parachute's space. Then, sitting on Cameron's lap, he flew back to base.

That night the squadron had a great celebration as the day's tally had taken them past the '100 enemy destroyed' mark—the first squadron in the desert to do so. The party was in their mess—a small and smoky tent—and they were presented with a German swastika flag by the wing commanding officer to mark the occasion. That day also marked the finish of Alan Rawlinson's brief but excellent leadership of No. 3 Squadron. He had been in the desert longer than any other pilot in the squadron.

These nights, and others like it, when resting after battle, gave Nicky a chance to question some of the more experienced pilots about air combat. Because of a type of humbleness and a desire to present themselves as low-key operators, Nicky initially found that it was difficult to wheedle information from them. However, once they relaxed, and the experienced pilots were sure they weren't thought to be 'bunging-it-on', Nicky found that they were free in imparting positive advice.

These occasions were also a chance for the squadron to have a few drinks and sing. Nicky hadn't brought his squeeze box to the Middle East, but his friend Freddy Eggleston had. Eggleston couldn't play well, so he strapped it on Nicky who from then on rarely took it off on these occasions, becoming known as 'Squeeze Box' Barr.

The first few days of December afforded some relief for the squadron as they flew back to Sidi Heneish for some recreation and re-training. Some of the pilots had been in action continually for weeks and were close to exhaustion. A dusty, cold, six-hour ride in the back of a truck transported some of these men to Alexandria and the promise of good food, some grog and nightclubs.

Life in the desert provided little in the way of comfort. Pilots slept on camp stretchers, two in a tent, with the floor composed of either sand or hard, gravel earth. There was a minimum of water for shaving and bathing and it could be extremely cold at night. The squadron cooks did their best to serve bully beef in appetising ways, and there was seldom any alcohol available in the mess, which consisted of two large EPIP (eight-person Indian pattern) tents joined together.

During this period, 11 new pilots arrived from Australia. They had not yet converted to Tomahawks and, due to the pressure of the war situation, training for them had to commence virtually on the job. Under the eye of the more experienced pilots, some of whom were a little nervous concerning their precious machines, the new men received an intensive conversion course. Many had to complete their training during squadron operations, an often dangerous situation.

On Monday 8 December, the squadron received news that the Japanese had bombed Pearl Harbour and the Germans had declared war against the United States. The initial reaction was generally one of shock, but this was tempered with some relief because of the belief that the American presence would eventually shift the balance of power in the desert and the war in general. There was some concern in north Africa that the US might divert sorely needed resources to the Pacific theatre of war instead.

The following day, 9 December, during his fourth operational flight, Nicky experienced his first real taste of combat. His was one of nine Tomahawks of 'C' flight led by Pete Jeffrey. Along with ten Tomahawks from No. 112 Squadron, under the command of Clive Caldwell, an Australian, they were to undertake a general sweep of the Tobruk–El Adem area. This was mainly to ascertain and test the enemy strength, both on the ground and in the air. They were also to report to the army any ground movements, as there was still a legacy of requirement from No. 3 Squadron to act as a type of army-cooperative unit.

In the early days of the Middle East Campaign, when operating in Syria, the squadrons would often fly in groups of three aircraft in close 'V' formation with one or two aircraft swinging backwards and forwards above the 'V', theoretically to guard from attacks from behind, the practice being pretty much a hangover from World War One. The No. 3 Squadron found this didn't work well here, so they experimented with different formations and manoeuvres, settling on a system where they divided into three sections of four aircraft, each four having a section leader and flying in a figure-four box formation. The leader of the centre section was in command of the operation.

The leader of Nicky's box was Eddie Jackson, and the other two pilots, like Nicky, were new recruits, Lou Spence and Don Knight. Jackson was one of three flying brothers and was tough and experienced. One of his brothers, John, had just left No. 3 Squadron to take up the command of the No. 75 Fighter Squadron in the Pacific Theatre.

As the squadron penetrated deeper into Rommel's territory they ran into tremendous fire from batteries of anti-aircraft guns which had sighted them. Nicky followed Jackson in a strafing dive right into the concussive path of the guns shooting back at them. To his horror, he saw the root-section of Jackson's wing blow out as it was shattered by a powerful shell. The plane rocked violently, and Jackson fought to regain control as other Tomahawks wheeled and howled down in turn, locking their sights onto the guns. As they screamed into the attack, tracers burst from their machine-guns, crashing a stream of lead into the guns, driving the crew, panic-eyed, into any nearby shelter.

Nicky couldn't get a burst off, as he protectively stuck close to his damaged leader and then escorted him back to the main body of the flight who were now continuing with the planned operation.

During the strafing action, high in the sun at about 12 000 feet, the two squadrons were being observed by seven Me-109s from 1/JG27, the opposing Luftwaffe Fighter Wing assigned to the area. (No. 1 designates No. 1 group of Fighter Wing 27—Jagdgeschwader 27 or JG27.) The leader of the group, Erhard Braune, an experienced German ace, waited until the squadron was at 1500 feet directly below them, then signalled for his group to swoop, as Nicky found out later.

Someone's voice rasped over the radio, 'Bandits, 12 o'clock high! Out of the sun!' By now, the squadrons had formed a defensive circle, the philosophy being a little like the protective circling of wagons in the old West. Nicky felt uncomfortable in this situation, and considered the pilots were at a decided disadvantage, suspecting that anyone attacking from above could simply preselect their target, dive down and pick it off, seemingly at will. They could then maintain the dive, then climb up for another attack, a little like a shark zooming through a circling school of fish.

Nicky felt tense, waiting for something to happen, but the instant he saw the enemy planes for the first time, apprehension was replaced by substance.

Confident of his own abilities, he was more than ready as he rechecked that the safety catch of the trigger was off. The Me-109s dived and screamed through the circle, selectively firing with precision at their predetermined targets.

About 50 metres over to his left, Nicky saw Dave Rutter's plane shake as the blast of a 109's guns brought an immediate belch of black smoke from the engine. He then watched as long tongues of orange flame came stabbing out with blowtorch intensity. Within seconds, the flames wrapped around the fuselage, forcing the plane into a death dive.

The 109s continued through at great speed, untouched. However as they bottomed out and banked to come back up again, one briefly moved through Nicky's line of fire. He squeezed the trigger, and watched annoyed as his bullets traced harmlessly underneath the target. Damn—he was too far away. He was perspiring freely now, both from the heat of the enclosed cabin and from his pulsing adrenalin. That and the smell of the cordite sharpened his senses and he resolved to try and approach closer before taking a second shot.

By now though, the formation had virtually dissolved, as

single individuals went chasing after the speeding Me-109s. Nicky dived closer to his mark, and when he figured he had the enemy in his sights and within range he would let go a burst of two or three seconds. Even though the guns were capable of firing continuously for about 11 or 12 seconds before the ammunition was expended, the intense heat generated would often jam the mechanism, so smaller more frequent bursts were recommended. Discipline was also required to contain the gun use.

The battle expanded to all corners of the sky as planes howled and roared in every direction. Individual clashes occurred as the fighters toyed and closed on each other, matching wits and tactics, all the while probing for a weakness. Once an advantage was pressed, chattering machine-guns ripped bullets into the opposing plane, a smoke trail signalling the final testament to a second's enterprise.

Nicky clung to his foe, darting, spinning and swirling, his hours of aerobatic training allowing his subconscious to assume control of the flying while he set his full concentration on his sights and on the plane in front. He was trying desperately to keep the black ball in his sights centred, indicating his plane was trimmed. Now! He would let go a burst—damn, too wide. A flick of the rudder. Again; another burst—he watched helplessly as the tracers spat under the plane in front.

The guns were loaded with a mixture of tracer, incendiary and normal explosive and one out of every six was armour piercing. He corrected his deflection a little and fired again, willing the line of tracers to finish in the 109 ahead. That was closer!

Nicky had been advised by the old hands that most air combats were over in one or two minutes—sudden and vicious. However, this conflict was extending noticeably as it took its deadly toll. After about ten minutes of nerve-wracking attack and evasion procedures, Nicky's ammunition ran out.

In the same instant, he also realised the sky had mysteriously emptied—the battle had moved on and he was alone—except, he noticed, for two 109s circling above him. Nicky's blood went cold. Quickly, he assessed his situation. He had lost his leader, he was alone way behind enemy lines, he was out of ammunition, fuel was low and his movements were being tracked by two 109s from an advantaged position—one, he found out later, was the hardened group leader, Erhard Braune.

The position was serious, but Nicky realised the German pilots could not know that he was out of ammunition so, playing it cool, he flew a little north until he could see the Mediterranean. To get home, he would have to fly east and keep the Mediterranean on his port or left side. There was no time to look at maps, so from these initial bearings, and an intuitive form of dead reckoning, he slowly began flying in large confident figures of eight, all the time steadily working towards his home lines.

The moments were tense and long. His eyes moved from the ground where he was searching for landmarks to the 109s hovering like eagles waiting to pounce, while his subconscious was willing himself over his own territory.

His ability to consistently remain conscious of his overall position and direction in relation to the enemy and to the ground must have impressed his enemy above. This skill—'situation awareness'—which normally only experienced pilots exhibited at such a high level of competence, may have prevented them from attacking. Whatever the reason, Nicky managed to keep them at bay until he was almost over his own landing field.

Quickly, he dived his plane to the ground, and thankfully crawled out, wet through with perspiration. He was mentally, emotionally and physically exhausted from the ordeal, his energy completely sapped. He had just experienced tough combat flying, involving as it does, among other stresses, extended periods of high G-forces.

The day's mission had been expensive for No. 3 Squadron. They had shot down one plane and claimed another two damaged. But even though No. 112 Squadron returned complete, No. 3 Squadron counted four of their planes missing, including their leader, Pete Jeffrey. At least three fires had been seen from downed aircraft over the area of combat and the squadron feared the worst.

Thankfully, Jeffrey arrived back later that evening. He had chased a 109 down low over the desert and had been gaining on it when his engine failed. He limped into Tobruk, where he brought it to life again with a plug change. 'Tiny' Cameron was also missing but both Rutter and Sergeant Rex Wilson were confirmed killed. Wilson had just been recommended for a Distinguished Flying Medal (DFM), having shot down eight enemy aircraft.

Nicky felt Dave Rutter's death very much. An outstanding individual, Rutter had been dux of Melbourne Grammar School. Nicky had known him since his Power House days. Dave had also trained with him at Point Cook and had only arrived in the desert five days earlier.

By now, Nicky and some of his newer pilot colleagues had discussed the day's events and were beginning to question certain tactics, particularly the defensive circle, concluding that it really wasn't successful. In fact, only the day before, sitting around their tent, Dave Rutter, Don Knight, Graham Pace, Lou Spence and Nicky had been quite adamant and unanimous about the need to recommend a change in this defensive circle tactic. As the official attitude was that the P40 Tomahawk was inferior to the Me-109, particularly at high altitude, this appeared to be the only ploy they could use. Nicky, Lou Spence and Don Knight sought out their commanding officer and expressed their views on this, to which he replied, 'Well, if you didn't like it so much, why didn't one of you lead off?'

That wasn't the answer Nicky wanted. Discipline was a strong component of their flying, and it would not have been proper for a junior inexperienced officer to lead off from a defensive circle; it had to be the formation commander. Nicky started to formulate the idea that even though the Tomahawk was a solid and magnificent machine, it was just not as good as the specifically designed Me-109 for this type of combat, especially above 14 000 feet. The Tomahawk was built for air-to-ground army-support operations—his logic supported a more offensive role.

Nicky began to change his attitudes and tactics, deciding from then on he would be more aggressive. Using a boxing ring analogy, he reasoned that if you sense your opponent is superior in any way, aggression will often take him by surprise. By the same token he realised that aggression should not be mistaken for overconfidence; brashness would not work either. Any offensive action must be tempered with a carefully thought out strategy. He was determined to experiment and build on this philosophy over the next few patrols, given the opportunity.

First Victory

By late November, Operation Crusader was having a considerable impact on Rommel's Army. When the British attack opened on 18 November, it achieved total tactical surprise. Armoured brigades, tanks, infantry and the Desert Air Force had combined to muster an intensive and co-ordinated massed attack against the Axis troops around the Tobruk fortress, making Rommel's situation critical. The battle had developed into one of attrition and in early December Rommel began to pull back to a defensive line at Gazala, west of Tobruk.

On the evening of 9 December, the enemy abandoned their positions around Tobruk and retreated towards Cyrenaica (Western Libya). Tobruk was at last relieved.

They had held out for 242 days, 55 days longer than the legendary Mafeking Siege of the Boer War, having resisted everything the Germans could throw at them. The German retreat was delightedly confirmed by Nicky from the air two days after recovering from his spat with Erhard Braune's Me-109s, when he took part in a patrol over Tobruk while giving protection to some Hurricanes from another squadron which were refuelling there.

There was no air activity but down below, particularly around the El Adem area and later around Gazala, he could see large fires burning on the ground, left by the retreating Germans who were pouring westwards. When retreating, a 'scorched earth policy' was invoked by the Germans—nothing was to be left that could be used by the advancing Allied army.

The retreat was good news, and it was a considerable boost to the Allied Armies' morale to at last be steadily advancing again. There was more good news on 12 December when 'Tiny' Cameron walked in from the desert after a harrowing three days of evading enemy patrols. There was also extensive fighting that day, both in the air and on land, as Rommel tried to consolidate a toehold at Gazala.

Across the extended battlefield that day, most squadrons of the Desert Air Force clashed with the persistent Luftwaffe, repeatedly strafing and bombing the retreating ground troops and motorised columns. In particular, during the heat of the battle, three squadrons of the South African Air Force (SAAF) lost four aircraft over the Derna Road area, which links to Gazala. In response to this combat, No. 3 Squadron and No. 112 Squadron took off on a morning patrol to sweep the Derna area.

As they approached the south of Gazala, the patrol sighted some unidentified aircraft which quickly climbed into cloud when the flight turned towards them. The patrol landed at El Adem, where they refuelled and were briefed for the afternoon's operations. They were to carry out a fighter sweep over the Gazala area to cover some Blenheims returning from a bombing operation.

The squadron took off and was flying in formation of three boxes again, with Nicky flying wingman, or No. 2, to Ed Jackson. The basic function of the wingman is to protect the stern of the more experienced leader to allow him to consider and then dictate tactics. To some extent, it is quite sacrificial, as the No. 2 places himself between an attacking enemy plane and his No. 1.

Ahead in the distance, Nicky could see some bomb bursts, which indicated that the German ground troops were probably firing at the Blenheims and their escorts, which they knew to be two squadrons of the SAAF.

No. 112 and No. 3 Squadrons flew higher so that if any enemy fighters were having a crack at the escorts or the Blenheims, they would be in a position to surprise them. Nicky scanned the skies, peering into the distance, but always alert for enemy planes surprising him from behind. He was grateful for the scarf Dot had given him—it was almost like a talisman for him now. He wouldn't fly without it. In fact, he realised most pilots flew with a 'good luck' charm of some sort on them, although few would admit to being superstitious.

A few minutes after the mission began, some small dots appeared ahead and were first recognised by Bobby Gibbes. Gibbes was an ace already and had fought through the Syrian campaign with No. 3 Squadron. He was blessed with particularly keen eyesight and excellent field vision. He had also developed highly sensitive survival skills, and was invariably the first to detect the presence of enemy aircraft and identify them. He intuitively realised the small specks were most likely the Blenheims. As the squadron flew a little closer, he could make out smaller dots which were twisting and turning, indicating that the SAAF Squadrons were in combat with attacking enemy fighters.

They were now at about 13 000 feet above Tmimi and were rapidly approaching the dogfighting mêlée ahead. The two squadrons were increasing their rates of climb in order to create an advantage when Gibbes called out over the radio, 'Bandits, coming in from behind.' For obvious reasons, planes normally fly in radio silence, the silence only being broken when enemy planes are sighted. The call immediately signalled that the squadron should take evasive action, scattering planes in all directions to get clear of the blazing enemy guns coming from their rear.

As the formation broke up, in the confusion and scramble, Nicky caught a glimpse of his friend Freddy Eggleston becoming involved in a midair collision with another Tomahawk, flown by

Robin Gray. As Nicky watched, wide-eyed, Freddy's plane whirled away in a tight turn. Nicky last saw him struggling to level the plane as he flew into a heavy cumulus cloud. He then saw Gray's plane dive towards a cloud. Gray, like Rutter, had only recently arrived with the latest batch of pilots, and was quite inexperienced.

Most of the formation had broken up by now, with the cloud cover confusing and protecting but also adding to the terror. In the excitement, Nicky had lost sight of his leader, Ed Jackson, who was busy having his own private duel with two Me-109s in another section of the sky. As Nicky could find nothing to shoot at, he pushed his stick forward and dived after Gray with the intention of protecting him and escorting him home. When he had almost caught up to Gray, at the level of the cloud base at 3000 feet, he caught sight of a Messerchmitt 110 above in the distance, flying towards him. The twin engined Me-110 was a versatile fighter with an extended flying range; not as manoeu- vrable as the 109, but nevertheless formidable.

Nicky's pulse quickened. There was no confining defensive circle now. He swung in from behind, aggressively pushing his plane to maximum speed. As he approached to within firing range, he quickly made sure his gunsight was absolutely right and checked the deflection angle and range. Committed now, he rushed in on the 110 from below and behind in a 30-degree attack angle. Beads of sweat speckled his forehead and ran down his neck, soaking his shirt, his concentration not wavering from the target ahead. The distance came flashing down in seconds—600 metres ... 400 ... 300 ... 250 ... the Me-110 loomed large in the gunsight.

His total concentration with his gunsight and the target ahead precluded Nicky from registering any emotion as he pressed the gun button. His eyes followed the white ribbons of tracers as they raced from the guns, then watched them chew into the Me-110. With satisfaction, he saw two large pieces of the Messerschmitt suddenly blast clear which were then whipped backwards by the slipstream. Maintaining the intensity he fired again, his bullets this time raking the fuselage and wing. Immediately, orange flames burst from the wing and thick black smoke poured out from deep gashes in the body of the stricken plane.

He knew he had badly damaged the crippled plane and pulled away, up and above the thickening clouds, and was suddenly lost to the battle scene. Rather pleased with his first encounter, he returned to LG 122 and was confronted by a glowering Ed Jackson, who asked, 'Where in the blazes were you?' Nicky explained that he had lost sight of him because of the thick cloud. Jackson, however, wasn't sympathetic. 'That's no good. Stick closer next time.'

Nicky realised Jackson was justified in reprimanding him. The wingman, No. 2, has the responsibility to protect his No. 1— that, after all, was the prime purpose of the box formation. Nicky resolved to do better. Later that evening, when filling out his report of the day's battle, he didn't claim the Me-110 as he couldn't be sure he'd finished it off, or even that there were any witnesses to ratify the event. However, RAAF command headquarters received a report from the army who confirmed Nicky had indeed shot the Me-110 down.

This information provided a lift for Nicky and the squadron as it was their only kill for the day, although Bobby Gibbes did damage a Ju87 Stuka. No. 112 Squadron fared worse, losing three aircraft for one Me-109 destroyed. Nicky's lift was shortlived when he found out that Freddy Eggleston, having pulled out of his dive earlier in the mêlée, had been seen taking part in a terrific dogfight, and was eventually shot down and captured. This was the price of war, Nicky was learning, and it was heavy. He and Eggleston had been good friends since Essendon. At least Robin Gray had made it home.

He would have a chance for revenge tomorrow.

The next day, Saturday 13 December, started quietly as Nicky's squadron spent most of the morning on standby. Standby was often stressful, and entailed patiently waiting around, fully kitted and ready for combat, generally lounging on chairs outside the 'ops' tent. Mostly the men talked quietly to each other, some played cards, others joked, but always they kept one eye on their planes, lined up ready to fly, less than a stone's throw away. Even though they tried to relax, there was always a degree of tension as they waited either for an assignment or for a signal to 'scramble'.

Men found different ways to cope with the stress of standby. Ed Jackson would often sit by himself playing solo. Nicky could tell he wasn't concentrating on the card games though; his mind was always deep in thought, preparing for the action to come or some other compelling problem.

Eventually, at four in the afternoon, the squadron was ordered to carry out a patrol over the Derna–Martuba area. Jackson led the formation of ten Tomahawks and for this, Nicky's eighth operation, Bobby Gibbes was his section leader. Some minutes after becoming airborne they approached Derna from the sea, flying below a thick layer of cloud at about 5000 feet, heading south. As they crossed the coastline, in the ten o'clock position ahead (twelve o'clock is directly in front, six o'clock behind) they spotted a V-formation of eight Me-110 bombers heading towards Alexandria. They were fitted with special reconnaissance cameras and were escorted by seven Me-109 fighters.

The Tomahawks were sighted before they could close, and the 109s swung around in formation to confront them—a chilling sight. The low cloud base prevented the 109s from creating an advantage, by allowing them to use their superior performance at height and also negated their 'pick and zoom' tactics, although Nicky realised the cloud could assist both sides with evasive tactics. Either way, Nicky wasn't going to wait.

He broke formation and thrust the Tomahawk forward to meet the 109s which by now had swung around to attack the Tomahawks from the left rear. Once again, the squadron split up as the sky erupted into a swirling mixture of fighter planes clawing at each other in individual dogfights.

In his direct vision, Nicky caught sight of a 109 sitting in a perfect quarter stern position, posturing to fire at a Tomahawk. Nicky saw his chance. He violently wrenched his plane around, banked, then climbed upwards, quickly reaching a position above the 109. Within a few seconds, he pushed his plane into a dive, rapidly shortening his distance to within 350 metres from the Messerschmitt. Although Nicky's shooting record had been adequate at training, he hadn't convinced himself he was an accurate shooter, so he forced himself closer to the 109, watching the plane fill his sights. At about 250 metres, he pressed the trigger. He followed the tracers spurting from his gun and was sure he'd hit the plane, but cursed to himself as he couldn't see any obvious or immediate effect on the 109. However, he was relieved to see the Tomahawk, which had been in the 109's sights, suddenly dive and turn off to port, apparently untouched.

The 109 pulled off from his line of attack and headed for the temporary shelter of the cloud. Nicky followed in close pursuit. The enemy fighter banked and wheeled in a hair-raising attempt to escape, with Nicky matching every turn.

By now, the cordite smell from the cockpit guns was very strong and Nicky's concentration was fuelled by adrenalin. It was close and hot in the confined space of the cockpit, but Nicky's main focus was on the plane ahead. His eyes narrowed; the distance closed, he was in range. He pressed the trigger again.

The 109 shuddered and half rolled. As Nicky watched, the plane flicked into a spin, a wisp of smoke trailing in its wake. He followed it visually until it crashed in flames into the ground, close to the burning wreckage of another Messerschmitt. There was also a burning Tomahawk some distance away.

His adrenalin still pumping, Nicky quickly searched the now almost empty sky. In the distance, all he could see were three 109s, so he climbed up into the cloud and flew south-east towards where he knew Gazala would be. It made sense to use cloud cover whenever it was available. Air fighting is not like land fighting where it may be possible to find even some small cover. There are no trenches or shields on a plane, just a thin skin of metal and glass. The real risk is that no one knows who is in the cloud, there is no visibility and one needs to be reasonably good at instrument flying.

After some moments, he dived just below the cloud and realised he was south-west of the Gazala inlet, a clear milestone carved into the desert shale by the Mediterranean. The pressure was off a little now; there were no fighters in sight.

From Nicky's position high above the vastness of the Sahara, running parallel to the coastline was the black ribbon of the highway leading to Gazala. In the distance, further along the road, Nicky noticed a swarm of Junkers Ju88 twin-engined bombers attacking an Allied truck formation. Some of the vehicles had crashed into each other and others were stranded in the clutching sand on the edge of the road. Some were stalled, and palls of black and blue smoke spiralled upwards, signalling their helplessness.

Nicky accelerated towards the marauding planes and stealthily moved inside the whirling formation. As he approached to within shooting distance, one Ju88, after levelling out from an attacking sweep, swung around full into Nicky's air space and raced directly towards him. For a milli-second, Nicky flew right through the German's gun sights. Horrified, he waited for a spray of bullets to come at him. Luckily he was through before the pilot could react.

Instinctively, Nicky now violently manoeuvred his Tomahawk to a position setting himself in line for a front-to-quarter attack. The German pilot would have seen him, but too late, he'd missed his chance. The side of the German's plane was perfectly exposed and presented a clear target. Nicky's bullets ripped along the plane's fuselage, cutting holes into it like a can-opener.

As the Junkers roared past him, Nicky slipped round behind the tail and swung into a position below the plane and prepared for a second shot. He fired again at close range and saw his bullets bite into the left wing. Immediately, the wing dropped away and tumbled into space, leaving jagged edges of metal protruding from the fuselage. Now, unbalanced and out of control, the Junkers rocked and then dived sharply, rotated, then quickly generated into a flat spin.

The action was all over in a few seconds—sudden and violent. However, Nicky realised there was no time to consider the victory, or even savour it, as he knew others in the swarm would quickly react and then concentrate on this infiltrator—a viper in the nest. Without waiting to witness the Junkers' final death dive, Nicky quickly shot up into the protective cover of the clouds again.

With some degree of security and satisfaction, he settled himself on instruments then, a few minutes later, dived below the cloud cover again for a quick look. North-west of where the bombed trucks were now recovering and assessing their damage, Nicky could see a black pall of smoke pouring from a crumpled plane fiercely burning on the ground; almost certainly the Ju88.

Back at base, Nicky was pleased once again to be the highest scorer with his two confirmed 'kills'. 'Tiny' Cameron had claimed a Me-109 and shared a second one with Tom Briggs, while Ron Simes and Bobby Gibbes had both damaged at least two each. However, Tommy Trimble had been shot down and was still missing.

The next day Nicky took part in a search for Trimble, but after 20 minutes of flying around over the battle area he was nowhere to be found.

The same day, 14 November, while Nicky was searching for Trimble, six Tomahawks from No. 3 Squadron took off on a 'rhubarb' (mission) over the Martuba area and became involved in a nasty dogfight with seven Junkers 87s which were covered by a flight of Me-109s. The 109s caught the squadron in a vice-like grip, attacking simultaneously from six o'clock and three o'clock, allowing little room for evasive action. The squadron claimed one Junkers, but Nicky was saddened to learn his friend Don Knight was shot down and killed and another friend Derik Scott was taken prisoner.

Every night, at 11.00 p.m., the Afrika Korp would broadcast the German news in English. It was always heralded by a rendition of 'Lili Marlene' and was very much propaganda material. Two days after this episode the squadron were tuned into the broadcast and were amused to hear how successful the Luftwaffe had been that day, shooting down five Tomahawks from No. 3 Squadron.

Alan Rawlinson laughed and said, 'We'd better go out and do a census.' The squadron had lost no planes that day.

In fact, it had been a good day. A very cheerful Tommy Trimble turned up out of the desert with an interesting story; one that Nicky took some note of as Trimble's situation could have related to any of them.

Trimble had been shot down in flames and suffered extensive burns to his face and hands. He was able to escape from his aircraft without being captured and, after wandering for a while, was helped by a Bedouin who fed him and tended his wounds with native herbs. At night, he was placed on one side of the chief's tent to sleep, while the chief's unattractive wife was positioned on the other side. To Trimble's amusement, the chieftain would lie in the middle with a cocked rifle at the ready. However, Trimble insisted, even without this deterrent, in his injured condition, and considering the wife's generally un-hygienic state, he wasn't the least bit tempted to make an advance. Trimble had been with the No. 3 Squadron as one of the originals and had seen a lot for his 20 years. He had done well and was duly posted home to Australia.

In general, Nicky was often puzzled and amazed at how depersonalised air combat was. He never really felt he was killing somebody; it was easy to convince himself that he was hitting a plane—no people involved. However, this perception was challenged almost daily as friends from the squadron—close colleagues Nicky had trained and bonded with, some during pre-war days—were either killed or taken prisoner. This necessary, although subconscious, protective deception was continually reinforced as, in the evening following a loss, the men did not allow themselves the luxury of grieving publicly.

They rarely dwelt on an incident, generally uttering a respectful comment followed by a determination to get on with the job. However, the loss was always felt, but was held deep down to be later retrieved when acceptance was possible. Along with this sadness, the men also registered a quiet gratefulness that they weren't themselves added to the statistics. Trying to depersonalise combat did not work very well in reverse.

FIVE
Enter the Kittyhawks

On 17 December, the No. 3 Squadron collected its new Kittyhawks. The conversion was fairly smooth as the Curtiss P40 Kittyhawk was a development of the basic Tomahawk design with certain changes and refinements. It boasted a new, powerful Allison engine, and all of the six .50 calibre machine-guns were in the wings, which presented a minor concern to Nicky. During test flights over the next few days, without the cordite stimulating his nostrils and the sound of the cockpit guns resounding in his ears, the quietness evoked an unsettling sensation that the battle might be somewhat remote. He had to override the impression that he was enjoying himself on an interesting and exotic flight.

Initially, he wasn't as impressed with the Kittyhawk's aerobatics as he had been with the Tomahawk. However, when he climbed to the rated altitude in combat—about 18 000 feet— with its excellent stability and with the supercharger working, Nicky gradually gained full confidence that the plane would be a reliable partner.

By now, in the troubled air, Nicky was feeling confident in his ability to fly and in his performance as a fighter pilot. He had developed a distinctive attacking style and maintained a constant eye for improving and sharpening his battle tactic skills. On the ground, under Rawlinson's and Jeffrey's leadership example, he was also maturing, impressing others as a strong team member who took his responsibilities seriously.

Others' confidence in Nicky was reinforced over the next few days as he took part in some reconnaissance missions plus some shadow shooting sessions which allowed him to test the plane to his satisfaction. Shadow shooting was a method of refining aerial gunnery techniques and involved the honing of deflection shooting skills by a pilot firing at another aircraft's shadow as it sped along over the desert. It was a technique developed by Nicky's Australian friend, Clive 'Killer' Caldwell, when he was flying with No. 250 Squadron RAF. (The two Australian Squadrons, No. 3 and No. 450 RAAF, and No. 112 and No. 250 Squadrons RAF formed the RAF's 239 Wing of the Desert Air Force and would often train, fight and socialise together.)

'Killer' Caldwell achieved wide fame when, in early December, he became the first fighter in the world to shoot down five enemy planes in one combat, two of them actually with one burst—all Stukas. By 20 December, his tally was 17 enemy aircraft and he became, deservedly, the Desert Air Force's leading ace. Curiously enough, he earned the sobriquet 'Killer' not because of his unbeaten record in air combat, but because of his love of diving low at speed to strafe enemy troops, airfields and transport.

At this stage he was commander of No. 112 Squadron and had formed a strong friendship with Nicky, cemented at parties such as Pete Jeffrey's and Al Rawlinson's farewell on the night of 23 December. These two admired leaders were going to be sorely missed by the squadron as they were both heading back to Australia and would establish the RAAF's first operational training unit at Mildura in Victoria.

The new command was taken over by a regular RAAF officer, Squadron Leader 'Dixie' Chapman, Nicky's former commander from No. 23 Squadron in Brisbane. Chapman was the most experienced pilot in terms of flying hours but he was inexperienced in combat, coming as he did straight from Australia. This sat a little uneasy with most of the squadron, as they felt that a competent leader should know more about what is involved in aerial combat, and experience this by flying for a time at No. 2 before leading the squadron into combat. Time would tell.

A boisterous New Year's Eve party heralded the end of 1941. With large supplies of grog and food being brought from Benghazi and NAAFI stores, the often riotous celebrations continued late into the night. The new year was welcomed with a blast of weapons of all types, fired into the black desert sky.

War waits for no one. The seedy revellers opened their eyes to the first sunrise of 1942. Nicky, a non-drinker when flying and one who was comparably fresh following the previous night's shenanigans, realised he was committed to a patrol that day. (Any pilot scheduled for operations the next day was not supposed to drink alcohol the previous evening—some complied, but not all.)

At this stage, No. 3 Squadron had moved forward to their furthest position west and was based at Antelat. They also had the use of another airstrip nearby at Msus. The army was deployed a little further forward at Agedabia where the front-line battle, as furious as it was, had stalled into something of a deadlock. Desperate for time, Rommel was being reinforced with supplies from Italy and Germany. This period coincided with the Luftwaffe developing many crack squadrons while the Italian's Regia Aeronautica were blooding a fine new plane—a Macchi model MC202 with a Daimler-Benz engine. At the same time, the Allies were experiencing difficulty coping with their extended supply line from the Nile delta and further afield.

The scene was set for a determined stand-off by Rommel as

he geared for a strong reversal and a second big effort to drive the Allies from Africa.

During breakfast on New Year's Day, Nicky and the squadron were surprised as they were treated to a rare early morning drenching, the rain quickly being absorbed into the parched sands. The desert here was gravelly with little topsoil to give purchase to the sparse vegetation, which was mainly patches of dense camelthorn. Rocky outcrops were interspersed with windswept sandy ridges and lonely deep wadis that wandered into the sea. Dotting the landscape was one small deserted Arabic mosque and occasionally a stone cairn to some ancient prophet inscribed with Arabic writing.

The refreshing rain quickly gave way to stickiness as the drying sun reminded the fliers where they were. Before long, the burning rays would make the aircraft white hot and almost untouchable—the temperature could exceed 51°C.

The first patrol was over the Agedabia area and was fairly uneventful, although they reported clearly on the enemy positions and activity below. Later in the day, Nicky was flying again with the full squadron of 12 planes, led by 'Dixie' Chapman.

Official policy considered one meaningful mission a day for one man was adequate. However, as Rommel increased his pressure this luxury was continually denied them as their own resources were tight. At this stage, the squadron had only 29 pilots on strength, having lost 21 the previous year, either killed, taken prisoner or missing, and were down to 19 serviceable aircraft, having lost seven in December alone.

As the squadrons were approaching Agedabia, 13 Ju87s were sighted about to bomb Allied troops in this area. They were escorted by ten Me-109s from JG27 and were, as before, as Nicky later found out, led by Erhard Braune.

Once again, there was turmoil in the sky as the planes closed, broke, then twisted out of formation. Much of this was due to the constant requirement for each pilot to check and recheck rear quarters, above and below, from an enemy attack. Immediately, fighters tangled like wildcats, rolling, spiralling and looping.

In an effort to lure the squadron away from the bombers, some of the Me-109s climbed into the cloud and were hotly pursued by 'Tiny' Cameron. On breaking above the cover, he frantically radioed that he could see them and called for help. Bobby Gibbes shot up to join him and found himself outnumbered. He quickly dived below the cloud right into the path of nine enemy aircraft coming at him in line abreast. There was no time to do anything other than to fly head into the lot, guns firing madly, then to feverishly climb into the filmy haze above.

Meanwhile, as the fighters were engaged overhead, the Ju87s had formed into a defensive circle about 1000 feet below the cloud. As Nicky watched, the bombers, with classical Teutonic precision, slipped out of this circle, joined up as pairs, then moved out in a V formation. Nicky pushed the control stick forward and dove after the huddling Stukas, heading directly for the leader of the last pair. Around him, other Kittyhawks were also now diving and attacking the disciplined formation, taking great care to evade the dangerous fire blasted back at them by the rear gunners in some Stukas. The Stukas were only fitted with one gun, but it was a powerful and deadly 7.92 mm machine-gun. Nicky noted that a number of the dive-bombers were not carrying a rear gunner.

Nicky increased the 'revs', steadily closing the distance on the last pair, then at about 250 metres he opened fire. Even though the noise was suppressed, unlike his old Tomahawk, he felt his own plane shudder a little in reaction as he opened up a withering barrage. He poured a hail of incendiary and explosive shells at the machine in front, watching them tear into the tail and streak along the fuselage. A split second later, flames streamed out, then spread to the motor. The pilot and gunner were not seen to bail out and Nicky watched it dive towards the desert, trailing smoke. Then, as the wind fanned the flames, the Stuka burst onto the desert floor like a giant sliver of burning steel.

Nicky pulled his plane into a really tight, steep turn and, with his confidence brimming, went searching for more of the enemy. Nicky's evasion tactics in combat included flying under maximum G-force, almost to the point of blackout; both plane and pilot were functioning under high stress levels, especially when flying in tight, while climbing and during diving turns. It was important for pilots to know their 'recovery rate', which in Nicky's case was quite short. He really was very fit and well.

By now Nicky was relishing his reliable Kittyhawk. He found in combat that it was extremely manoeuvrable at speed and responded to his will. Under G-force, while combat flying with maximum revs and fuel mixture, it was satisfyingly stable. To Nicky, it felt 'chunky'.

By now, the Stukas had reformed into a ring closer to the ground. Nicky zoomed back into the very active circle where other Kittyhawks were creating more havoc. The symphony of singing Allison engines playing against the characteristic whining roar of the Ju87s filled the sky as Nicky saw several wounded Stukas spiral to the earth. A couple of times, a Stuka would momentarily sweep across Nicky's sights and he would unleash a burst.

Down below on the battlefield, he knew the Allied soldiers would be cheering. The hated Stukas had a history of shrieking out of the sky in a terrifying dive, then dropping 908-kilogram bombs that had 'screamers' attached to them for effect. They had been dubbed the 'Shrieking Vultures' because, with their under-carriage extending like grasping claws from their 'gull' wings, they looked for all the world like vicious birds of prey.

Nicky saw his chance as he pulled up under one in a savage, climbing turn, then rolled up behind him. He felt he wouldn't be able to get the pilot, who was protected by a heavy plate behind his seat, so he aimed under the fuselage. The bullets crashed along the metal which connects the wing to the fuselage then chewed forwards to the motor. The Stuka wobbled as the bullets hit home, then the stricken plane suddenly rolled onto its back, flames now racing to the rear along the fuselage and pouring smoke from the tail. During this time, the battle had been fought closer to the ground, and at 900 feet the Stuka nosed towards the desert floor with its engine now pouring a plume of black smoke.

Nicky had fired his last bullet and suddenly felt quite vulnerable. He quickly climbed away, not waiting to witness the enemy complete its death dive. As he retreated over the battle-field, he counted five fires burning on the ground below. However, before he could escape the scene, two 109s spotted him. Urgently, he headed out to sea and even though the 109s chased him for a while, he outdistanced them as he quickly gained speed in a steep dive to ground level, then eventually flew back to base. It had been a long, muddling scrap, and again Nicky was completely exhausted.

When these mêlées were over, such was the amount of energy expended that Nicky rarely had the need for rocking to go to sleep.

In the meantime, after 'Tiny' Cameron had dived back down through the cloud from chasing the Me-109s early in the foray he had been unable to relocate the squadron. He was aware that the enemy aerodrome was based at Agedabia so he flew there, then circled in light cloud above the drome to greet the returning planes. As they landed, he attacked one Me-109 with its flaps and wheels down. It crashed in flames and some others were damaged also. He then flew in cloud to the enemy satellite drome nearby and claimed a further two Ju87s as 'probably destroyed'.

Overall, it had been a good start to the New Year for the squadron as they claimed five enemy aircraft destroyed, two 'probables' and four damaged. The only loss, and the first

Kittyhawk from the squadron to be shot down, was 'Dixie' Chapman, who reported in from the desert some time later.

Nicky was feeling pleased and confident with himself now as he felt he could effectively 'mix it' with the best of the enemy pilots. In fact, he was aware that his tenacity was gaining him a reputation with some for bordering on overconfident.

To Nicky, this was just not the case. He had accumulated enough experience to consider that he had to take the fight to the enemy. He had decided to be deliberately aggressive, but controlled. At night, he and a few of his colleagues would regularly discuss tactics in his tent, highlighting the need for this change. They would violently flail their arms in all directions as they replayed battle scenes, often poking their fingers through the tent ceiling.

Every night, he would also put his thoughts on paper to Dot. Before 'lights-out', he would bring Dot up to date on what was happening—within the limitations of the censor, of course. As well, Dot would write to him daily and volubly, bringing him news of his family, his twin brother Jack and his ailing mother. Dot visited her regularly, even more than Jack had, and gave her Nicky's news.

Dot continued to live at home with her parents in Malvern. On most weekends, she joined other helpers at the Albert Park headquarters of Power House, which provided assistance and friendship to Allied personnel.

Because of the uncertainties in the mailing system, Nicky and Dot both received their mail irregularly, and often in batches. Their style of communication allowed them to be together in a way, and they were never far from each others' thoughts.

Nicky was bonding well with his ground crew at this stage. He spent as much time socially with his personal armourer, Felix Sainsbury, his engineer, 'Kaiser' Wehrman, and his airframe mechanic, Ray Dunning, as he did with the aircrew.

He was given early lessons in the importance of teamwork as he acknowledged the significance of these men. Along with the radio operator, he considered their enthusiasm and efficiency to be absolutely critical to the overall success of any mission.

Nicky took part in several missions over the next week—mainly bomber escorts, patrols and sweeps over the Agedabia area—but did not personally encounter any enemy aircraft. He was having a rest day on 8 January when the squadron destroyed seven enemy planes over Agedabia. On the following day, while he was on escort duty with seven Maryland bombers over Marsa el Brega, a lone Me-109 surprised the squadron and shot down two Kittyhawks. One was flown by his friend Geoff Chinchen, who managed to crash-land at Msus and survive. The other was flown by Ron Simes, who was killed after bringing his score to six the previous day.

This possibility of being shot down or killed at any time concerned most pilots, as did the overall fear of warfare. Earlier, Nicky knew he would experience fear, possibly even abject fear—any reasonable person could expect that. The fact was, he just wasn't sure how deep his fears were or how he would react to a given situation. After discussing it with other pilots, he realised it was definitely a normal part of combat, and this helped to reinforce his long-term conviction and faith in himself that he would be able to manage it. However, until he had actually been tested, worry about the unknown and how he would handle it made him anxious and uncomfortable. Thankfully, after the first few combats he gained enough confidence to satisfy himself that he could manage it, and this made subsequent combats easier.

By early January in 1942, Nicky was becoming fairly at ease with the knowledge of fear, and also with his experience of coping with it, and even though he tried not to show his anxiety (and he wasn't always sure he succeeded in this) he was beginning to realise it was probably healthy to possess a certain amount of fear; rational fear, after all, is most likely the remnants of a necessary primitive protective mechanism.

At first, he was often mesmerised by people who showed no fear. However, he learned to be critical of such individuals as he could see they possessed a tendency towards a reckless attitude to life, with the potential to unnecessarily endanger themselves as well as the rest of the squadron. In effect, he considered they lacked a sensitivity that was necessary for war, and for survival. Split-second reactions, so important in combat, were aided by this sensitivity born of fear.

Nicky was intuitively developing a philosophy of controlled aggression and was determined to take risks in combat only if he had balanced out the known factors and if he considered he was mentally adjusted to control them.

Nonetheless, he did appreciate that this 'fearless' style did wondrous things for morale and, in a way, encouraged leadership qualities in others. However, he also considered this 'fearlessness' could be dangerous when allowed to dominate.

On another level, he pondered that a man who feared nothing probably loved nothing. What could give such a man joy in life?

His next patrol, on 11 January, would test his philosophies to the limit.

SIX

Senussi Adventure

Squadron Leader 'Buck' Buchanan, Commander of the RAF's Blenheim Bombers No. 14 Squadron was a man who appeared to feel no fear. He sported a dark Errol Flynn-type moustache, impressing Nicky that he could be as derring-do as any of the characters ever portrayed by Flynn. On the morning of 11 January, he organised for his squadron to carry a passenger of similar ilk to himself. Her name was Eve Curie, a war correspondent with Time-Post Publications. Curie, daughter of the famed Madam Marie Curie, possessed an audaciousness and degree of dash to match Buchanan's and she was to fly in his plane. Earlier, she had applied considerable pressure on RAF Headquarters and had prevailed on them to allow her to witness and experience a front-line bombing mission. With only 15 minutes warning, Buchanan called representatives of No. 3 and No. 112 Squadrons for a briefing of his intentions to bomb one of Rommel's advance bases, El Agheila, near Agedabia. During the course of the briefing, he meticulously stressed his desire for everybody to adhere to his plans for the raid and advised the gathering, 'I always come back.'

Just before lunch, Nicky roared off as part of a formation of 20 Kittyhawks from No. 3 and No. 112 squadrons flying escort for Buchanan's six Blenheim Bombers. As they approached El Agheila from over the ocean in preparation for their planned run south over the target, Nicky noticed Agedabia down below.

From the air, Agedabia presented as a group of little white buildings, surrounded by nothing but desert sands with the blue Mediterranean in the distance. Not a lot of ground action appeared to be evident, although a great deal of weaponry blasted up at them, pockmarking the sky.

Then Bobby Gibbes reported one, then two Me-109s diving at their formation from out of the sun. The Messerchmitts attacked the top cover of fighters who briskly evaded the assault, then gave chase.

In the meantime, Buchanan, in the lead Blenheim, had his bombs 'hang-up' at the release point over the target. Instead of gaining speed in a shallow dive and haring down to the desert and getting away, contrary to his original plan, he turned 180 degrees and set on to the target course again. The other bombers continued through, released their load, then headed back towards base on their scheduled flight path.

Meanwhile, the escort formation, still orbiting above, was forced to wait and protect Buchanan for his second and un-programmed bomb run. Nicky circled, waiting, then at 13 000 feet over El Agheila, time ran out as the sky erupted with planes. Messerschmitts from Erhard Braune's JG27 and Macchi 200s, 202s and Fiat G50s from the Italian Air force thundered out of the blue and caught the Allied squadrons from nine o'clock level and twelve o'clock high above.

By now, all Allied pilots were using an aggressive attitude in defence, not the defensive circle formation of 1941. Nicky eagerly joined the other Kittyhawks as they reeled off to en-counter the attacking planes. Once again, the sky was a blur of motion, sound and split-second action.

With his left hand, Nicky switched his fuel mixture to full rich, which ensured maximum power during combat. (Normally he would cruise on a mixture designed to conserve fuel.) His left hand would never leave the throttle or the adjacent lever which controlled the fuel mixture. His right hand was totally free to fly the plane and to fire the guns, the trigger positioned underneath his thumb on the top of the joystick. He climbed quickly towards the sun, searching for an advantage, levelled at 14 500 feet, then focused below on one of two Fiat G50s which he had seen earlier and were climbing after him.

Nicky could feel the adrenalin rush as he applied absolute concentration to aligning the nearest one through the centre of his ring sight. As the plane zoomed upwards, it presented him with a clear frontal target. Nicky pressed the trigger.

He poured a few seconds' burst into the left quarter of the G50 as it flew directly across his fire. The rounds slammed into the nose and raced along the cockpit where the glass exploded. The plane shuddered and jerked violently upward and to the right, forcing it to flick into a roll. Thick white smoke streamed from the wing root and the plane fell off into a downward spin. Briefly, Nicky saw the pilot whisked from the shattered cockpit, pull to a jerk as his parachute opened, then watched it gently lower him away from the seething action.

By now, the battle had disintegrated into a tremendous free-for-all. Nicky swung his Kittyhawk around, head and eyes swivelling, searching for the Blenheims and the rest of the squadron. Suddenly, from his peripheral vision, he noticed a Kittyhawk quickly losing speed in a steady dive. It was one of his colleagues from No. 3 Squadron, as denoted by the squadron's letters 'CV-E'. The plane was being hotly pursued by an Me-109, which was lining up to score a certain conquest. Nicky tried to get an intercepting shot at the 109, but he was too far away. He was on maximum 'revs' in an attempt to hook on behind, but by the time he had reached the scene, the Kittyhawk had crash-landed near a beach at Marsa el Brega. Nicky was a little perplexed as he hadn't seen the German fire at the Kittyhawk pilot or witness him take evasive action; he simply appeared to crash-land—engine failure maybe?

The Me-109, in the meantime, was considering the Kittyhawk to be his 'kill'. Nicky later found out that the plane was flown by Oberleutnant Hugo Schneider, a nine-victory ace from 1/JG27 who had claimed victories on the day when Dave Rutter, Nicky's friend from Power House, was killed the previous December. Schneider circled the downed plane once, then waggled his wings in a self-laudatory victory salute.

Angered, Nicky pulled back on his throttle then gave chase to the demonstrative German. He quickly drew in from behind, arcing his plane up slowly in a climb, then rolled steadily as the distance narrowed between his fighter and the enemy plane. At about 250 metres, Nicky poured bullets into the wing, some hitting the fuselage. Abruptly, a splash of flame burst through the wing, spread wildly, and in a few seconds the Me-109 seemed to turn into a flame thrower. Brilliant fire streamed into the wind from the wing and along the fuselage. The plane twisted wildly, then dived towards the desert, crashing in a trail of smoke. There was no chance for Schneider to escape.

Earlier, Nicky had noticed two Me-109s hovering nearby, but now the air appeared clear, so he flew back to the beach at Brega where the Kittyhawk had gone down. By now, the pilot had climbed out of his crashed plane and was standing by it. Nicky recognised him as Bobby Jones by his white gloves. (Some pilots wore lightweight gloves under the heavy leather gloves to keep their hands cool, but most were dark-coloured.) Because they were many kilometres behind enemy lines, and Jones would surely be taken prisoner, Nicky decided to attempt a rescue landing. The terrain nearby seemed suitable.

Nicky lined up his intended landing strip, reduced power, then lowered his undercarriage. He was in the process of lowering his wing flaps to begin his landing glide when he noticed Jones, next to his plane, pointing to about ten o'clock above. Nicky turned in his seat and cursed his vulnerability. There was a 109 coming in on him very fast, all guns blazing, possibly one of the two he had noticed earlier. Luckily for Nicky, the pilot must have been inexperienced as he couldn't press his advantage. With a resounding roar, he overshot Nicky and desperately attempted to climb away, now realising his own precariousness. In the same instant, Nicky reacted. He pulled the flaps and wheels up, pushed on absolutely full throttle, wrenched back on the stick and braced himself. The powerful motor discharged a trail of blue smoke, lifted the Kittyhawk upwards and thrust it forward.

The violent surge quickly closed the gap on the 109 now losing its speed in a climb. Within seconds, the German plane filled his sights. Without hesitating, Nicky fired the six .50 guns, shattering the Messerschmitt's tail and damaging the fuselage. Immediately, smoke poured out through the wing mounting. Within seconds, flames, fanned by the slipstream, seared backwards, emitting a bright red glow inside the now curling black smoke.

The crippled plane fought to stay aloft for some time, but crashed some distance away, unseen by Nicky. In fact, Nicky's attention had been diverted as he caught sight of a second Me-109 which was now directly overhead and climbing into the sun.

As Nicky found out later, this plane was flown by Oberfeldwebel Otto Schulz, an ace from II/JG27. Schulz already had nine victories from the Battle of Britain and had fought in Russia. Even though Nicky had picked up considerable speed since his abortive landing attempt, he was still flying relatively slowly, compared to Schulz. Nicky raised the nose and gained some distance, then fired a brief burst at the Messerschmitt's underbelly. His gaze followed the tracers then bullet holes as they penetrated the metal skin, but there was no obvious immediate reaction.

Schulz then wheeled his plane around hard. He possessed a speed and height advantage, and positioned himself perfectly for a quarter attack on Nicky's plane. He fired and Nicky felt the bullets rattle along the Kittyhawk's fuselage—kathump, kathump! Nicky didn't think he had been hit in the engine, but the plane suddenly lost power. Maybe the engine wasn't responding after the effort of coping with the prolonged intense demands for full power. He lost altitude. Then nothing responded. He was still under 1000 feet and there was no time to lower his wheels or turn the flaps down. (Fighter planes have trimming flaps which help to adjust the plane to a horizontal position if it goes into a dive.) They were activated by a switch and controlled both ailerons as well as elevators, but nothing worked. Nicky was going to have to belly-land. In preparation, he flicked the master switch off, turned the ignition off, checked the tightness of the harness, then braced himself.

The fighter landed with the sound of crumpling metal. A parching cloud of dust swirled around the plane as it continued to career for some distance, grinding the metal underbelly into the sandy shale. Nicky was concerned that the plane might cartwheel or even burst into flames. He desperately wanted to get out. For what seemed an eternity, the plane skidded and rocked out of control, screeching incessantly as the metal ripped a large gash in the earth. Finally, it slithered and grated against an incline to a dead halt.

Mercifully, it didn't burst into flames. Nicky worried that the hatch might have jammed on impact, a common occurrence, but it slid back cleanly. He crawled out, trying numbly to assess his situation, when he noticed the Me-109 circling, as if it might land. It didn't, then Nicky realised it was going to blow up his Kittyhawk. As the 109 came round in a circuit and lined up for a strafing run, Nicky reasoned he wasn't far enough away to be safe if it did blow up. He decided to make it tough for the pilot and unsettle his aim by running directly at the Messerschmitt as it zoomed in low towards him and the Kittyhawk.

Nicky sprinted towards the attacking Me-109. He was back on the athletic field again, but this time he was sprinting for his life. He lifted his knees and hands high, trying to gain purchase in the sand, his legs working like pistons, willing himself forward. The plane started firing. Nicky sidestepped as he watched the 20 mm shells spitting at him, firing beautifully through the nose of the 109.

The bullets smashed into the ground just ahead and to the left of him, crashing and shattering nearby rocks. The explosion caused splinters of rock to ricochet into his legs. He collapsed and dropped to the ground as a searing pain surged through his lower limbs.

The cannon fire continued to zip through the sand, spurting dust skyward and pockmarking the earth, tracing a lethal path to the wrecked Kittyhawk. An instant later, the plane was enveloped in flames and then exploded with a convulsive detonation that rocked the air. The pilot completed a quick circuit to supervise his handywork, while Nicky waited to see what he would do. The blast had thrown him into a dense clump of camelthorn and he lay there motionless, forgetting to breathe, wondering whether the pilot would try for a second run at him. To his relief, he flew off, albeit rather unsteadily, as his left wing was drooping. Nicky hoped this had been caused by his own fire. In any case, Nicky assumed the German only intended on making sure the Kittyhawk wouldn't fly again.

For long moments, Nicky lay still and contemplated his situation. It had all happened so fast and he was disoriented. In the space of a few moments, he had shot down three enemy planes and had been downed himself; he had crash-landed, been strafed, then skittled, and he was still alive. Wonder of wonders. He began to feel some elation even over the severe pain of his wounded legs.

As he was bleeding profusely, his first task was to arrest the haemorrhaging, then to excise the rock splinters from where they had pierced his shins. Then he began to consider his next step. He was behind enemy lines, wounded and without food and water. The molten sun gloated over him. The endless desert wore the blank look of death. What next?

After some moments, Nicky suddenly realised he was not alone. About six Arabs had materialised out of the arid surrounds and were observing him from a distance. They seemed friendly, and two came forward. They noticed his damaged legs and by now Nicky realised he also had some shrapnel in his left elbow. Communicating with them through a rudimentary sign language, some of the Arabs left and came back with some dressings. They looked to be stolen German dressings. 'Justice,' Nicky thought. They carefully applied some local herbs and medicines to the wounds, dressed them, then assisted him to walk to their tent, which was some distance away towards the sea.

During the walk, they were forced to hide in a wadi as a German patrol was moving through the area, possibly investigating Nicky's crashed plane.

Nicky was at least 30 kilometres behind enemy lines and, from the air, he knew there was a great deal of enemy activity in this area. He had little hope of regaining his squadron without the help of the Arabs. On top of these concerns was the fact that in the Sahara a person sweats about two gallons of water a day—four if walking. Without water, after two days he would not be able to stand. His core body temperature would have risen so that his central nervous system could no longer control heart rate or breathing; he would drift into a coma and death would quickly follow.

His rescuers offered him some camel milk, which he disliked, but he was so thirsty he drank it anyway, appearing most grateful. At the Arab encampment, a typical group of desert tents complete with family members, goats, camels and other assorted animals, an Arab chieftain emerged and placed Nicky into one of the drops of a large tent.

This Arab could speak some basic Italian, as could Nicky. He learned the people who he was with were the Senussi, a peaceful and almost courtly tribe of Arabs. They had a great hatred for the Italians as in the early days of their occupation, to instil fear into them, the Italians had taken some elders of the tribe and dropped them from an aircraft at about 3000 feet.

Nicky produced his 'goolie chit' to prove his heritage and loyalties. The Arabs understood it and appeared genuinely pleased, laughing among themselves. They redressed his wound, then fed him. That night, Nicky slept in a large tent, a camel one side, and an extended Arab family the other—shades of Tommy Trimble. Next day, Nicky rested while scouts carried out a reconnaissance of the area and planned his evacuation.

Early the following morning, Nicky was dressed in white Arab robes and a burnous—a headpiece—and mounted on a camel. He was made up to appear as a family member, one of seven, complete with three children. If apprehended, the story was that they were in transit to an oasis to the south.

Even though Nicky's wounds were still giving him some pain, after some time he got used to the rhythm and became rather comfortable atop his noble beast. A camel moves in three planes, up and down, side to side and forwards, much like a ship at sea. Nicky's camel was guided by one of the Arabs, walking in front. Twice a day, they would stop to milk, then feast on some nourishing dates.

The front-line was fluid at this stage, as evidenced by continual cannon fire from all horizons. This created in Nicky a consistently high level of anxiety and, as the journey continued eastward over the next three-and-a-half days, the fear was often raised to a critical level as the area was heavily patrolled by German and Italian scout cars.

Once the 'family' was apprehended by an Italian patrol car, and twice by German scouts. The Arabs handled them all with assertive courteousness, although during one incident there was some real drama, producing a few moments of acute nervousness for Nicky. One German officer wanted them to dismount for a weapons search. The Arab luckily convinced him otherwise, and the entourage continued on their way.

At night, they would sleep in the open, the black crystalline sky brilliant with stars. The hard bed made for fitful sleeps, but the discomfort was offset by the sight of the moon creeping across the sky, suffusing the rugged desert landscape with an ethereal light. To Nicky, there was some security watching the familiar Orion the Hunter wheeling above him, still aiming at infinity.

During this time Nicky became very conscious that by now he would have been posted as 'missing'. His deepest thoughts were with Dot and his family. He believed no one had seen him shot down, and the battle was such that, to the observer, he might not have survived it. Surely there was no worse category than 'missing'? Even 'missing believed dead' would probably be easier for relatives to cope with. He was intensely frustrated and well aware of the emotional impact the message would have on those close to him at home.

During his journey, Nicky observed Rommel's heavy buildup of Axis troops, noting great numbers of enemy tanks, personnel carriers, guns and infantry groups. He was also interested to notice the amount and diversity of wildlife springing from the supposedly 'dead' desert. He spotted lizards, birds, small animals and even a wild pig foraging in rubbish left by the armies. Most times, however, he gazed across a seemingly lifeless shimmering, mirage-infested desert.

Finally, on the fourth day, while traversing no-man's-land,

the 'family' were questioned by a British scout car, mounted with a machine-gun and manned by four British soldiers.

At first, Nicky was slow to reveal himself. It could be a trick—Germans dressed up as Brits. He realised this was probably not the case after he heard their accents. However, the Brits were suspicious of him, looking as he did like an Aryan who was trying to speak educated English, brushed with an Australian twang. Eventually, with some relief, he convinced them of his identity then, with the camels at the trot for 20 minutes, the scout car escorted the group to advance British Intelligence Headquarters.

Here, lengthy interrogations by Army Intelligence officers thoroughly debriefed Nicky and his escorts. Combined, they were able to pass over extremely valuable information concerning the enemy buildup, their positions and strength.

In fact, even though the British Intelligence were aware of the increase in enemy activities, they were surprised at the rate their new information revealed it was happening.

When Nicky asked his Arab saviours what reward they would like, all they requested was some tinned fish.

'Is that all you need?' he asked through an interpreter. 'Surely I can do more to repay your kindness. I can never fully repay you as I would never have made it back, but I must be able to show my gratitude in a more tangible way.'

'Thank you, but we have all we need,' came the soft reply. 'We do not like the Italians.'

Nicky arranged for the fish and also appropriated some blankets for the children, as he noticed they appeared cold at night. Nicky questioned again whether these gifts were adequate, but indeed that's all they wanted. There was much laughter and goodwill all round. Nicky farewelled his friends, savouring the lesson he'd received in humility. It would not be the first time he would experience kindness in this war.

Feeling huge gratitude, he watched them ride off. Just before they disappeared over a little ridge, they turned and waved, then merged into the sun-scoured reaches of the desert.

Some time later, Nicky was returned by a staff car to his squadron, some 70 kilometres distant. Here he was immediately admitted to sick bay, which was a tent erected beside the medical wagon. Nicky was placed in an annex and examined by the squadron medical officer, Tim Stone. The doctor considered Nicky would need specialised treatment, so he arranged for him to be admitted to the Scottish General Hospital in Cairo.

While waiting for his transport, Nicky, with his sheikh's persona and unique story, became something of a celebrity and was welcomed back by his friends. He was particularly touched at the concern displayed, not only by the pilots, but by his ground crew, including the armourer, engineer and airframes man, who all asked pertinent questions dealing with their personal areas of expertise.

'Great to see you Nicky. Hope my guns didn't let you down,' enthused Felix Sainsbury.

'Nope, they fired beautifully,' replied Nicky, then added to 'Kaiser' Wehrman, his mechanic, 'Sorry about wrecking another motor on you, Kaiser. Put it on my tab.' Nicky had already burnt out several other motors.

'Come to think of it,' he quipped to Ray Dunning, his airframe mechanic, 'you'll need a bit more than glue and wire to repair this last one. I'll see what I can do to the next one. Put it on my bill also.'

The repartee between them reinforced the feeling to Nicky that these men—in fact, the whole squadron—were as brothers. They cared for each other and had bonded out of mutual respect, united for a common cause. Ranks weren't that important—respect was so much more a matter of what you were than who you were.

As a postscript, Buchanan and Eve Curie got back safely and in good order.

SEVEN

Cairo

Nicky welcomed the idea of a break in Cairo. His friend Geoff Chinchen was recovering there from wounds collected after his crash-landing, and he looked forward to joining him.

To get there, the RAF Transport squadron had acquired along the way a German Junkers Ju52, a three-engined transport plane, and Nicky was informed by the commanding officer, 'I have some brass visiting here and they have to return to Heliopolis [Cairo Airport]. If you can fly this thing, you can have it. Be ready at 6.00 a.m. tomorrow.'

Nicky agreed. He had never flown a three-engined plane before, but didn't consider it would be that difficult. Next morning, to his surprise, there was a full complement of about 20 passengers on board, including a couple of English wing commanders. Nicky climbed into the cockpit and another pilot sat down next to him.

'You my No. 2?' Nicky asked.

'Yes, sir.'

'Can you read German?'

'A little, sir.'

'Better get these engines going, then.' Nicky was happy with the motor in front, but was a bit doubtful about the ones on each wing.

'They don't normally trust me with anything more than one engine,' he grinned to the co-pilot.

With some luck, they managed to coax all the motors into life. Fortunately, Antelat possessed a long airstrip, and it allowed them to get airborne without too much trouble, therefore saving Nicky from experimenting with the flaps. (Flaps are mainly used for short take-offs, or to act as a brake to land.) He was also spared the trouble of retracting the wheels, as they were fixed.

After a few minutes, the three BMW motors settled into a steady rhythmical hum. Soon Nicky could hear the passengers singing in the cabin. It was a comfortable trip, and after an hour or so Cairo came into view. Preparing to land at Heliopolis, Nicky pulled the throttles back, cutting his speed, then shakily touched the wheels onto the strip. To his dismay, he realised the plane was going far too fast; it was never going to stop in time. He gunned the motors and the plane lifted, skimming a hangar. The acting flight engineer commented dryly, 'We'd better go around again, sir.'

Nicky circled, then brought the Junkers on line again, a little slower this time. The wheels touched down, kicking up dust, but once again, he realised there was no way he was going to stop in time. He fired the motors for the second time and the plane roared upwards.

He glanced briefly behind him into the fuselage, and was met with 20 pairs of staring white eyes peering back at him, transfixed. One of the wing commanders, quite disturbed, came up front and asked, 'Is your name Barr?'

'Yes, sir.'

'How many hours have you got on this plane?'

Nicky checked his watch. 'About an hour and 20 minutes, sir.' Nicky barely suppressed a smile.

The wing commander went pale. 'Do you realise you are endangering the lives of His Majesty's officers and servants?'

'Not purposefully, sir. The last thing I want to do is endanger my own.'

Nicky banked and wheeled for a third attempt. This time, he cut the speed way back, far more than he was used to—which was normally 110 mph when landing fighter planes laden with ammunition and fuel.

The wind changed, causing him to drift suddenly, narrowly missing one of the hangars. He corrected his flight, then finally placed her onto the ground, fighting for control as the renegade Junkers rolled to a halt not far from the control tower. Shakily, his passengers crawled out, with Nicky tactfully following at a distance. However, the wing commander wasn't going to leave it there.

'Stop where you are Barr. I'm placing you under arrest.'

Next moment, Nicky was surrounded by several MP's.

Nicky was a little bemused. The wing commander was a charming Englishman who was playing the game by the book. In effect, he did have some justification at being upset, as Nicky's lack of skill with the plane had endangered them all. However, Nicky explained why he was coming to Cairo, and that he had been the only available pilot.

'Well, you'd better get yourself to hospital,' the wing commander ordered. 'Nevertheless, I'm going to inform your squadron commander to confine you to barracks for 30 days.'

Nicky smiled. 'Certainly, sir.' He realised the order would have no meaning back at the squadron—the 'barracks' were so huge.

Nicky continued to the Scottish General Hospital where he underwent two minor operations and a course of the new and recently refined precursor to antibiotics—M and B 693. The staff and treatment were first class and he was also much fortified by the traditional Scottish porridge. Nicky felt quite at home with the Scottish and Gaelic accents, as his mother spoke with a strong brogue. He also enjoyed the company of a great number of Australian Army chaps who were convalescing there. As well, he was reunited with Geoff Chinchen.

On discharge, Nicky and Chinchen spent much time at the Gezira Club, a posh upper class institution complete with palatial gardens and, to Nicky's delight, a swimming pool and springboard. Their convalescence was based on the Australian Houseboat, moored on the Nile, and they watched the feluccas as their lateen sails billowed and played against the light. Nicky felt, once again, the war was a long way off.

This was about to change dramatically. On 12 February, Nicky picked up a new Kittyhawk from Heliopolis and flew straight into one of the most terrifying experiences of his time in the Middle East. He was met back at No. 3 Squadron by Bobby Gibbes whom he shared a tent with that night. Gibbes had been a good friend of his since Point Cook days and at No. 23 Squadron in Brisbane. He was a first class example of the rugged Australian character— independent, tenacious, and cool and level-headed in combat. He was small in stature, but sturdy. Nicky always enjoyed his sense of humour and dynamism, and that night, just on dusk, Nicky was catching up on No. 3 Squadron news when Germans cruising above in Ju88 bombers dropped some incendiary flares right over their camp, brilliantly highlighting their tent like a beacon.

A few seconds later, they heard a sound which turned their blood to ice—the whistling of bombs directly overhead. Nicky raced out of the tent and was almost blinded by the brightness of the flare. It was gently swinging above, hanging in space from a parachute. Suddenly, Nicky felt naked—as if he was exposed to the whole German Army. Both he and Gibbes dived into the slit trench beside their tent, just as a clutch of 500-pound bombs crashed within 100 metres all around them.

One landed nearby with a great thud but mercifully didn't explode on impact. With cold fear gripping them, one thought raced through their minds: did the bomb have a delayed reaction fuse? And if so, how much time did they have? If it exploded now, they would be buried alive. If they made a dash for it, and it went off, the end result was unthinkable. After a minute, the all-illuminating glare died, leaving the men anxiously peering into the stygian blackness. Seconds ticked by, the suspense unbearable. Nicky was shivering, from fear he suspected as much as from the cold.

There was nowhere to go, no place to hide, no in-range or out of it—no truly safe haven and there was nothing he could do about it. He was overcome by a feeling of utter helplessness. He jumped out of the trench, then commanded his feet to move even faster than they did when the Me-109 had strafed him the previous month. After what seemed an eternity, he eventually sprinted to an area of relative safety, gasping in great relief. A few minutes later, he was joined breathlessly by Gibbes. The two of them were still shaking some time later.

Next day, when the armourers defused the bomb, they were intrigued to learn that the fuses had been tampered with. Inside was a piece of paper on which was written 'from a friend'. Nicky and Gibbes had difficulty imagining a 'friend' existing in the midst of German attacking planes. (The 'friend' was almost certainly a foreign slave worker employed in a German factory who had neutralised the fuse as an act of sabotage.)

One pleasant finding for Nicky on his return from Cairo was a large batch of letters from home, and from Dot. How normal and reassuring they were, serving to strengthen even more his resolve to get this war over with and return home.

Over the next few days, Nicky learned that as an aftermath of the air battle on 11 January, Bobby Jones had been taken prisoner. In the same battle, 'Tiny' Cameron had also been shot down—for the third time—and was also made a prisoner. Nicky wryly mused to himself that he hoped Mademoiselle Curie had a good story.

He also found out that a few days after his return from the desert, while in Cairo, Rommel had begun his second offensive to wrest North Africa back from the Allies. The battle had escalated quickly to the point where Benghazi was recaptured on 29 January. By 7 February, Rommel had almost taken Gazala, recovering nearly all the ground the Allies had won during Operation Crusader. Further, the situation for the Allies was a little more desperate now as the Sixth and Seventh Australian Divisions had left the Middle East in January to confront the Japanese in New Guinea. Meanwhile, the Ninth Division were holding guard duty in Lebanon in case Hitler approached the Middle East through Turkey. (Australia's other Division, the Eighth, was involved in a desperate holding action against the Japanese in Singapore, but by 15 February, they had been taken prisoner—18 500 of them along with 112 000 British personnel.)

By the end of January, No. 3 Squadron had lost 13 more planes. The battle was hotting up and the retreat was quickening. The Allies' own propaganda, disseminated on the radio in the news programs, saying that 'The Allies were doing quite well and were involved in a strategic withdrawal,' was wearing very thin to the men in No. 3 Squadron. This type of information gave tacit support to the belief that the Allies had everything under control. In fact, the situation in the Western Desert and Malta was extremely critical. Other than a successful commando raid or two, the Battle of Britain and the Syrian Campaign, the reality of it was that the Allies, after more than two years of war, had achieved nothing that could be crowed about.

Make no mistake about the situation at this time. Hitler, the successful conqueror, was receiving the full support of his people, as was Mussolini in Italy. The Third Reich and a New Roman Empire looked like real possibilities. It would require decisive defeats to change all that!

EIGHT

Gambut

On 26 February, Bobby Gibbes was deservedly promoted to squadron leader of No. 3 Squadron. Dixie Chapman's performance had been suffering; not from lack of courage, but from his lack of hard combat experience. This had been affecting his leadership. Ironically he was promoted to wing commander, then transferred to a squadron not in operations. Gibbes, while surprised at his own selection, moved into the position with great energy and objectiveness. He was a popular choice, and Nicky especially was pleased. He respected him and knew they could work well together. Gibbes always let the squadron feel they were contributing something worthwhile. Leading by example, his message seemed to be, 'Let's go and fight. Get this thing over with, and get back home.'

One of Gibbes' first pleasant jobs was to inform Nicky he had been awarded an immediate Distinguished Flying Cross (DFC). The battle on 11 January had brought Nicky's confirmed victories to eight, gained in 16 combats from a total of only 22 operational flights.

'A wonderful effort,' Gibbes congratulated Nicky.

Nicky's citation referred not only to his flying achievements, but also to the value of the ground information given to Allied Intelligence as a result of his five-day Senussi adventure.

On top of this, Gibbes promoted Nicky to senior flight

commander, in charge of 'B' Flight. This meant he would lead the squadron when Gibbes did not fly.

For the next few weeks, the squadron took part in regular sweeps, mainly escorting bombers over the El Adem, Tobruk and Tmimi areas. During this time, even though some members of the squadron encountered the enemy and registered some impressive victories, Nicky didn't personally intercept any enemy aircraft until 8 March.

On this day, Nicky, for the first time, was leading planes from both No. 3 Squadron and No. 450 Squadron. Six Kittyhawks from each were taking a freelance sweep over the battle area with no specific target. They were flying some distance behind enemy lines, about 24 kilometres west of Tobruk, looking for trouble. Just before dusk, they found it.

The day was still very hot and the cockpit was like an oven. Nicky was perspiring freely, soaked in sweat. Then his heart thumped wildly as, dead ahead at about 2000 feet below him, he saw the sky was suddenly full of planes. Streaking towards Nicky's planes were 15 Stukas on their way to a bombing mission, escorted by two Me-109s and 13 Italian Macchis.

The Macchis were flying in two echelons of nine MC200s and four MC202s. Amazingly, they did not immediately appear to recognise the Kittyhawks as being enemy aircraft, as they made no move to attack.

Seizing the advantage, Nicky quickly called for No. 450 Squadron to act as top cover while he signalled for No. 3 Squadron to stir up the hornet's nest, to dive for the kill. The six Kittyhawks dropped their noses and screamed in behind the still unsuspecting Macchis.

Within a few seconds, the Italians realised their mistake—too late. Immediately, there was a frantic twisting and turning as more than 40 planes vied for predominance. Nicky dropped his plane behind the scattering Macchis and levelled out behind several MC202s. Directly in front of him one of the 202s, rolling desperately to evade Nicky's impending attack, attempted to move in a wild half turn loop.

The plane's belly flashed in front of Nicky, and he made it line-astern like the hunter he was becoming. He snapped out a short burst and watched the shells crash into the fuselage then smash into the motor. A burst of flame and smoke exploded outward from his engine. The stricken plane rolled, pouring thick black smoke in a long trail as it spiralled towards the ocean. Nicky didn't wait to see it crash; there were too many planes filling the sky to contend with. His victory was confirmed by his wingman, No. 2, Sergeant Beard, who witnessed the Macchi diving into the ocean. Beard then shot down an MC200 himself.

Nicky continued to chase and attack the Macchis as Allied and Axis planes rolled and sawed in confusion across the sky. Intermittently, Nicky would line up a target and fire short bursts at it. At the end of the day, he was credited with one 'probable' MC200 and two 'damaged' MC200s as well as his MC202 'kill'.

It was a most successful mission for him and his two squadrons. They had shot down seven Macchis and two Stukas for no loss of their own. That night they heard that No. 112 Squadron had later met the surviving planes of the enemy formation and had exacted a further toll, claiming a Stuka and an MC200.

Back at base, Nicky was absolutely exhausted again, feeling the effects of tremendous tension generated by manouvring with so many planes in the sky. He was not concerned that after each combat he felt 'washed out'. He expected that—short, highly concentrated periods involving life and death were bound to sap the energy. His recovery rate was good and to this point, there was no accumulation of 'tiredness'.

Overall, he was very satisfied, not only with the number of victories accredited to the squadron, but also with the knowledge that they had turned the enemy squadrons around without allowing them to drop a single bomb on target (some were jettisoned).

However, the general pressure did not let up. The next day, as Rommel continued to press forward, the squadron moved back some 300 kilometres due east, to a field set up earlier by Fred Rosier at Gambut Main. It was a little east of Tobruk, not far from El Adem, and was set on the crossroads of the old Senussi trade routes.

For the next few weeks, No. 3 Squadron mainly carried out bomber escort patrols, including a successful Boston Bomber mission over Martuba Airfield, a large Messerschmitt base. As they flew away from the drome Nicky noticed, with some pleasure, four large fires raging from the base. He was also pleased to record that Geoff Chinchen and Tom Packer shared a confirmed 109 conquest.

However, the main task over this period was to protect the British Fleet which was taking vital fuel, ammunition and food supplies from Alexandria to Malta. Lying in the central Mediterranean astride the enemy sea–air route to the Afrika Korps, the defenders of Malta had long been a thorn in Hitler's side, creating a stubborn resistance to everything the Axis forces could throw at them. It was critical for Malta to stay in Allied hands in order to slow Rommel's flow of resources moving down from Europe.

The large convoy consisted of four Merchant Navy vessels, 17 destroyers and four cruisers. For these missions, the Kittyhawks were fitted with long-range fuel tanks. As well, the fleet always had four Beaufighters flying in close escort to protect them from submarines. It was harrowing work as the fleet was spirited right past enemy-held Benghazi, increasing the opportunity to be found by German reconnaissance patrols.

On the first day of this mission, Nicky flew two sorties amounting to six hours and five minutes, an exhausting day in a fighter plane. There was always tension in the air. Once, while flying through thick cloud at 18 000 feet, Nicky broke through the top layer and, to his great surprise and horror, over to his right, he saw the thickest Balbo of enemy aircraft he had ever seen—well over 100 planes. To his relief, he saw they had missed seeing the convoy, which was protected by the heavy cloud, and they were flying in the other direction. Nicky zipped down into the cloud quickly and disappeared from their view.

On the third day, after flying 370 kilometres out to sea, fatigued and almost out of fuel, he barely made it back, landing with only 30 gallons left in his tank.

During this time, Nicky shared his tent with Bill Dargie, the official war artist commissioned to record the Middle East battles. Dargie had been chronicling the various branches of the defence forces, and was now to spend time with the air force. The two quickly became firm friends, and Dargie convinced Nicky to pose for him.

Dargie insisted Nicky wear his flier's goggles, helmet and leather coat, which was appropriate for the coolness of altitude, but at ground level the warmth and Nicky's general fatigued condition ensured drowsiness. Dargie's finished oil painting evoked this somnolence, depicting Nicky with his eyes closed.

'It'll probably hang in the War Memorial in Canberra,' Dargie said. Then he added, smiling, 'If anyone complains, I'll open the eyes for you.'

As a means of explanation to a potentially curious viewer, Nicky, with some licence, wrote in the top left-hand corner, 'Sorry, I fell asleep.'

Towards the end of March, as a reward for getting the fleet through, the exhausted No. 3 Squadron was given a much needed two weeks' leave.

Nicky spent a relaxing fortnight in Cairo and Alexandria and, on his return, continued to enjoy a relative respite from intensive combat. No. 3 Squadron spent most of April out of operations, regrouping at Sidi Heneish.

Here, over a few weeks, they retrained, re-equipped and also prepared a new batch of sergeant pilots. On 26 April they moved forward again to Gambut Main. Unfortunately, a few minutes after the squadron was airborne, Nicky's No. 2, Sergeant Beard, developed engine trouble, and when he tried to turn back, his plane tragically spun into the ground and burned. He was killed instantly.

To Nicky, there were still too few answers about how to deal with this type of sudden death, and nobody was immune. A fortnight later, Geoff Chinchen led 12 planes in a sweep over the forward area when they were attacked by two Me-109s. Nicky's friend, Graham Pace, was shot out of the sky and killed on the first attack. Acceptance was never easy.

During this last month, as both sides rebuilt again, there had been a general lessening in hostilities. By early May, however, Rommel was ready for another offensive. He now had about 130 Me-109s in his Luftwaffe formations, as his III/JG53 had returned from Sicily and Crete.

As May passed, both air action and land action intensified, with Nicky leading sorties over Gazala, Bir Hacheim and El Adem.

Once again, Martuba, the large Messerschmitt base, was selected for special attention by the Allies. On 22 May, Nicky was leading four Kittyhawks from No. 3 Squadron as part of a diversionary force, including planes from No. 3, No. 265 and No. 450 Squadrons. They were to fly ahead of nine SAAF Boston Bombers in a freelance sweep designed to draw enemy planes away from the following bombers. In turn, the bombers were given close escort by Kittyhawks from No. 112 and No. 250 Squadrons.

At about 50 kilometers east of Tmimi, the diversionary group was attacked by four Me-109s from II/JG27. The Messerschmitts streaked out of the sun, completely surprising No. 450 Squadron who were flying top cover. Two of the Me-109s dived straight onto the squadron, decisively ripping into two Kittyhawks which, within seconds, were sent spiralling to the ground in flames.

The other two 109s screamed through No. 450 Squadron and levelled out below No. 3 Squadron. Nicky pulled the nose of his Kittyhawk up, searching for height, as other planes violently manoeuvred in all directions. Below him, Nicky noticed one of the Messerschmitt pilots had focused on him and was racing his 109 in a spiral climb roaring up after him.

Nicky snapped his plane around into a tight maximum 'G' turn, almost standing the Kittyhawk on her wing, and came out directly on the tail of the surprised Messerschmitt pilot. A swift look behind to see whether his own tail was clear and Nicky closed the distance on the enemy fighter. Nicky opened fire 200 metres away with his six guns, raking the plane with a blistering fusillade. Amazingly, Nicky didn't notice any damage, but the 109 slowly rolled over and arced gracefully onto its back. A few seconds later, it crashed into the desert, destroying itself in flames.

Swinging into a wide, climbing turn, Nicky headed back to the main fight. The battle was still at its height. Bobby Gibbes had shot down one of the other Me-109s earlier, and Nicky could see the other two searching for blood. He raced after one of them and managed to get some bursts into it, damaging it.

Very quickly, however, the formation split up. Gibbes, with Nicky and some of the other Kittyhawks, flew to 15 000 feet over Gazala and waited for the bombers on their way home from Martuba.

The bombing assignment had gone well, creating much damage. However, the Kittyhawks escorting them were met by

Messerschmitts from I and III/JG27, and lost three for one Me-109 downed.

The drama wasn't quite over for the day. When Nicky arrived back at base, he couldn't lower his undercarriage for landing. He didn't remember being hit, and feverishly worked the auxiliary pump to lower the wheels by hand. Luckily, the pump worked and the wheels lowered, shakily, ready for landing.

As the Kittyhawk touched down, Nicky felt the wheels shudder. Immediately he was aware of the tail crashing into the ground, spinning out stones and sending up blankets of dust. He fought desperately to prevent it from skidding sideways, and eventually brought the rollicking machine to a slow crawl.

At this stage of the campaign, in order to improve the rate of turnaround—that is, the speed at which the squadron could be in the air again—one of the ground crew for each plane would be placed at the end of the landing strip. As a plane landed, the pilot would bring it to a halt, then the crewman, using the landing wheel for a step, would lift himself onto the wing with a half twist. He would ease along the wing, away from the arc of the propeller, then sit on the leading edge, often with his feet dangling in the spaces between the three .5 machine guns protruding from the wing. He would then assist the pilot to taxi to the fuel and armoury areas, while keenly listening for any impediment to the motor's performance as well as undertaking a preliminary assessment of the plane's airworthiness (bullet holes, etc.), situations he could immediately report and commence the necessary repairs on. At the same time, he was always thankful his pilot had returned and not missed the pick-up, as it was usually a long, hot dusty trek back to the workshop zone.

On this occasion, as Nicky began to taxi his damaged plane off the runway, Ray Dunning, waiting at the edge of the strip, stepped onto the still-moving wheel and crawled onto the wing. He manoeuvred to his usual position, his legs straddling the centre gun, and gave Nicky a cursory check to see that he was all right.

In fact, the operation had been long and tough, and Nicky was fairly exhausted. Dunning then quickly scanned the steaming plane, mentally noting any obvious damage, then directed it back to its parking bay.

As soon as the Kittyhawk rolled to a stop, Felix Sainsbury, the armourer, boarded the other side, also noting Nicky's condition. He was prepared to assist him from the cockpit if needed. (A regular event across the landing field.)

After the motor was silenced, Dunning called dryly to Nicky, 'I hope you're in better shape than your plane, sir. We've almost got a new one ready for you. I might just have enough time to inscribe the squadron insignia and the devil on it. I don't think we'll get this one airborne for some time.' Then he added, smiling, 'Hope you got a couple of Jerries to even the score.' Wry humour sustained these men.

Sainsbury continued, 'In that case, I don't suppose it matters if you've got any ammo left. Have you?'

Nicky was about to answer as he took off his helmet. He was perspiring and tired from the events of the day. Then, the scene was set for a near tragedy. Unthinkingly, he placed the helmet on the control column, forgetting he had not switched his guns off!

The guns exploded into life, blasting flame and smoke from the wings, the bullets whining out into the desert.

Nicky was shocked, and immediately focused on Dunning, who though shocked too, gave the thumbs-up sign. He was okay. Luckily, no one else was hit either.

Sainsbury commented dryly, 'Well, I guess there's no ammo left now.'

When Dunning unsteadily alighted from the plane, he was heard to say, laconically, 'I think the boss was trying to shoot my dick off.'

Someone observed, 'He's a terrible shot. He shouldn't have missed at that range.'

And he didn't. Dunning produced a small leg burn from the heat of the gun. Yes, just near the groin area.

NINE

Operation Venezia

At Gazala, the opposing armies had been confronting each other for three and a half months across an immense minefield running from the sea to Bir Hacheim, more than 70 kilometres to the south. On 26 May the ever-aggressive Rommel launched Operation Venezia, an all-out attack on the Gazala line. This would bring important ramifications for Nicky and the No. 3 Squadron.

On this day, No. 3 Squadron was called at 4.15 a.m. The morning stillness was broken by the first splutter of an engine then, one by one, a dozen Kittyhawks, sounding like the powerful tattoo of thousands of war drums, throbbed into life as the ground crew inspected and warmed the motors. Nicky placed his flying gear in his plane, then returned to the operations room. With Bobby Gibbes, he had a cup of tea only, believing that if he received a bullet in this area, less damage would be done if his stomach was empty. At 7.00 a.m., the first rays of early sun glinted on the Kittyhawks as they taxied to the landing ground from their dispersal points. The dust swirled like a mini cyclone as they lined up in order to take off.

The engines were quieter now, throbbing restlessly and waiting for the unleashing that would send them high into the morning clouds, soaring above the sun. Then the tone changed. It became harsher, more strident and demanding of the air. It built to a clamour of controlled thunder and the Kittyhawks rolled forward. Swiftly the planes gathered speed—then they were up. The flight lifted into the air, then glided into formation. Within seconds, they became mere black specks in the west. Gibbes led the full squadron as it powered towards a scramble above El Adem. After climbing to 15 000 feet they commenced to patrol the area. Within a few minutes Gibbes saw and reported four Ju87 Stuka bombers escorted by six Messerschmitts approaching their squadron at about 4000 feet above their level. He immediately ordered a turnabout, which meant each aircraft carried out a fast 180-degree turn, then climbed up on a parallel course about a kilometre from the enemy.

The bombers also started to climb on sighting the Kittyhawks, but not quickly enough. Gibbes led the top cover of six aircraft on a sweep above the bombers to clear the fighters, while he ordered Nicky to take the bottom six to confront the bombers.

Gibbes managed to get three or four bursts into a Me-109, then swooped down to have a go at the Stukas. The bombers, meanwhile, had released their bombs and dived to escape to the east. A Stuka is not as fast as a Kittyhawk and Gibbes yelled over the radio, 'Forget the fighters, get the bombers.'

The Stukas were flying in a tight diamond box formation and Gibbes focused on one aircraft flying in the tail of the diamond. In desperation, he carried out two or three attacks on the plane from unorthodox angles, trying to avoid the withering crossfire set up by tail gunners of the other Stukas. It appeared he had killed the rear gunner of the plane he was shooting at, as it suddenly stopped firing at him. He then concentrated his fire on the starboard side of the engine and within a few seconds had it smoking strongly. Then one of the rear gunners from another Stuka caught him in his sights and riddled his Kittyhawk, setting it on fire.

That was the last anybody saw of Gibbes. His plane spiralled out of the battlefield zone.

In the meantime, the rest of the squadron were not having much success. Nicky had fired at five enemy aircraft with no visible result. The only confirmed hit was Bobby Gibbes' 109 which was listed as a 'probable', but Gibbes was most likely downed himself.

When the squadron returned to base and it was certain that Gibbes had not returned, RAF Headquarters in Cairo ordered a reconnaissance patrol to search for him.

With great concern and urgency, Nicky led a flight of four planes in a 30-minute grid sweep retracing Gibbes' flight path over the battle area. To Nicky, Gibbes was the best pilot he had ever flown with. He was an excellent leader and by now a close friend.

'Hell, we have to find him,' he continually pushed himself. 'We need him.'

There was a definite risk involved in these searches, but there was no man in the squadron who wasn't willing to gamble all to find Gibbes.

At all times when flying, a certain vigilance is required against an enemy air attack, and there is always a need to be alert when flying over anti-aircraft gun emplacements.

As the search continued, Nicky remained hopeful that Gibbes would be alive somewhere. Knowing his skills, both as a pilot and as a genuinely resourceful individual, Nicky felt he would probably be all right. But even though Nicky's flight examined several downed planes and checked out other burning pyres, to his distress they could find no trace of Gibbes.

That wasn't the end of the day's flights. For some time, No. 3 Squadron's Kittyhawks had been fitted with bomb racks under the fuselages and had been practising dropping 250-pound (113-kg) bombs. That afternoon, Nicky led the full squadron of 12 aircraft on their first bombing mission. They came in low over Tmimi and scored four successful direct hits on the dispersal area. It was a good result and it meant bombing was going to be a viable addition to No. 3 Squadron's commitments.

By the time the squadron arrived back they had received the good news from RAF Headquarters that Bobby Gibbes had been found by a British patrol, west of El Adem. He was all right, but had sustained a fractured ankle and was to be treated in Cairo. Nicky was happy that Gibbes was safe and some time later he marvelled at Gibbes' story.

When Gibbes' plane was set on fire, flames roared out of it, forcing him to dive for protection. Frantically, he turned his petrol off, hoping that the fire would go out. However, by the time he had glided from 6000 to 4000 feet, the fire was burning more fiercely than ever. As flames started to lick around him, he realised he had no option but to bail out.

He levelled his plane to reduce his speed, adjusted the trim to create a nose-down attitude, undid his Sutton harness and put his hand on the top of the canopy. On releasing the stick, he shot out like a cork from a bottle. He was now clear of the aircraft, but on the way through the tail fin struck him a savage blow on his thigh, just above his left knee.

Gasping in pain, he almost panicked as, in the same instant, he also found the aerial had wrapped around him. Clawing at the wire, he managed to get free, but hesitated before pulling the ripcord of his parachute because his fear of being strafed on the way down. Even though both air forces considered themselves chivalrous enough not to take part in this practice, there had been precedents. In October the previous year, one of No. 3 Squadron's pilots had been attacked by four 109s and his harness shot off in midair. Consequently, the pilot fell 4000 feet to his death without a parachute.

Gibbes found himself tumbling aimlessly towards the

ground, then he pulled on the ripcord. The parachute opened, snapping him up with a jerk. Below him he watched his own aircraft plunging down, a mass of flames. It crashed into the earth with a mighty burst of flame and black smoke.

Gibbes was gently swinging in a world devoid of all sound, contemplating where he might land. Then suddenly, he heard the roar of an aircraft's engine coming towards him. He went cold. 'My God, I'm going to be strafed.'

Desperately, he pulled on his parachute shrouds to create a wider swinging momentum in order to make for a more difficult target. The noise from the approaching aircraft built to a crescendo, then abruptly ceased as it culminated in a loud explosion.

Confused, then with great relief, he realised that he wasn't being attacked by a 109, but had simply heard the roar of his own aircraft in its flaming downward plunge. That, followed by the blast of its crash, had taken a few seconds to shoot back up to him.

Suddenly, the desert grew closer at frightening speed. Like a flash, it occurred to him he had never been given lessons on how to land in a parachute. Too late, he gave a shout of fear as he hit the dirt, crashing heavily and falling sideways.

A burning pain emanated from his left leg as it buckled under him. He could tell it was probably fractured by the nasty bend in it. With some relief, he realised he was otherwise safe for a while, but he was very disoriented and wasn't sure of his exact position. Would he be picked up by an Allied patrol first? He took the boot off from his injured foot and waited. He had actually landed between both forward lines, and before too long was picked up by a British bren gun carrier.

Later the same day, Nicky heard through a memo from RAF Headquarters that he was to be the new squadron leader. Even though the announcement of his own promotion initially excited him, the situation also presented him with some degree of apprehension. He had never sought promotion. It was enough to be out there fighting. In fact one of the aspects of being a fighter pilot which had originally appealed to Nicky was the individuality and personal responsibility that this role accorded. He would be in the plane on his own, making his own decisions and depending on himself for survival.

As he obtained rank, and therefore responsibility, he realised he did not particularly enjoy it. As the commander of a flight he could not fly as he would want to. He had lost the freedom he relished as a 'sprog' (lowly rank), and indeed he had felt safer while flying as a pilot officer. As the whim took him, he could suddenly roar ahead full bore, or drop into a spin if he wanted to. Now he had to consider the full squadron flying behind him. He had to slow down so that he wouldn't leave his number four man behind. And it also meant he would have to distance himself from friends.

He wasn't really certain he had the skills to be squadron leader. There was such a high attrition rate that his rise through the ranks had been swift. He didn't really feel like an 'old hand'— he was still learning. Now he would have to be responsible and make decisions for other men whom he had come to respect, any number of whom he considered would have made an excellent leader. The squadron had great depth and so many pilots had the potential to accept the responsibility of command. Some were gone—Don Knight, Freddy Eggleston, Graham Pace and Peter Giddy—but still around and setting outstanding examples were others like Geoff Chinchen and Lou Spence.

Though still daunted at the prospect of becoming leader, an unrelated incident ironically gave him strength to help him accept the challenge.

Towards the end of that same long day, he received news that his mother had died. She had been ill for some 18 months, so the news was not entirely unexpected. Nevertheless, the reality of the news still shocked him. He needed time and some solace. He excused himself and retired to his tent. His mind raced as he tried to comprehend his mother's death, then reconcile his loss. It was to start Nicky on a process of prioritising the value of war, and a search for other ideals.

At the same time, he had to consider the implications of his new appointment. His mother had always encouraged him to 'do his bit'. Promotion would not have been important to her but 'getting the job done' was. He ached for home—for Dot.

He was moved to write a letter to his brother Jack, something he rarely needed to do. Somehow, the two were so close, normal communication wasn't required. They had always been aware of the other's thoughts and feelings. The exercise of writing to Jack soothed him.

He yearned for the war to be over. Perhaps as squadron leader he could make a difference. He searched deep inside and resolved to get on with his new responsibilities.

Knightsbridge

Nicky's term as squadron leader almost finished as quickly as it began. The following day, 27 May 1942, the Allied Air Units were given a simple directive: to carry out as many strafing and bombing attacks as possible on the advancing enemy. This read as, 'Stop them at all costs, anyway you can.' No. 3 Squadron were to concentrate on the enemy columns south-east of Bir Hacheim, mainly flying freelance missions.

Nicky led his squadron for the first operation of the day. From the air, he witnessed the sad sight of the British Eighth Army in retreat—'strategic withdrawal' was the military term—ruefully marvelling at the masterful mop-up job Rommel's crew was performing. The Allies did not have a unified front-line, but the push was culminating at a fortification dubbed Knightsbridge by the British soldiers. A Free French brigade, as part of the British Eighth Army, was resisting gallantly at Bir Hacheim and was preventing Rommel from forcing his way around this flank.

The battle hotted up and the combined Axis armies threw everything at the brave Frenchmen. The war zone was to earn the name the Battle of the Cauldron because of the seething battles fought there. Nicky's No. 3 Squadron whined in over the enemy positions, then levelled out, their sights fixed on the enemy trucks, gun positions and columns of German soldiers.

The Kittyhawks dropped their bombs, shattering and exploding army trucks and tanks and sending up large clouds of dust and smoke as the impact rocked the area. They then wheeled around and screamed in again for the attack, blue flames bursting from their machine-guns, causing panic-eyed men to desperately propel themselves out of the line of fire.

As the planes sped off through the morning haze, they left columns of smoke billowing from upturned vehicles and troops lying dead and wounded. Abruptly, a little distance away, Nicky's plane spluttered and lost power. It was overheating and Nicky quickly realised he would not make it home. He had just flown over Sidi Rezegh and began searching for a reasonably cleared area to attempt an emergency landing. He realised the enemy would be in the area, but he had to risk this possibility.

Nicky observed that the desert below was littered with the carnage and debris of war, some vehicles still smouldering. There was not much sign of life, except for a couple of villages further east on the coastal strip, and occasionally a holy place dotted the landscape.

He found an uninhabited, wild-looking area relatively out of the battle zone and, spotting a likely landing site, deliberately decided to bring the plane down in the regular manner (as opposed to attempting a belly landing). He quickly jumped out, feeling quite vulnerable and lonely, and immediately levered the cowling off the motor. He went straight to the air cleaner, a Vokes model.

The Vokes was generally regarded as a very efficient cleaner and was often the only thing that helped the aircraft's engine to survive, given the problems with dust and sand inherent in desert fighting. The downside was that it did reduce the motor's effectiveness minimally in terms of horsepower, a trade-off the pilots were happy to concede. Nicky expected and hoped that this would be the problem site.

In the meantime, one of his squadron members, Keith Kildey, flew his own Kittyhawk down and landed beside him. He cut the motor so they could talk, then pulled the canopy back.

'Are you all right?' he called.

'Thanks. I'll be okay. I think this is the problem,' replied Nicky, pointing to the cleaner. 'Get back up and fight the war.'

Kildey gave him the thumbs up sign, turned his plane into the little wind available, and took off, forcing a stream of dust behind him. He had only been gone a few minutes when Nicky looked up to the horizon and noticed a patrol car coming towards him. He froze. He could see it was a German motorised scout car and was approaching quickly. It was about a kilometre away, and getting close enough for a machine-gun to render some damage to him and his aircraft.

Feverishly but methodically, he found there was sand in the air filter and quickly removed it. However, he realised there wasn't going to be time to replace the cowling.

He briskly raced ahead of his plane and cleared the make-shift landing field of some light camelthorn bush that was lying in his intended take-off path. He then raced back to his plane, climbed up onto the wing and got into the cockpit. He strapped himself in, then stabbed the self-starter. To his great relief, the motor burst into beautiful life. He revved it and gunned the plane over the rough desert sand. Without a hitch, the Kittyhawk took off and quickly left the makeshift runway and the fast approaching Germans behind.

Despite Nicky's safe return, it had been an expensive mission. The squadron had lost one pilot, Sergeant Norman, as he dive-bombed a tank, and lost two more planes, one to a ground trooper's chance rifle shot and one to an Me-109.

On his return to base, Nicky filled out his normal fighter pilot's combat report. After detailing his observations, he quite validly reported his impressions to RAF Headquarters in Cairo, via his Intelligence Officer, that he didn't think the Allied forces, from the air, were presenting as a unified front-line.

He was tactfully informed that the top brass didn't think he had the maturity or experience to assess this type of observation of the larger scene.

Rebuffed but undeterred, over the next few days Nicky led and directed his squadron with alternate intensive bombing and strafing raids. He concentrated as many attacks as possible against defined enemy targets, particularly over Bir Hacheim and the Cauldron area, as well as the supply line along the coastal road.

On 28 May, the squadron flew 35 sorties, on 29 May, 17. Once again, exhaustion was a constant companion. The pilots continually received devoted assistance from all members of the squadron to stay in the air. As CO, Nicky had a tent to himself and a batman to assist with his gear and general day-to-day management details. His name was Leo Freeleagus and Nicky found him to be a very caring and cheerful fellow, as well as being something of a resourceful character. He always ensured Nicky was cleanly dressed, even if the shorts and shirts he wore were someone else's. Whenever Nicky was scheduled for an early morning operation, Freeleagus would dutifully wake him and have a cup of hot coffee ready inside his tent.

On 30 May, the morning of the fourth day of the raids, Nicky's batman placed his boiling-hot coffee on the ground, but Nicky was struggling to wake after his exhausting schedule. Freeleagus had no sooner left the tent when a 109 strafing raid commenced. Six of the Messerschmitts materialised out of the western sky, screaming in low like sinister black spectres.

Nicky instinctively dived from his stretcher to the ground the instant he heard the familiar whine of the Messerschmitts, followed by the staccato blast of their guns. The planes opened up a withering fire, shattering the morning stillness and raking the camp with 20-mm cannon shells. Explosions followed as the bullets ignited petrol dumps, whistled into tents and crashed into engineering installations. The frightening effects of the eruptions were amplified by the closeness of Nicky's tent, as bullets cut through the canvas walls like a knife and embedded in his recently vacated stretcher.

Suddenly, he felt a sharp stinging pain in his right upper thigh, causing him to roll in agony around the tent floor. He uttered a suppressed groan of pain as his fingers groped in the dark and located a hot sticky mess emanating from his hip area. Sensing the worst, he cursed his bad luck and tried to remember, through the pain, where the doctor's tent was. In his hysteria and panic, he thought he might have been mortally wounded.

He was set to scream for help. However, on discovering he could move his leg fully, he cautiously decided to pursue a closer examination. As his adrenalin settled, he found, with much-growing relief, that the wound probably wasn't invasive. The truth was that he had incurred nothing more than a severe skin burn from rolling onto his cup of coffee!

He allowed himself a sheepish smile and was grateful no one had witnessed his dramatic performance, worthy, he considered, of the great actor, Lionel Barrymore.

Word of this incident did get round, causing a degree of humour among his squadron members. In future, Freeleagus made sure he delivered the coffee out of Nicky's reach.

The bottom line was that during this strategic retreat period, the squadron did not get too much peace; enemy raids were a common occurrence and caused a great deal of damage to equipment as well as adding to the underlying stress and anxiety of the stretched men.

That wasn't to be the end of the day's drama for Nicky. Outside, the Battle of the Cauldron was raging, and he would soon be part of it.

ELEVEN

Battle of the Cauldron

Towards five o'clock on the evening of the base attack, Nicky was leading four Kittyhawks from No. 3 Squadron and six from No. 250 Squadron. His thigh was still stinging from the early morning's misadventure, but his attention was now diverted to the Cauldron battle area coming up. As they approached the war zone, Nicky saw pillars of smoke and stabbing flashes of shell-burst over a wide area below. It showed the line of the barrage and the extent of the heavy, front-line fighting.

In the sky, somewhere just ahead, Messerschmitts from 111/JG53 and 1/JG27 were engaged in a deadly skirmish with a squadron of Boston Bombers which were escorted by Kitty-hawks from South Africa's No. 2 Squadron. Nicky's Kittyhawks were flying in pairs and his wingman, No. 2, was a fine young pilot from Cooroy in Queensland, Sergeant McDiarmid.

When they were over the thickest area of the battle scene, Nicky ordered No. 250 Squadron to cover his No. 3 Squadron while they dived to release their bombs. Down below, all defence areas were saturated. The Germans were firing off a terrific number of rounds from their 88-mm anti-aircraft guns and were effectively covering the sky. Flying here was dangerous; strafing was going to be particularly hazardous.

Nicky's four Kittyhawks roared in low. Focusing on selected targets, they screamed into the teeth of the anti-aircraft barrage, then released their bombs. Nicky pulled out of his dive and, looking quickly behind him, noted with satisfaction the smoking devastation caused by their attack. He pulled the joystick back further and reached for height. As he did, he called for the No. 250 Squadron Kittyhawks to dive in turn to drop their bombs.

Before Nicky had a chance to level out, someone called over the radio, 'Bandits at 2000 feet'. Eight Me-109s were approaching in formation of twos, the first four quickly homing in on No. 3 Squadron. Further back, two other Me-109s were acting as escorts for 15 Ju87 Stukas preparing for a dive-bombing attack. The eight lead Messerschmitts were from 1/JG27 and were clearing the area prior to the intended bombing raid. They were fresh from dealing with the South African Kittyhawk squadron and the Boston Bombers, leaving 17 of the Allied planes smouldering in flames.

The sky, once again, became full of whirring planes, but Nicky concentrated on the four 109s coming directly at him. These four had climbed to achieve height advantage, and the first two dived at speed towards the squadron. In a fraction, Nicky twisted out of their way, rolled and came up beneath one of the second pair of 109s as it lunged after their leader. Its belly and tail loomed large in Nicky's vision and was instantaneously framed in his sights. He pressed the trigger and watched the tracers crash along the length of the fuselage.

A puff of smoke poured out of one wing mounting, and the plane immediately lost power. It steadily dropped towards earth, trailing a small plume of white smoke, then moved out of Nicky's vision. He was sure he'd got it, but he realised now that his own No. 2, Sergeant McDiarmid, had gone missing while defending Nicky's tail. Damn. He couldn't see him.

With the sky and ground still erupting around him, Nicky called to his squadron to reorganise, saying, 'No. 3 Squadron, fall into position behind me. There is our target down below.

Some heavy armour and troops. Follow me and shoot anything that moves.'

In turn, the Kittyhawks streaked from their formation and concentrated their attack on a heavily grouped section of artillery.

Nicky could see German tanks and armoured cars were supporting the artillery and were engaged in a vicious land battle as well as defending the skies. He pushed his plane into a powerful dive and chose his target—a battery of 88-mm artillery guns. He screamed in low, barely noticing the desert flash up towards him, while he fought to hold the plane steady with his right hand. When less than 100 metres from the ground, Nicky began to level out then, with full concentration on the target ahead, he squeezed the trigger. He watched his tracers stream out towards the enemy installations.

In the same instant, the full battery of 88-mm guns opened up. Orange flames and smoke propelled the blast directly at his plane. He caught the complete concussive force front on, momentarily shocking him. The shells zipped harmlessly underneath his plane, but in that instant, like a mighty hand, the powerful energy from the blast took control of the plane and spun it like a toy.

The Kittyhawk completely swivelled on its longitudinal axis, so that Nicky suddenly found himself being flipped upside down. There was no time for analytical thought—hours of reflex aerobatic training and hardened battle experience were about to pay off.

Spontaneously, his practised fingers frantically worked the joystick, coaxing the renegade plane to respond. Within another instant, he had righted the aircraft.

He was now powering along about ten metres parallel to the desert floor, the roar of his plane engine echoing loudly back at him, filling his ears. Sun-scorched earth and sparse camelthorn weed flashed past his eyes as he fought to keep the plane from diving. With all the resultant forces grabbing at his Kittyhawk, Nicky felt like he was floating. It was an unreal sensation, as if he was living the seconds in slow motion.

The controls conceded a little; the impact from the blast must have interfered minimally with the tail elevator controls. The nose of the plane dropped a fraction and within another flash, the propeller whirred, then splintered as it sliced into the desert floor at speed. Sand and dirt sprayed wildly, lashing a wild dust screen back over the cockpit. The engine and cowling then crashed into the earth, ploughing a trough through the shaley second layer.

Once again, Nicky was on a roller-coaster as his plane rocketed for long seconds on its belly, the grinding metal screeching as it bounced across rough rocky outcrops. Abruptly, the rocking wildcat finished its run by crashing into a low ridge of upraised earth. The impact expanded the restraining harness around Nicky's shoulders, forcing his head to whip forward. His forehead bashed with a resounding thunk onto the gun sight. At the same instant, his knee smashed against the instrument panel.

Dazed, he forced his body to move and to respond to the emergency. He shouldn't be in the plane. It might burst into flames, or he could be subjected to enemy strafing runs, as last time, or targeted by enemy artillery. He had to get out—now! He forced the canopy open, and groggily jumped onto the ground and stayed there.

Immediately, he was confronted by an unexpected sensation—as well as enduring the Sahara's sting, his senses were shocked into reality as they were overwhelmed by the tremendous level of noise that existed on the battlefield. His private war in a fighter cockpit was relatively quiet, but this was frightening. Above him, Kittyhawks and Messerschmitts were roaring around each other, machine-guns blasting, Ju87 Stukas were screaming into dive attacks, unleashing their shrieking bombs, and artillery from both armies were lashing each other with a thunderous fusillade, as well as pouring lead into the fuming sky. To Nicky, the ear-splitting sound was completely intimidating. He could feel cold fear racing to invade him—to engulf his senses. He had to get away from here. This must be the centre of the Cauldron.

To Nicky, it was hell on earth. He fought back waves of almost abject fear, and once again he was grateful no one could witness his deepest gut reaction.

After some moments, he calmed himself and tried to assess his position and situation. He realised it would not be safe anywhere near the crashed plane, but at the same time it would not be prudent to stand up or even kneel as there was too much fighting going on. Once again, he wondered at his amazing luck and that he was still alive. He had suffered a bleeding nose and was slightly dazed from his accident. His leg was also bleeding but he was otherwise all right, although he felt he needed reasonably urgent medical attention. He realised now he had managed to crash in no-man's-land, somewhere between the two warring belligerents, and was aware that both sides might send out search parties for him.

To his worry, he could see in the distance some German motorised patrols from the Afrika Korps moving his way.

The battle seemed to be at full pitch, and the noise and the prospects of capture maintained his fear at an intense level.

Then, briefly, there was a lull in the noise level, and he became aware of the crackling sound of a loudhailer, calling from somewhere. A pukka English voice was saying, 'Keep down. Stay where you are!'

He couldn't isolate where the voice was coming from, or even how long it had been calling him, but he immediately responded to this advice.

'You are in a minefield. Stay where you are. We'll try and get you out.'

There was no way Nicky would move after that. After about half an hour, he heard the loudhailer again. It was now less than 200 metres away and he could thankfully see a party of about five men working towards him, clearing a track through the minefield. He could also see the Germans getting dangerously close. He willed the British soldiers to move faster, much faster.

The British soldiers were from the Royal Gloucestershire Regiment and the Seventh British Hussars—the 'Cherry Pickers' as they were known because of their tradition of wearing cherry red trousers. Nicky was aware then that their artillery and infantry were firing at the approaching Germans. He and the five men marking out the track kept low as they were caught in the crossfire. Bullets and shells whistled across their heads and exploded on either side of the minefield.

Eventually, to Nicky's great relief, the British team arrived first. At last he could get out of this hellhole. With their assistance, he began crawling through the maze, taking great care to move only within the track that had been marked. He was keen to get out in a hurry; but it seemed to take an interminable time. Several times he tried to move quickly, but the loudhailer would tell him to keep down.

By now, Nicky realised that he was bleeding from his eyes, ears and nose. Eventually, gradually, he was safely led out of the minefield. After thanking his saviours, he was immediately taken to the CCS (Casualty Clearing Station) adjacent to the regiment.

The station was already under a lot of pressure, inundated with casualties from the raging battle outside. When a doctor eventually examined Nicky, he considered he had been seriously concussed, enough that he recommended a complete checkup. The doctor cleaned Nicky's head wounds and also dressed his bleeding leg wound, sustained when he hit the instrument panel in the cockpit. He then arranged for a vehicle to drive Nicky to the Tobruk Military Hospital.

While Nicky was waiting for transport, the doctor smiled at him. 'You're going to have to sing for your supper. We're flat out here. Can you lend a hand?'

The medical orderlies needed assistance with wraps-ups after amputations and all types and degrees of surgery. Wounded men were lying in stretchers and beds waiting to be tended. Nicky saw at close quarters the human price of the terrible carnage of war. There were some horrendous injuries, particularly as a result of exploding and burning tanks. Most of the walking wounded were assisting the medical staff.

The doctor asked Nicky to assist while he operated on a tank officer whose lower jaw had been completely shot away. The man was having difficulty breathing as his throat was filled with blood and mucus, and he kept swallowing his tongue. The doctor asked Nicky to help restrain the man while he injected a local anaesthetic into his throat. The patient's breathing settled almost immediately and the doctor performed a tracheotomy.

Nicky followed every procedure with a degree of fascination, although deliberately keeping himself a little detached. He didn't completely trust that he could manage it. However, at the end of the operation, he was both pleased with the result and with himself.

'Thanks,' the doctor said. 'He should pull through'.

With some annoyance, Nicky understood that he would once again be placed on the missing list. The only consolation was that he would not be out of touch for five days like last time. His family would soon know he was safe.

When Nicky arrived at Tobruk, he was examined by medical experts, both Australian and British. After a thorough testing, he was hospitalised overnight for observation and was cleared the next morning. The army drove him the 30 kilometres to his squadron where, as squadron leader, nobody would know of his condition. When he learned that his wingman from the previous day's mêlée, Sergeant McDiarmid, had been killed, he glossed over his medical state briefly with his medical officer, Tim Stone. 'I'm OK, Tim. Bushy-tailed and bright-eyed. I'll be flying tomorrow.'

He was upset at the news of McDiarmid and he was keen to get back into the air. Besides, he was going to make sure his active flying command lasted more than five days.

TWELVE
Bir Hacheim

The next morning, 1 June, Nicky did feel fine. He had no headaches, giddiness, nausea or loss of balance. All his symptoms as a result of the crash had gone and he was confident that his medical testing had been thorough. He took his position as squadron leader very seriously, and if there was any possibility his health could endanger the squadron, he would not fly.

Today, however, he was emphatic that he could. In fact, he needed to fly. Back in Power House days he had reasoned that after a disastrous fall while performing a high-risk dive, the sooner he took to the board again, the better. He figured the same philosophy should apply here. The longer he had to analyse his position, the harder it might be to get back in the air. He was ready now, and he felt good; he was fit again.

As it turned out, all planes were grounded that morning as a severe sandstorm halted all operations. A *khamsin*, or dust storm, could last three or four days, and generally created uncomfortable hothouse conditions. As the wind roared in, it swept up sand and sent grains billowing across hundreds of square kilometres. The temperature soared, sapping energy and life, and soldiers of both sides gasped for air through makeshift sand masks.

The scorching air, filled with swirling particles of sand, hit the skin and eyes like razors, getting into clothing, bedding, food, engines and machinery, and every personal orifice that wasn't kept closed.

While he waited for the storm to abate, Nicky retreated to the squadrons' operations tent to confront another problem. During the last month, eight aircraft had been lost or written off. As a result, several pilots had been killed or taken prisoner. Further, a handful of men had been stood down medically.

The whole squadron was under stress and the medical officer, Tim Stone, was alert for signs of exhaustion or 'operational tiredness'—a form of battle fatigue. As well, Bobby Gibbes had stood down a couple of pilots for 'unsuitability for air combat'. The squadron was desperately short of pilots.

Nicky remembered there had been five pilots who'd trained with him the previous October at Khartoum and who had been destined for No. 3 Squadron, but didn't turn up. He considered if he could find them they might be able to help. He phoned Group Captain Bill Duncan in Cairo, the liaison officer for all RAAF personnel in the Middle East. Duncan knew the air force well. He had been a RAF officer before the war but then retired and had owned several copra plantations near Rabaul. Now, brought out of retirement, he filled his position with enthusiasm and competence.

'Bill, I need reinforcements,' Nicky pleaded. He recited the five names to Duncan. 'These characters have never shown up at the squadron. Do you know where the hell they are? I want them,' Nicky demanded urgently. 'I need them. Also, there must be some other Australians floating around the Middle East who were trained with the Empire Training Scheme from Canada or Rhodesia.'

'Yes, Nicky, you're right on all counts. There were some from the training scheme, but the casualties in all squadrons are the same as yours. There's nothing special about No. 3 Squadron. I'm sorry,' Duncan informed him firmly.

Undeterred, Nicky continued, 'Fair enough. That means I'm not getting any replacements from there. But what about the fellows from Khartoum. Where are *they*?'

'I'm not too sure I know. I think some actually went back to Australia without any active service, and I believe with a promotion. I'll check up on them for you. At the same time, I'll see what I can do about replacements.'

This revelation was distressing to Nicky. The system wasn't supposed to work that way. His men were doubling up and even trebling for sorties in a day. Exhaustion was compounding human error and lives were being lost. He considered the pilots who'd trained with him in Khartoum were rorting the system. He thanked Duncan, and warned he'd call every day until he got some replacements.

The *khamsin* settled a little towards the afternoon, but the conditions were still hot and sticky. However, by about 6.30 in the evening, it had cooled and Nicky led six Kittyhawks from No. 3 Squadron and four from No. 112 on a mission south of Gazala. Radar had recently been introduced to the army and they had reported enemy aircraft about 30 kilometres south-east of Gazala. However, in these early days, their reportings were not always accurate and by the time Nicky and his formation arrived there the sky was empty.

Nicky elected to fly deeper south, and after a further ten minutes, while cruising at 7000 feet, 12 enemy aircraft were sighted at the three o'clock position. Nicky's formation had intercepted a bombing raid consisting of four 109s from 111/JG53 which were escorting eight bombers—four Me-110s and four Ju88s. Immediately, Nicky sent the Kittyhawks from No. 112 up as top cover, as simultaneously the Me-109s and 110s broke off from the Junkers and swung into a position directly astern of No. 3 Squadron.

Nicky called for No. 3 Squadron to whirl around to face them and, as one, with the evening sun flashing off their wings, they wheeled towards the enemy. Ahead of him, a 110 skidded into Nicky's space, coming directly at him. Nicky kicked the rudder bar and yanked the stick over hard.

Instinctively, as the enemy plane lined up with the black ball centred in Nicky's sights, he let off a burst at the front quarter as it roared closer to him.

The 110 flew right into his shells. Nicky saw strikes crash into the port wing and then noticed flames sear out of an engine. The bomber flipped wildly through the air and then dropped towards the ground, trailing a fast growing plume of black smoke.

As usual, Nicky was soon soaking wet. He had been in the air a long time already and the setting sun concentrated and magnified the evening heat, causing a furnace effect in his cockpit. He tried to wipe the sweat away from his face but there was no time. There would be more enemy planes.

He swung his Kittyhawk round, expecting to find other bombers, but the sky was empty; they had melted into the haze of the evening sun. Then, suddenly from above, three of the 109s dived through the top cover of No. 112 Squadron and dropped right past Nicky. Nicky hooked onto the tail of one, as other Kittyhawks joined in; another line-astern chase.

The golden sky sparkled with metal flashes as Kittyhawks and Messerschmitts seesawed across each other's flightpaths, leaving no shadows on the dark and brooding desert floor below.

Again, Nicky went through an eternity of diving, looping, skidding, rolling, stick over, back, forward, right and left, kick the rudder bar, take more 'G', skid her around. From the corner of his eye, Nicky winced as another Kittyhawk appeared beside him. Bright, flashing tracers. A 109 burst into flames not far from him, swooping and rolling crazily.

Then Nicky drew in closer behind his 109. He had narrowed

the gap and was looming onto the 109s port quarter. At about 300 metres he steadied, then his bullets raked the fuselage with a long, deadly burst. Flames immediately thrust out of the under-carriage and the 109 quickly lost power. Once again, Nicky didn't wait to see its dying throes. He was exhausted. G-force combat does that to a person.

By the time No. 3 Squadron had returned to Gambut, they had been in the air for over two hours but had shot down a confirmed three 109s, including one for Nicky. He was satisfied that the 110 he had left in flames was confirmed as a 'damaged'.

The sandstorms were still a problem over the next few days and No. 3 Squadron did not fly again until 4 June, although elsewhere in the desert the battle raged up and down the line. The quieter period for No. 3 Squadron gave Nicky a chance to work into his role as squadron leader. It was his first venture in-to the area of delegating responsibilities and, in his favour, the staff who administered the squadron were extremely competent and dedicated. Efficient systems were already in place and it required only minimal administrative duties from Nicky.

One obligation which he did insist on personally was to write the appropriate letter to the next-of-kin in the instance of a death of a squadron member. He knew this duty was often carried out by an adjutant in other squadrons, but to him, as he knew all these men personally, he felt the only letter the next-of-kin should receive should be a personalised one from the squadron leader. He was also keen to make sure that the deceased's belongings were properly gathered up and looked after. (If a 'missing' pilot had not turned up after three months, the gear would be placed in storage at RAAF Headquarters in Cairo.)

In his letters to next-of-kin, Nicky would try and comfort the recipient by stating his great sadness about the loss to him personally, and also to the squadron. He would talk about the importance of the job the deceased had been doing and how he considered that the relatives would like to know that the member had 'gone out happy', keen in his work.

Unfortunately, one aspect which made Nicky's job a little tougher was the reality of the escalating war in the Pacific. As the menace of a Japanese invasion threatened Australia, Nicky became aware of the detrimental effect that this news was having on some of his squadron members. Adding to this distress, the Sixth and Seventh AIF Divisions had returned to help protect Australia, and many loved ones and friends back home were unable to accept the reasons given for No. 3 Squadron's continued presence in the Middle East. They wanted their men back home—now. Adding weight to their arguments were reports of heated parliamentary debates and local media articles drawing graphic attention to this fact.

During these moments, Nicky appreciated and was comforted by his continuing letters from Dot. In turn, he would express his concerns about the situation in the desert and gain strength from her ongoing commitment.

Nicky often found himself counselling distraught personnel who had been advised by their wives and sweethearts that their relationships had been irreversibly damaged—the women were not waiting.

This situation was serious enough in itself, but the negative effect on morale was intensified as these men were also under extreme pressure from Rommel's dominant strategies and the force in his Panzer (tank) Divisions.

Some of the immediate fears of the impending Japanese invasion were calmed a little as the squadron received the welcome news that the Japanese had been stalled during the Battle of the Coral Sea in May, and had been soundly beaten at the Battle of Midway in the Pacific Ocean. Between 4 June and 7 June, the Japanese lost four aircraft carriers and many irreplaceable pilots. This would give the Allies time.

And Nicky needed time—and men. At this stage, the battle along the Gazala Line had intensified around Bir Hacheim. Earlier, British Eighth Army strategists had ordered their units to build a fortified chain of defences dotted over what could have been, if joined up, a unified strong front-line from Gazala to Bir Hacheim.

Unfortunately for the Eighth Army, Rommel did not attempt to take on these series of strongholds, about six altogether, all at once. His policy was to concentrate on one fort at a time, to devastate it, then move onto the next. Right now, the British armoured units, which were equipped with newly arrived American Grant tanks, were desperately trying to hold Rommel's Panzer Divisions. Army Headquarters called for aerial bombardment to try and trap Rommel in the Cauldron.

The Intelligence Officer from No. 3 Squadron reported to Nicky that RAF Headquarters had given him clearance to fly all day. The directive simply told him to get up in the air and strafe the enemy and drop bombs whenever and wherever he thought it would do the most good. Nicky called the squadron together and relayed this message to them.

'All right fellows, we have been given the green light to fight this war on virtually our own terms. Let's get out there and show 'em. We will concentrate mainly on the Bir Hacheim area and the Cauldron. Let's kick these bastards out so we can get back home.'

For 12 intensive days, the squadron united in one of the strongest, most protracted and desperate periods of battle they had encountered. From 4 June to 16 June, they flew 350 sorties, raining blistering bombs and strafing attacks from El Adem to Bir Hacheim. Time after time, the Kittyhawks roared down the strip, their blue exhausts illuminating the wings and fuselage, their bombs hugging the undercarriage. As one, they unflinchingly staggered through the protective flak defining the battle zone, then wheeled over the battle site, hurling their defiance into the teeth of Rommel's armour.

Day after day, they dropped hundreds of bombs on tanks, motor transports, armoured cars and anti-aircraft installations. They would then streak across the desert and strafe lines of troops, motor vehicles, tents and gun positions. The devastation and terror was complete. Troops reeled wildly under the impact of the bullets of the six heavy machine-guns. Tracers spat through the air and hurled dirt upwards as they moved across the ground and poured onto the guns.

Within seconds, the impact of the bullets would ignite ammunition dumps and fuel supplies and explode into a roaring ball of fire. Tanks and vehicles would be left upturned and in flames, leaving ribbons of black smoke spiralling skyward, signalling the devastation. It was a period of convulsive horror.

While involved in this carnage, the Kittyhawks were regularly challenged by Messerschmitts and Macchis, resulting in many savage dogfights. Between 2 June and 10 June, the Luftwaffe flew 1300 sorties against Bir Hacheim. Incident piled on incident, story upon story as the two armies collided. On 9 June, No. 3 Squadron scrambled to a mission south of Bir Hacheim where, at 7000 feet, they intercepted seven 109s. Instantly, planes broke out of formation all over the sky, swirling from ground level to a high thin cloud layer during a wild running encounter.

Several Messerschmitts dived underneath Nicky's plane, threatening to catch him from below. Nicky snapped into a tight sliding loop and rolled onto the tail of a 109, then squeezed out a burst as soon as the plane came into the range finder. The 109 rolled away and the bullets met only empty air. Nicky went into a left vertical spiral, and kept closing the distance, trying for a clear shot at the plane's belly. The 109 tried to match the turn, and for just a moment, his underbelly filled the range finder and Nicky squeezed out a second burst. The shells exploded along the fuselage, but the plane dived, speeding out of range, trailing a long smoke plume. The other Messerschmitts quickly followed, leaving the scene. As no one witnessed the 109 actually crash, Nicky was credited with a 'damaged'. In retreat, an army's opportunity to confirm destruction of enemy aircraft is greatly lessened, as much of the fighting takes place over enemy territory.

On 12 June, No. 3 Squadron escorted a squadron of Hurricanes over the El Adem area and recorded a successful bombing mission, obliterating long lines of motor transport and leaving a thick concentration of tents in flames. Unfortunately, with the increase in sortie activity there was also an increase in the chance to lose planes and squadron members. On this day, three planes were badly damaged, including one forced into a crash landing and one shot down in flames.

During battle, it was not always easy to see how other members of the squadron were faring. After a mission, as the planes flew back towards home, Nicky always glanced around the sky to gather some idea of who might have been lost, carefully searching and hoping everyone, especially his close friends, had made it. As with most pilots, on the return journey, he generally experienced a light-hearted exuberance in celebration of the fact he had made it through safely. However, it was not until the planes had taxied into the dispersal area, and enough time had elapsed for stragglers to arrive, that he could be assured of his squadron's safe return.

This same day, 12 June, his heart dropped as he realised his friend Geoff Chinchen, a most resourceful and reliable flight commander by this stage, did not return. Fortunately Chinchen had been seen parachuting from his burning plane and was later found to have been taken prisoner—a sad but hopeful consolation.

During this period, the pace did not slacken. As the planes landed, the mechanics, fitters, engineers, riggers and armourers worked furiously to maintain and keep the squadron in the air. They would tirelessly repair damaged structures, refuel the engines and replace the ammunition. Working through the day and often the night, they were regularly strafed by enemy fire. They resolutely shared the same deprivations as the pilots, caused not only by the war but by the unrelenting heat and dust of the desert. To Nicky, the success of his squadron regularly pivoted on the efficiency, fortitude and attitude of his wonderful ground crew and staff members.

Unforgiving pressure continued until it reached a peak on 16 June. On that day, the squadron, with just 14 aircraft, set an operational record, flying 69 sorties and dropping 61 bombs.

Nicky commanded six flights himself, which was acknowledged as a record at the time by any fighter pilot from any air force. His day started with him and Lou Spence—who flew five missions himself on that day—undertaking a reconnaissance flight over the Sidi Rezegh area. They observed a motor transport column moving behind 15 German tanks. Streaking out of the morning sun, they scored direct hits on two of the tanks, exploding them into a roaring mass of flames, then strafed the column of motor transport, leaving a wake of destruction behind them.

The area had become a cauldron of smoke and flames, fuelled by burning oil. As they flew low over the scene of the carnage, the terrible smell of putrefied flesh seeped into the cockpit as the slaughter continued, causing Spence to vomit into his lap.

On their return, Spence was still upset and shared his feelings openly. 'Hell Nicky, we did a lot of damage then. What a ghastly horror.' However, he realised the job had to be done.

After a quick refuel, Nicky led the squadron while they escorted another squadron of Hurricanes over Bir Hacheim. From the air during the previous few days, Nicky had clearly read the battle. A division of Free French Army troops had been hammering bravely at Rommel, and even though the Frenchmen were putting up a game resistance, the withering onslaught of the German tanks was cutting them to pieces.

The Hurricanes had been fitted with specially modified Bofors guns under the wings to counter the tanks. However, the extra weight seriously slowed the Hurricanes' speed. Moreover, when the guns were fired, the planes almost dropped out of the sky. The engineers had removed a part of the recoil section of the gun and used the planes' weight to act as the spring device. The effect was alarming. Nicky admired the bravery of the pilots as the Hurricanes lumbered in to account for at least six destroy-ed German tanks. However, their diminished manoeuvrability made them easy targets for the anti-aircraft guns. Slow and sluggish with their heavy armament, the Hurricanes wallowed helplessly in the air at low levels, unable to escape the slaughter. As Nicky watched, the deadly 'ack-ack' shooting hit and ignited some of the Hurricanes flying below him. Several of them exploded in a ball of fire, disintegrating in a burst of light.

For their next run, Nicky advised the Hurricane pilots to climb higher to gain speed. This proved extremely effective as ten planes dropped their payload directly over the centre of an Italian lorry unit brimming with infantry. The attack paralysed the column, leaving burning and upturned lorries sprawled in their wake and the road littered with dead men.

After lunch, just before 3.00 p.m., Nicky flew his fourth mission of the day. This time, he lead seven Kittyhawks south-west of Sidi Rezegh where the squadron encountered some more motor transport and troop carriers. Nicky had just released his bomb and was circling, preparing for a strafing run, when four Me-109s streaked out of the western haze, attacking the Kittyhawks head on.

Nicky was at some height and quickly came up into a firing position in front of the 109s at high speed. Nicky watched his closing distance—400 metres ... 350 metres ... 300 metres ... the range diminished in a twinkling. Looming in a camouflaged mass, the Me-109 filled Nicky's sight at 200 metres. A short burst from all guns. His bullets streaked down the fuselage of the 109 in a long side sweep. Nicky saw flashes as his bullets ignited small fires in the engine area which then seared out from behind the cowling. Pieces of the tail flew off and hurtled into space, whipping into the slipstream.

Nicky broke away instantly after firing and whirled his plane in a tight 'sliding' loop. He was preparing to line up for another run, however the 109 was nowhere to be seen. It had melted back into the haze from where it came. Nicky was credited with another 'damaged'.

On the return flight to base, Nicky experienced an unusual situation. Usually air-to-air combats are rather impersonal; Nicky generally managed to convince himself that he was merely shooting down a plane, not a person. In some respects, this philosophy was obviously a protective device to guard against the vicious reality of war. However, in this instance, his perception was about to become very personalised.

The haze, which often covers the desert, steadily thickened into cloud and Nicky and his squadron disappeared into its friendly concealing greyness. After some moments of peacefully flying blind and savouring the lack of stimulation, Nicky suddenly burst into brightness and found himself alone in a large bubble of clear sky, surrounded by cloud on all sides. To his surprise, over to his port, Nicky saw that he was not alone. He was, in fact, flying in formation with a German in a 109. For a few seconds, side by side, less than ten metres apart, the two planes flew in a bizarre parallel formation, the pilots' eyes meeting in glances across the narrow space between their planes.

He wore a helmet, but strangely the goggles were across the forehead. Nicky could see fear in the German's eyes, and he realised he too would be showing similar signs. Here was a real person—like himself—displaying the same primitive, yet very human, reaction. The impasse turned into a long minute. Both pilots knew that to pull away would allow the other to fire a shot. Eventually, the stand-off ended when they both flew into a cloud and were lost to each other.

Towards the end of this longest day, Nicky went up for his fifth mission at 4.30 p.m. leading nine Kittyhawks. The squadron located Rommel's headquarters north-west of El Adem at a location provided by the Eighth Army, and carried out a bombing and strafing raid. Six 250 pound bombs crashed at various sites around the Nazi establishment, throwing up explosions of dirt, flames and clouds of dust. Six ghastly pyres flared in six huge, debris-strewn craters and six pillars of black smoke united in a single, swirling path above the scene. The squadron then left a final message for Rommel by streaking across the perimeter and delivering a shattering strafing run, reducing many tents and installations to flaming ruins.

On the return flight to base, the squadron was intercepted by four 109s, and several of the flight members became engaged in close, desperate duels. One of his pilots, Sergeant Ross Biden, with engine problems, attempted to carry out a forced landing—his third in five days; such was the intensity of these encounters. He was at very low altitude and unable to release his bomb as he nursed his aircraft some distance behind the squadron. Unfortunately, as the plane touched down, it disappeared in a blinding explosion, blown into tiny pieces of wreckage as the bomb, one with an extended nose striker, went off with a shattering crash. The roaring mass of flames disappeared in a searing burst of light, as it disintegrated into the desert.

Several other planes did not return from this mission, so Nicky took off at dusk for his final flight of the day to search for them. It was a lonely flight. Shadows of small clouds rose and fell across the rippled sand dunes and mingled with the longer shadows of approaching evening. The perceived peace and solitude of the desert starkly contrasted with the signs of the day's combat. Sad plumes of smoke wisped skywards, marking the last stand of burnt-out tanks, gun installations, vehicles and planes.

Nicky flew low over bullet-riddled lorries with the palm and lightning forked swastika of the Afrika Korps stamped on gaping doors. He searched among overturned ammunition trucks, left scorched and twisted, and flew over derelict, blackened motorcycles; blood in the sand.

Nicky found Biden's plane, then landed to identify it. He also established that Sergeant Ryan had been killed. Nicky did not need reminding of the heavy price for this war.

The sacrifice did not go unnoticed at the top level either. To Nicky's great pleasure, he received a personal note from Air Chief Marshal Sir Arthur Tedder, Commander in Chief of the Middle East Air Force—a great honour. It read:

> *Congratulations on most efficient and successful fighter operations past two days. The bombers did very well because of the secure protection by 450 and No. 3 Squadrons. The fighting by No. 3 Squadron was particularly grand. You have put the Germans back a good pace and we must keep them there. Tedder.*

With great delight, Nicky took the message around to the various messes—the pilots' mess, the sergeants' mess and the ground staff's mess. Each reading was greeted with riotous cheering, as if they had won a football grandfinal.

This, after all, was what they were fighting for: to kick Rommel out of Africa.

THIRTEEN
Sidi Rezegh

War is never static for long. The next day, on 17 June, the over all battle picture swung decisively back in Rommel's favour. Despite a determined, collective will to push him back, Rommel's generalship and the power of his attacking armour were simply too overwhelming for the British Eighth Army. Even though No. 3 Squadron flew nine sorties that day, they were forced to retreat further back to Sidi Rezegh, 80 kilometres east of Tobruk.

During one sortie they lost another Kittyhawk, shot down in flames, but its pilot, Sergeant Hooke, returned later on foot. Nicky later learned that Oberleutnant Otto Schultz, the German who had shot Nicky down earlier, was killed this day, shot down by a Kittyhawk from No. 274 Squadron. He had just been decorated with the Knight's Cross and had amassed 51 victories. Another German pilot who had terrorised the desert skies, the ace Marseille, shot down six aircraft this day. Over the months he had taken part in some memorable duels with the Allied pilots, one in particular with 'Killer' Clive Caldwell of No. 112 Squadron, resulting in a moral victory to Caldwell. The victories this day brought Marseille's score to 101, and he was immediately called to Berlin to be awarded the Swords of his Knight's Cross with Oak Leaves—a Luftwaffe hero.

That same evening, Nicky needed some peace and solitude.

He regularly found it wandering in the desert on sunset. Nicky had discovered the colours of the desert; every hour brings a different tone to the sable hues, the sun touching patches as with a golden wand. Yet the sunsets and dawns can be magnificent.

On this particular evening, the sunset was unforgettable. It was like an immense silver and pink quilt, which hung overhead like a canopy, through which the early stars twinkled. It slowly changed to a vivid scarlet, the soft pastel shades being replaced by bold reds and fiery pools of crimson.

Nicky was compelled to be creative. He rested against a handy ridge and etched a poem in his logbook. He titled it 'Meanderings'.

Only the wind has life,
It wanders through this arid land,
Then does some dancin'
In the sand!
A sand, a grain of it in fact,
So seemingly lifeless, inert—basically!
When joined in fellowship by a trillion friends
And melded by oceans on kindly winds,
And even when it rains—occasionally!
Then, our desert sand embraces movement, life, serenity,
A rapturous calming therapy—gratuitously.

Nicky dated it '42 then, typically, needing some humour, he added:

My lines rarely scan,
So should their meaning not be clear
That is, remain a blot!
Then take me out and have me shot—immediately!

On 18 June, Nicky was recalled to RAF Advanced Headquarters in Cairo to report on the outcome of the preceding two weeks. He was introduced to the room of gathered officers by Air

Commodore George Beamish, RAF. Beamish was well known to Nicky by reputation as he was a rather legendary figure in rugby circles, having played for Ireland 17 times. He was a bear of a man, in character as well as stature, and towered over Nicky. He placed his large hand on Nicky's shoulder in a mock-intimidatory gesture and, when introducing him to the officers as another international rugby player, he smiled and said, 'I always eat little boys like you.'

Nicky accepted his patronising tone in good spirit, then, in cavalier mode, unflinchingly stood his ground with his address. His first protest was that he was desperately short of pilots.

'I am sure you are all aware of the pressures Rommel and his advancing army have placed on us. Some of my pilots are completing upwards of three and four missions a day, and operational tiredness is becoming a real issue to us. I would respectfully like to remind you that we need pilots—now. I don't know where they will come from, but I do know that there were at least five pilots who trained with me at Khartoum who are now "missing". They would be a great help if they could be found. However, my most pressing problem is accepting the changed role that No. 3 Squadron is being forced to play. It is on record that we have justifiably earned the reputation of being a specialised fighter squadron, particularly with our claim of achieving the highest number of air-to-air victories in the desert theatre.

'Even though No. 3 Squadron pilots have become both skilled and experienced in bombing and strafing, the energy spent on ground attack operations is removing them from the tactic they do best, air-to-air fighting. Here is the dilemma. Our army is in retreat and the Luftwaffe are having a field day. I must point out that squadrons with lesser air victories are being pitted against the Germans and I consider it makes more sense, in these desperate times, to utilise my No. 3 Squadron for air-to-air fighting.'

Beamish and the command listened and treated the requests seriously. They would certainly consider this point of view. Beamish said, 'I'll put your ideas to the AOC [air officer commanding]. In the meantime, you're in Cairo for a night, come and join us at The Dungeon.'

Nicky was pleased. The role of negotiator was a new experience for him. He considered he had been treated fairly.

'The Dungeon' was a nightspot under Shepheards Hotel, a Swiss-operated hostelry with grand accommodation and sumptuous meals. In the evening, as a cooling breeze drifted in from the green River Nile, the mood of Cairo mellowed as defence force officers and their ladies went dancing or dining. Soldiers of lesser ranks or gentility released wartime tensions in haunts like the Melody Club, where the band was protected from brawlers by a barbed wire fence, and the highlight of an evening's revelry was often a performance by a belly dancer.

The Dungeon was more atmospheric and intimate. Its steaks were tender, its wines French, and the companionship warm. This night, the place was filled with soldiers from the Free French Army, relaxing and recovering after intense weeks at the front. Some were still displaying dramatic evidence of the raging battle they had just left, either on crutches or wearing slings or bandages.

For a blistering two weeks, in an epic struggle, the besieged Free French brigade had gallantly defended Bir Hacheim, the outpost that blocked Rommel's drive towards Tobruk. The stubborn garrison scorned Rommel's call to surrender three times, until they were eventually ordered by Ritchie to evacuate. The proud brigade withdrew under fire at night, leaving behind heavy casualties of almost 1000 of their compatriots.

In the foyer of the hotel, which was in blackout, Beamish introduced Nicky to a French officer. The three of them moved downstairs, then settled into seats around a table. They ordered drinks and, through the smoke-filled atmosphere, they relaxed and reflected on the events of the last few weeks. There was a floor show in progress, everyone intent on enjoying themselves, albeit briefly, away from the horrors of war.

Suddenly, the lights dimmed, the room hushed, and the spotlight fell on a beautiful French woman. She had flawless skin and her flaming red hair was caught in the glare of the single beam. To complete the mood, Nicky could see she was wearing a French military uniform. The nostalgic sound of an accordion filled the room. She began to sing, standing motionless.

From the opening notes, her soft tones were charged with emotion. Her Piaf-like voice trembled as it speared unveiled sentiments deep into the Frenchmen's hearts. She sang a French loyalty song dear to the hearts of all Frenchmen, 'J'attendri' ('I will wait').

Nicky briefly glanced around the semi-darkness of the room and watched the dramatic effect of her words as they fell across the audience. Everywhere, tough but passionate Frenchmen wept openly and unashamedly, allowing the phrases to release previously restrained emotions. It was a most poignant moment.

As the song further evoked sentiments of patriotism and loyalty, Nicky felt a lump appear in his own throat. He swallowed hard, fighting to control his own feelings, his eyes stinging with unshed tears. He was deeply moved by the unbridled display of caring and grief and it was a necessary reminder of everything good and decent in the human spirit. In the middle of an ugly war, it would nourish him for some time to come. These Frenchmen were something special.

By now, Operation Venezia was having its full effect on the Allies. The balance of the battle remained firmly in Rommel's favour. After subduing Bir Hacheim in mid-June, he had pushed his Panzerarmee Afrika tank unit north along the Gazala Line, one by one knocking out the remaining forts. With the Gazala Line in shambles, he stood outside Tobruk again. By 18 June, Tobruk was once more under siege as Axis forces gathered around its perimeter.

On 20 June, the Afrika Korps and the Twentieth Italian Corps—with the crucial assistance of the Luftwaffe—began an assault on Tobruk. With a devastating combined barrage from tanks, artillery and bombers, followed by intensive hand-to-hand infantry fighting, the Allied garrison was quickly overrun. There was no counterattack. Tobruk surrendered.

Within 24 hours, Rommel had captured his prized Tobruk along with 35 000 men, a great number of vehicles and tanks, provisions and ammunition, and enough petrol to restart his drive towards Egypt. The following day, Hitler rewarded Rommel by promoting him to Field Marshal, and Italian Dictator Mussolini arrived, complete with his splendid uniform and white horse, ready for the expected victory through to Cairo.

In the meantime, No. 3 Squadron had been flying missions over Rommel's headquarters and spearheads, and had generally been assisting with the defence of Tobruk. Unfortunately, from the air, Nicky had noticed much panic on the ground as the Eighth Army retreated in some disarray. German spearheads were everywhere, forcing Ritchie to move his army further east and set up defences at Mersa Matruh. On 23 June, Nicky flew to Sidi Heneish to prepare for the squadron to withdraw there the following day.

Nicky was still without any pilot replacements and his men were now consistently showing signs of battle fatigue. No one was immune, as was typified by one of Nicky's close friends, Reg Pfeiffer. Pfeiffer had arrived in the Middle East a few weeks after Nicky and, like Nicky, had taken part in his share of life-threatening adventures. During their time together, they had often competed against each other, playing golf and tennis in

Cairo, as well as sharing the stresses of desert living and facing the almost daily combat rituals with a degree of enthusiasm and humour.

However, as the intensive campaign ground on, Pfeiffer disclosed he was becoming increasingly more distressed. At the thought of impending battle, his stomach would cramp and tie in knots, and he began experiencing nightmares. On the morning of 24 June, while waiting to scramble, he told Nicky of his fears and his reluctance to fly.

Nicky confided to Pfieffer: 'There wouldn't be one man here who doesn't feel this way. I was going to chuck it in myself two weeks ago, so don't feel bad about it. I guess it would be abnormal to feel any other way. However, we have to go on. There is simply no one else. We are the last line.'

Pfeiffer gained some confidence from Nicky's personal revelations, and his encouragement assisted him in meeting his responsibilities. He took to the skies with renewed courage.

Their mission that day was to carry out a reconnaissance of the forward area. Rommel's troops were in the process of crossing the border into Egypt and Nicky, leading six Kittyhawks, had orders to search for the spearhead, as well as to report on and protect any Commonwealth forces who may have escaped from Tobruk.

The squadron was flying just below patchy cloud at about 3000 feet, some distance south of Bardia. As they flew over an area known as Maddalena, Nicky noticed a great deal of enemy activity down below. Suddenly the sky was peppered with explosions of black smoke as heavy anti-aircraft fire rushed up to meet the planes. The barrage plastered the immediate sky around them, causing the Kittyhawks to buck wildly as they manoeuvred through the concussive airspace.

Temporarily distracted, the squadron was stealthily intercepted by ten enemy planes—six Me-109s, two Fiat G50s and two MC-202s. The planes had quietly materialised behind them, probably emerging from the cover of cloud, and quickly closed on the Kittyhawks. Someone yelled wildly over the radio, 'Bandits behind, watch it!' Immediately, the Kittyhawks shot out of formation and spun, looped and twisted back on themselves to confront the enemy fighter planes yelping at their heels.

Nicky swung into a grinding turn. At full power, he screamed in a tight circle and came out behind a G50. The G50 pilot was absorbed with another Kittyhawk which he had lined in his own sights, and probably did not notice Nicky. The Kittyhawk, flown by Sergeant Fox, pulled into a steep turn and desperately tried to shake and evade the G50. The G50, however, followed close on his tail, with Nicky sticking like a limpet to the Italian. The G50 fired, and Fox's Kittyhawk staggered and went down, out of control, tumbling and smoking and dumping debris.

Closing now like lightning, Nicky's fighter shook briefly with the burst of gunfire and the Fiat nosed up suddenly. Nicky's burst had thundered into the Fiat's engine compartment and, with a rolling-out-movement, the stricken G50 went diving down underneath Nicky. Out of control and smoking heavily, it shed chunks of its structure as it slowly inverted onto its back. For some seconds, it flew upside down then, still inverted, rushed headlong to its final impact. The Fiat disappeared into a ball of flame and disintegrated into fragments as it smashed into the desert floor.

Rolling into a shallow turn, Nicky found a 109 rushing in to fill his windshield at close range. He fired again and saw pieces blast away from the Messerschmitt. He'd hit it, but it wasn't mortal. Nicky's engine was screaming and his Kittyhawk was shuddering as he tore around at full throttle, but there was no chance to fire again. The 109 had merged into the quiet safety of the cloud.

Over to one side, Nicky caught sight of Sergeant Boardman firing at close range on a 109. Boardman raked the

Messerschmitt, which burst into flames then fell out of the sky joining a graveyard of four other planes left smoking around the battle site.

Nicky's plane was now seriously overheating and he banked away from the conflict. He quickly ascertained he wouldn't make it back to base, selected a suitable landing site and once again force-landed his damaged plane. Meanwhile, Sergeant Boardman was following not far behind on his way home and noticed the stranded Kittyhawk.

Even though all Allied squadrons had only recently received a directive not to land behind enemy lines to save another pilot (the risk of loss was too high), Boardman risked a court martial and landed beside Nicky, such was the commitment of these pilots towards each other and their cause. Nicky assured Boardman he was all right, and insisted he fly back to base. Some time later, after his plane had cooled down, Nicky managed to take off and return himself.

Nicky claimed one enemy fighter destroyed and one damaged during this combat, but was only credited with one confirmed conquest, the G50. This brought Nicky's cumulative victories to 12 destroyed, three probables and eight damaged. In one of the vagaries of war, the results of battles relied on cross-referencing with other squadrons and pilots, RAF Headquarters Intelligence and Army reports. Up to now, Nicky's combat reports showed he only claimed six victories, and he also claimed nine probables and eight damaged. During intense battles, particularly when the odds are stacked against a pilot, Nicky reasoned there was no merit in waiting around to confirm if his target had crashed or not. Official confirmation often had to wait for other witnesses to report the incident. (The only two Allied pilots who recorded more 'kills' in the Middle East were Nicky's friend 'Killer' Clive Caldwell of No. 250 Squadron and then commanding officer of No. 112 Squadron, who had been credited then with 19 and three shared victories, and Squadron Leader John Waddy, also of No. 112 Squadron, who eventually claimed 15.5 kills.)

That afternoon, the squadron moved back to Sidi Heneish. The following day, 25 June, Ritchie and the Eighth Army had set up positions in Mersa Matruh Fortress. Mersa Matruh was previously a quiet Mediterranean resort town and had been prepared and laid out as a fortress by the Italians in 1940 as they were advancing into Egypt—before the Sixth Division threw them out. The garrison was then used by the Allies mainly as a provision depot and port for ships taking troops and supplies to Tobruk while under siege in 1941.

Rommel's reconnaissance troops had closed up the Matruh defences and prepared to attack it the next day. In the meantime, some top level politicking saw Ritchie relieved of his command by Auchinleck, who placed himself in command. On the same day, the Australian Ninth Division, indignant that others had lost in only a day the Tobruk fortress they had bled to hold for eight agonising months, received orders in Lebanon to prepare to move to Egypt as soon as possible. They were determined to have their revenge on Rommel.

Nicky flew two missions on this day, both over Rommel's spearhead west of Matruh, bombing and strafing the advance troops.

For Nicky, the next day would change everything.

FOURTEEN

Mersa Matruh

It was about 9.30 a.m. on 26 June 1942. The eight Kittyhawks of No. 3 Squadron were approaching Sidi Barrani, about 130 kilometres east of Matruh. On the horizon, steadily metamorphosing through the morning haze, were rows of tanks, army trucks and vehicles. The squadron was approaching one of the spearheads of Rommel's large grey army which was posturing around Matruh's perimeter.

The image of the emerging tanks was menacing. The tanks which led the way formed the chilling shape of a large spear as they cut a swathe through the desert. From his cockpit Nicky could almost smell the black exhaust fumes pouring from the growling diesel engines. He could sense the clanging of the caterpillar treads as they charged relentlessly through the dusty, stark landscape.

He focused on one of the leading tanks, dropped the Kittyhawk's nose and streamed out of the sky. In well-rehearsed precision, the squadron followed, keeping in strict formation, then they released their bombs on the closest enemy target. Once again, explosions thrust dirt and smoke skywards as the bombs found their mark. Sheets of flame enveloped several tanks, leaving them crippled and their drivers burnt and dying.

As usual, the squadron followed this routine with a strafing run to complete their damage, spraying their deadly message among the panicking infantry. The Kittyhawks then banked to prepare to return to base. As they were leaving the scene, 28 Me-109s and Macchi 202s wheeled in from the sea, spotted them, then gave chase.

As the Kittyhawks were low in ammunition and fuel and they were heavily outnumbered, there was no point in confronting the enemy planes in open battle, so Nicky quickly moved the squadron towards home. The enemy kept them in sight and followed at a safe distance, allowing No. 3 Squadron to land at Sidi Heneish.

As soon as the last plane had landed, the Messerschmitts and Macchis dived out of the high morning sun. They raced over the camp area, strafing the airfield and gun installations causing a great deal of damage during their once-over skirmish.

Six of the undamaged Kittyhawks were quickly refuelled and Nicky led them up again. They joined No. 450 Squadron as escorts for 12 Boston Bombers and carried out a raid over the same area as the earlier mission. Once again, they were intercepted by Messerschmitts—nine of them—and a steaming air battle boiled across the skies.

Nicky could not get a good line on an enemy plane, but the 109s exacted a heavy price for the bombing raid, shooting down two Bostons and two Kittyhawks from No. 450 Squadron.

No. 3 Squadron escaped serious damage, but the pressure did not let up. They had no sooner returned from this mission when orders came through for them to get aloft immediately. They were to escort the Bostons again as over 100 enemy transport vehicles had been observed moving through a place called Mingar el Amar, west of Matruh. While waiting for his plane to be refuelled and his ammunition to be replaced, Nicky was assisted into his harness by his batman, Leo Freeleagus. Freeleagus was also a general 'roustabout' and would help out whenever he was needed.

Nicky was tired now. This was to be his 84th combat flight

and his third that morning. He was happy for the assistance and appreciated Freeleagus' cheerful banter.

'If you don't come back Nicky, what will you leave me?' Freeleagus quipped.

'You can have the lot, Bambino,' Nicky laughed, using Freeleagus' nickname. 'Incidentally, I couldn't find my scarf this morning. Do you know where it is?' Nicky asked.

'It was pretty unhygienic, so I rescued it for the laundry.'

'Okay, thanks. Look after it for me,' Nicky smiled, not displaying any outward concern that the incident could be construed as an omen. He closed the cockpit and taxied ready for take-off. Within a few seconds, Nicky was airborne and leading the remaining five operational Kittyhawks towards the El Adem area. They were soon joined by a handful of Kittyhawks from No. 450 Squadron and the ten planes moved into formation around the Bostons.

From his cockpit, Nicky focused on the now familiar scene. Somehow, he was still bemused at the lack of reality of the whole drama. He looked at the fighters lined up each side of him and at the same level as the bombers. They did not seem to be moving, but were poised in midair, rocking gently, rising and dipping easily on the invisible swells of air.

Completing the illusory effect and perpetuating the moment was the dramatic setting of the Sahara itself, its vastness and wildness often too large to contemplate—a place where nature ruled with a vengeance.

By 12.30 p.m., the bombers were approaching their target area. Down below, Nicky could see long lines of transport vehicles laden with troops and supplies steadily moving towards Mersa Matruh. The Bostons aimed their bomb sights on the transports and proceeded to unleash their deadly cargo.

Then, once again, the call came over the radio, 'Bandits, two o'clock high.'

For the third time that day, Nicky was attacked by Messerschmitts. A swarm of Me-109s from 111/JG27 dived out of the high noon sun and ripped through the escort planes. Nicky later found out that among the 109s was Oberleutnant Werner Schroer, an ace with 61 victories to his credit in Africa.

Men from both air forces moved inexorably towards a showdown. Nicky could see several clashes occurring in the air across the battle front, but once again he couldn't sustain a telling attack himself on an enemy plane. He was aware several Kittyhawks had taken some damage from the initial onslaught, but luckily they all stayed airborne.

From his position, Nicky could see that the Bostons had released their payload and had turned for home. While the Me-109s were regrouping, Nicky swung his Kittyhawk around and quickly prepared to escort the bombers from the conflict area. After some moments, to his consternation, his motor started to lose power.

Nicky began to drop behind a little, slowly moving out of formation. He was slightly unnerved as they were kilometres behind enemy lines and he knew there was still four Me-109s hovering in the vicinity to pick up stragglers. The squadrons were still maintaining radio silence, so he reasoned his best chance, in case of attack, was to gain some height in order to utilise the assistance of speed with a dive. The Kittyhawk excelled at this as there was so much weight in front. By simply dropping the nose and increasing the 'revs', the plane could really pick up speed.

Nicky levelled at 12 500 feet and searched the skies for the Messerschmitts. Suddenly, while he was weaving to create a more difficult target, a 109 dived out of the sky above and shrieked passed him. It was a blood-curdling, screaming dive and Nicky gasped as the plane whipped right across his immediate vision then disappeared in a blur beneath him.

Normally, Nicky would have given chase but as his engine was not performing, he dropped to 10 000 feet and maintained his course towards home. Then, just as suddenly, a second Messerschmitt swung in from behind.

It was Oberleutnant Schroer. Schroer roared in as close as he could then, at 30 metres, he caught Nicky square in his sights. He unleashed a terrific fusillade that raked almost the entire length of the Kittyhawk. It was a perfect rear-quarter shot. Schroer's cannons exploded first right on to the rudder. Nicky immediately lost fore and aft control as the bullets severed connections to the tail fin.

Ray Pfeiffer, Nicky's friend, who had been having difficulty returning to the skies only a few days previously, was flying just a little to one side of Nicky. He witnessed the strikes chew into the thin metal of the fuselage and race along the port side of the Kittyhawk. The bullets then crashed into the cockpit and finished by smashing into the engine. Licks of orange flame darted and spat from beneath the cowling, escaping to form a trail of black smoke which quickly whipped into the slipstream.

Pfeiffer suspected Nicky had been wounded, but he couldn't assist him as he was being attacked himself by a third Me-109. He wheeled off to confront his own assailant.

Particles of glass shattered inside Nicky's cockpit as the bullets crashed into the armoured-glass windscreen. Sinister-looking spider-web cracks radiated from the window but the protective glass absorbed most of the impact. Two 20-mm cannon shells smashed into his left leg. He sucked in deeply, but felt no pain—nothing—just shock. He didn't have time to register exactly where the bullets had hit or the extent of damage as his concentration was abruptly diverted to another emergency.

His nostrils burnt with the acrid smell of cauterised electric wiring and his lungs began to fill with choking black oily vapour. Glycol smoke streamed from the motor and oil smeared over the windscreen, blocking his vision. The motor was failing. The nose of the Kittyhawk dropped and arced into a steep dive. Fierce wind suction had drawn flames from the exhaust stubs and other parts of the burning plane back into the cockpit.

At the same time, he was aware the flames were also licking around his feet. Now they were probing underneath his seat, igniting the parachute pack. He could smell flesh burning and was aghast to notice his left leg and the skin and fat on his left forearm was on fire. The wish that he'd worn a long-sleeved shirt that morning flashed through his mind.

The plane was now diving at a remarkably high speed. He would have to bail out, but was reluctant to do so at such a high altitude as, like Bobby Gibbes before him, he couldn't be sure a German pilot would not try and use him for target practice. He resisted trying to open the canopy for just a few more seconds.

Nicky was also concerned that the canopy might not open, and even if he could force his way out, he realised his left leg was not working and he might not be able to push himself out of the plane. He may have to try and roll the plane and fall out. Because of the steep angle of the dive, there was a danger of hitting the tail on ejection.

Nicky quickly realised he wasn't going to have the indulgence of that option. The flames had now caught the parachute and he could feel the heat searing his body and face. His eyelashes were burning and the cabin smoke was seriously interfering with his breathing and vision. He had to get out—straight away.

He struggled with the canopy. It wasn't going to open. His efforts to release the canopy were hampered by the increasing speed of the plane, which flattened him against the armour plating frame of his back seat. He wondered for an instant what the terminal velocity of the plane would be. He had been here before—with the Wirraway in Brisbane. This terrifying notion spurred him to try harder to force the canopy.

After what seemed an eternity of intensive effort, the canopy shot back. Immediately the gale-force slipstream howled and tore around the cockpit. He quickly disconnected his oxygen and radio cords, then unbuckled his seat harness.

In despair, he found his unresponsive left leg could not push hard enough to allow him to eject. As well, the increasing eye-ball popping impact of the building G-forces crushed him further against his parachute. He was effectively immobilised, while everything around him was happening at a furious pace.

Battling a rising tide of panic, with all his fading strength he pressed on his right leg. After what seemed like another lifetime, he slowly edged up out of the seat. Within another instant, the hurricane-force winds, whipping past the canopy, suddenly sucked him free of the doomed Kittyhawk.

Sky, earth and planes flashed before Nicky in a wild kaleido-scope as he tumbled earthwards. For some seconds he free-fell through space, savouring the fact that he was still alive and relishing the cold air as it revived his senses. Luckily he had shot well away from the tail, and was relieved when he noticed the rushing air had also extinguished the flames on his body. He was also grateful to see that the fire which had been raging on his parachute harness was now only smouldering and the harness cords were still holding.

Once again, he debated with himself how long he should free-fall before he pulled the ripcord. He didn't really know what height he was at. Besides, his line of vision was greatly impaired—the pressure that had sucked Nicky from the plane had damaged a blood vessel behind the eyes—he could not see the ground.

He was also aware of the taste of blood in the back of his mouth. What was that from? He shouldn't delay anymore—he pulled the ripcord. There was a rustling of silk and cord followed by a plumping sound as the parachute unfurled above him. To his great elation, Nicky felt his shoulders pull up and shake with the jolt. The bruising jerk shook every joint in his body as he was jarred upright in the parachute harness. He couldn't focus on anything clearly, but he knew he was floating down.

His first impression was how quiet it seemed after the combined noise of the aircraft engines, the gunfire and the roaring blaze in the claustrophobic confines of the cockpit. It also felt peaceful after the confusion and uncertainty of the previous few moments. The only sound was the gentle whisper of the air flowing through the silk above.

For a few brief seconds, his traumatised mind tried to contemplate his situation. Yes, he was alive. He had serious third degree burns on his legs and arms, bullet wounds to his leg, a seared face and damaged vision. As well, he was steadily and harmoniously spiralling to earth and he was deep behind enemy lines. But he would live to fight.

For one blinding instant, his mind flashed to Dot again, realising the concern she would feel when he was posted missing for the third time. He also realised he could hear no other planes in the vicinity so probably nobody at No. 3 Squadron would know his eventual fate. Suddenly, he laughed to himself, 'That bloody Bambino will take all my gear'—and then, 'I hope he looks after my scarf.'

The ground was fast approaching as a blur. A strong crosswind unsettled him as his left leg was dangling; in fact he could not feel it at all. The landing could be tricky. He considered the leg would not be much use, particularly if he hit the ground at speed.

An instant later, he crashed into the desert while the parachute was still in its high pendulum phase, catching all the force on his right leg. He landed heavily but, to his relief, safely. Before the wind could catch his parachute and drag him along, Nicky pushed the release button in the centre of his chest, releasing the harness. He then collapsed and sprawled onto the desert floor.

He was exhausted, in shock, and grateful he wasn't still on fire. Adrenalin suppressed his pain and he hugged the ground with gratitude. He hoped he was alone as he needed time to recover. He lay there dazed, moving in and out of consciousness. In this twilight state, he was vaguely aware that he was attempting to reassure his mother that he was all right, that he was doing the best he could. He then blacked out.

Some time passed before Nicky awoke to a voice. It was like a whisper, and it was in Italian, 'Lui é morto.' In his dazed state, he remembered dimly back to his student days. His friend Freddy Eggleston had bought a book for the two of them, *How to Learn Italian in Six Easy Lessons*. Vaguely he recognised the words as meaning 'he is dead'.

Nicky thought the voice was referring to somebody else—it could not be him. He was then aware the Italian soldier was taking his pulse. However, the pulse was impeded as some shrapnel was pressing hard against it. Next thing, Nicky felt somebody was taking off his watch. He raised his head, incensed that he was being written off. How dare they try and steal his Rolex. He began to posture in retaliation at the figure, but his eyes could only note shadows and blurred images. He then passed out completely, lapsing into a deep coma.

In the meantime, the remaining planes of No. 3 Squadron had flown safely back to base. They reported directly to Wing Commander Rosier.

Reg Pfeiffer said, 'Nicky's gone, sir.'

'Did he get out?'

Keith Kildey replied, 'I saw his chute open, sir, and I know about where he could have landed.'

Rosier thought for a moment. 'How many serviceable planes have we?'

'Four, sir.'

'Go back up and see if you can find him.'

Within minutes, the four planes had been refuelled and were searching over the battle area. They sighted a great number of German armoured cars patrolling all around the site, then just ahead, crumpled on the desert floor, Pfeiffer pointed out a bundle. It was Nicky's parachute harness, still dumped in a pile where he had discarded it. The Italians had taken the parachute as the silk was a treasured trophy.

There was no sign of Nicky.

FIFTEEN

Tobruk

Nicky very slowly and painfully attempted to move and open his eyes. Through a sea of fuzziness, he became aware that he was lying on a stretcher in a medical tent. As the blurred images of the scene around him cleared further, he could make out other injured men waiting on stretchers for treatment. He was bathed in sweat and every movement hurt. Outside, tendrils of oppressive heat still pushed down from a brassy afternoon sky, and he was grateful to be under cover.

Vaguely, the last thing he remembered was lying prostrate, crumpled on the desert floor. He had no recollection of being gathered up, transported and set-down in the tent. Now, in his semiconscious state, he was becoming aware of pain—deep, serious pain.

A young German doctor—a charming yet business-like major—appeared at his side and asked in perfect English, without a trace of a German accent, 'Young fellow, how are you going?'

'I don't really know. Where am I?'

'You're in an advanced German casualty clearing station, not far from Mersa Matruh. We'll have a look at you.'

The doctor examined him carefully and with some degree of compassion, although Nicky passed in and out of consciousness several times during the assessment.

'It doesn't look too good now. Might be a bit better after we clean it up. Haven't got much of your ankle left, the foot and Achilles tendon are badly damaged, and there's a "plug" in your leg—a fragment of something, probably from a 20-mm shell—and I don't know how deep it is. Might save you a lot of pain along the way if we take the foot off.'

Nicky wasn't too impressed with that suggestion. He realised he wasn't in the best mental condition to clearly comprehend the full implications of amputation. With a degree of wry humour, he asked, 'I don't suppose I could get a second opinion?'

The doctor appreciated his comment and laughed gently.

Nicky tried again. 'What are the chances of keeping it?'

'There is a hope. Depends a lot on your own wellbeing. I can encase the leg and foot in plaster,' the doctor explained. 'It may heal. Our next clinic can assess it from time to time.'

'Let's go for the cast.'

Nicky surprised himself by not being as concerned by both the extent of the injury and the possible outcomes of any treatment as he thought he would be. He now recalled his realisation almost immediately after he landed that he had sustained a serious injury and he knew instinctively that running and rugby would be a thing of the past. He would never know how well he'd stack up against the best rugby players in Europe.

It pleased Nicky that he could be comfortable with his fate as he had never considered himself to be a realist to that extent, rather a bit of a dreamer and an optimist. However, the decision was cut and dried, and instead of feeling depressed he was actually relieved about his situation.

Nicky moved in and out of consciousness until later in the evening when, as searchlights played across the evening sky, he entered into a deep sleep.

When he eventually and slowly emerged from his coma, his burns had been dressed and his ankle and leg were firmly encased in plaster. He noticed now that the clearing station was full of German and Italian soldiers as well as Allied prisoners. In fact, the patient on the stretcher next to him was a German tank officer, recovering from burns and a leg amputation. Outside, the walking wounded were everywhere.

While in the desert, Nicky had gained a smattering of German and the tank officer had an average command of English. They befriended each other and Nicky found out the German was to return to his home north of Hamburg for treatment. In turn, the officer expressed regret that Nicky would not be able to return to his own home for treatment. Nicky marvelled that he and this former adversary were capable of shelving their enemy roles and could consider each other simply as human beings, suffering together the misfortunes of war.

When transport became available, Nicky, the German officer and a number of wounded and sick soldiers were placed on the iron tray of a captured Eighth Army 3-ton truck and transported to Sollum, then on to Tobruk. There were no ambulances available and the journey was hot and long, made more bearable for Nicky by lengthening periods of unconsiousness.

Although initially impressed by the positive outlook of his German friend, Nicky became disturbed when he noticed his condition deteriorate during the rough journey. To Nicky's distress, the man died before reaching Tobruk—here was a man in desperate plight, an enemy, who had showed him compassion.

Nicky also received a lesson on expendability as he witnessed his captors carry out a quick solution to a nasty problem. Along with Nicky's German officer friend, six Allied prisoners also died during the difficult trip and were simply cremated by the roadside, with little ceremony other than the collection of 'dog tags'.

The truck finally manouvered its way through the rubble-littered streets of Tobruk and finished at the hospital on the perimeter of town. After being transferred to a stretcher on the floor among German and Italian wounded, Nicky became incredibly thirsty. An enthusiastic Italian wardsman introduced himself as Bruno and passed Nicky some water.

Showing off his Italian, Nicky responded with, 'Bravo, Bruno.' Bruno burst out laughing and went off in search of food. Incredibly, he returned with a tin of pears from Ardmona, a packing company in Victoria.

'Would you like a pear?'

'Si. Grazie,' Nicky answered. As the burns on his hands had been covered and prevented Nicky gripping anything, with good will and some humour, Bruno fed him.

'Do you like it?' he asked.

Nicky nodded.

'The nectar of the gods.' Bruno gave him more.

Nicky knew then that even though he was with the enemy, here was another man who was compassionate—an Italian who could laugh with him.

Bruno cleaned the crusty dried blood and mucous from Nicky's eyes and ears, and immediately he started to hear and see better. But he was exhausted and he needed to sleep, so for the next week he remained on the floor and simply rested.

With Bruno's care, Nicky's health steadily picked up. At the end of the week he heard that at least 40 prisoners had died in Tobruk over the previous few days from dysentery and lack of proper treatment, and he felt himself fortunate. The next day, Nicky noticed they were cleaning the ward—perhaps to curb the infections?

'What's up?' he asked Bruno.

'Mussolini is coming to visit Tobruk.'

And indeed, later that day, Mussolini arrived complete with entourage and supported by propaganda depicting him resplendent in fascist uniform with a dazzling array of medals on a magnificent white horse. As Italy's fascist dictator for 20 years,

Il Duce had ruled with an iron fist and commanded respect from his army.

Standing on a box in the ward, he took a position in front of Nicky to deliver his speech, polished heels at Nicky's eye level. He shouted, ranted and postured for some time and Nicky, with his broken Italian, understood most of the rhetoric. He told those assembled that it wouldn't be long before they would be in Cairo and onward, heading to a glorious victory. He spoke of his dream of the New Order and re-establishment of the Roman Empire, to which there was great applause.

Then he focused on Nicky, quite a pathetic looking individual by now, sick, unshaven, burned and in a generally decrepit condition. 'The Allies must be in a very poor way indeed to have someone like this as a major,' he gestured flamboyantly. (There were no squadron leaders in the Italian Airforce—they used army ranks.) Everyone laughed. Nicky understood and didn't like it—he disliked anyone who shouted, and here was this pretentious little prig, this jockey-sized pantomine character performing just as the Allied propaganda said he did. It was said that a film had already been made of Mussolini and Rommel leading a victory parade in Alexandria and Cairo.

Nicky muttered under his breath, 'I'll show this pompous little bastard.' Upsetting as it was, Nicky realised that parading a downed enemy presented an excellent opportunity for a politician to bolster his own success. So convinced were the injured Italians and Germans they would soon be in Cairo that they asked Nicky where the good night clubs and entertainment venues were, and how they could best avoid VD.

By now, Nicky had befriended another Afrika Korp officer. He too was a tank commander, an Austrian, and was in a bed next to him, his knee cap blown off. Curiously enough, he was also a doctor and spoke good English. He told Nicky he wanted to do postgraduate studies in surgery at Edinburgh and was keen to practise his English on Nicky. He also had news for Nicky: 'We are going on a ship to Italy and you are going with us.' Nicky was pleased as it had not been much fun on the concrete floor.

Nicky, his Austrian friend and another officer were carried down to the wharf in stretchers and placed on board the hospital ship *Città di Trapani*. Highlighted against the bomb-damaged ships in the harbour, Nicky noticed the huge red crosses displayed on the ship. Bruno carried one end of Nicky's stretcher and gently lowered him onto the deck. As Nicky turned to shake Bruno's hand and thank him, he was touched and surprised to notice Bruno was crying. During their small time together they had generated a strong friendship, and Bruno had shown him great kindness. Nicky smiled in appreciation and shook his hand warmly. When Bruno had gone, Nicky realised he didn't even know Bruno's last name.

Out at sea, the ship moved very slowly. Nicky and the two Africa Korp officers were placed mid-ship below deck and were concerned at the slow progress. Suddenly, an announcement came over the loudspeaker, first in German, then Italian: 'Action stations. We are being attacked by a submarine.'

Nicky's Austrian friend translated, then added, 'We're not in the best situation in this ship with that happening. We'd better get up top.'

The three men crawled up to the crowded deck where the crew insisted a torpedo from a British submarine had crossed their bow. Nicky moved to the rail and searched the ocean but could find no substantive evidence of the submarine or its torpedo.

While on deck, in the distance Nicky caught sight of an apparition that looked for all the world like an angel. He saw a man with both arms in plaster, forearms and elbows locked upwards as wings. The man had been burned on his arms and chest and the configuration was designed to keep his arms from contacting his body. Simultaneously, both men recognised each other. The man was Rudy Leu, known to all as 'Roo Loo', a laconic, laid-back character and an airman. Nicky knew him well; they had flown together many times.

Leu was an Englishman who had migrated to Australia and had been working as a jackeroo when the war broke out. He joined up immediately and became a member of No. 112 Squadron. Neither knew the other had been shot down.

'What the hell are you doing here?' they chorused in unison.

For the rest of the trip they supported each other. It was good to have a friend. The journey took five days and the ship was cramped, slow and potentially dangerous. Hygiene was very poor and in the wretched conditions many men died en route. They both agreed it was a 'misery ship'.

As they approached Naples, the men noticed the harbour was clogged with destroyers, ocean-going liners, tankers and other vessels of war. The wharves were lined with hustling electric dockside cranes and supplies. The industry of war overshadowed the sleepy ancient city perched on the cliffs surrounding the harbour. Nicky had trouble reconciling the scene with his expectations of the romantic village that gave birth to the Neopolitan love song. The meaning of the old Italian proverb 'See Naples and die' now had a more sinister ring.

The day was hot and sticky, although a small sea breeze did offer some relief. On docking, the sick and wounded were laid out on stretchers along the pier, the well-worn cobblestones offering a small clue to the antiquity of the town. Into their midst came a fine looking woman, the Princess of Piemonte. Incongruous with the scene around her, she was beautifully attired and gave a welcome address to everybody, friends and foe alike. Nicky was impressed; she was most charming. A few sugar lollies were distributed to some stretcher cases.

From here, the prisoners were gathered onto the tray of a

lorry and driven to the prisoner of war hospital at Caserta, on the escarpment almost 35 kilometres north-west of Naples. It was an uncomfortable drive, but eventually Nicky was lifted from his stretcher and placed in a ward bed. He settled quite well for a few days but then developed an increasing pain in his leg. Over the next few days he lapsed in and out of consciousness until an Italian doctor eventually decided to remove the plaster.

The smell was ghastly, causing Nicky to be very concerned about what may be left of his leg. However, all the doctors started pointing and appeared very happy with the result. They told him he had a very clean wound, due entirely to an infestation of maggots. The thought was repulsive, but Nicky was grateful for the outcome. The doctors then inserted probes into the wounds and removed the majority of the foreign matter which had been blasted into it. They retrieved remnants of leather (from his desert boots), a piece of sock, a fragment of plane, a piece of a 20-mm shell and some felt wadding (used in a cannon shell as a sealant between the bullet and the gunpowder, often adhering to the shell when fired).

They also cleaned and dressed his other wounds and burns, although it became obvious his captors were light on medication, particularly anaesthetics and antiseptics. Over the next few days some burn scabs became infected and although Nicky didn't feel too seriously ill, he was graded as such.

But his condition quickly deteriorated due almost entirely to neglect. In fact, death was eternally present in the crowded hospital. They were losing about 35 patients a day, many from dysentery due to poor hygiene. It was decided that Nicky's condition was serious enough for him to be sent to the Italian Ospitale Clemintino at Bergamo, about 50 kilometres north of Milan and just south of the Swiss Alps.

It was a two-day train ride of 750 kilometres and Nicky was provided with one piece of bread and two bowls of boiled rice.

Travelling with eight other prisoners, it was an uncomfortable and long journey and Nicky was not well.

His friend Roo Leu was also travelling with him, minus his wings (looking angelic never suited him, Nicky joked), and he too was unwell. The beauty of the Italian countryside was mostly lost on them as the train passed spectacular mountain scenery where steep ravines and streams crashed into the sea, and later, on the northern coastal plains, through peasant farm lands rich with olive groves and vineyards. Always on the left was the sparkling blue Tyrrhenean Sea, and through the opposite window glimpses of red-roofed villages in the folds of hills and along river valleys.

One particularly distressing event occurred towards dusk of the first day, when halfway between Naples and Rome the converted passenger train was attacked and the glass window adjacent to Nicky was shattered by a large rock. Stones were thrown along the whole length of the carriage, showering prisoners with slivers of glass. Two were killed, either by the glass or the stones.

The desire to harm the prisoners was borne purely out of a wish for revenge by Italians whose relatives had been killed by the Allies, and they knew this train was coming through.

The rest of the trip to Bergamo passed in a daze for Nicky as his condition deteriorated further. He was not alone in his plight—by the time the train had reached its destination, four prisoners had died.

SIXTEEN

Bergamo

Bergamo is centred around an industrial and agricultural region close to the Alps and was famous in history as it stood on the Old Silk Road. Indeed, even up to recent times just before the war it had provided silk for England.

Bergamo's Ospitale Clemintino was a large two-storey building, constructed in brick of solid Italian masonry, in keeping with the pompous neoclassical style of the town. It had been designed and utilised as an old peoples' home and was run by an order of nuns trained to care for them—*una comunità religiosa*. It quickly became obvious to Nicky that these nuns were unconditionally devoted to caring for people, particularly spiritually.

Nicky was placed in the care of an energetic young sister. She was petite, with a tiny face and frame, yet Nicky soon found she possessed a determined inner strength. Under her care, with rest and good food, Nicky's health steadily improved. He shared jokes with her and would affectionately call her *La Sorella*, short for *La Sorella del cuore buono* (the sister with the kind heart).

She called him *Birichino* (naughty boy)! He was impressed by how she would conduct her rounds at all times of the day or night, even when she should have been resting. Nicky would often chat with her at two, three or four in the morning while she was carrying out these unrostered checks. By then, everyone was calling her *Bambina* (little girl) as she was so elf-like.

Even though Nicky's general health began to prosper, his progress was hampered by a persistent infection in his wounded instep where the fragment of a 20-mm shell was still lodged. An Italian doctor, searching with probes, could not extricate it. Adhesions had locked it in.

Then, for all the wounded prisoners, a stroke of luck occurred. Into Bergamo came four of the top medical specialists in their field—two British and two Australians. They had been captured at the fall of Tobruk and quickly started to make a difference to the health of the prisoners. With the sisters' support, they were able to acquire alcohol and other medications to use as anaesthetics and perform surgery.

Supporting the commandant and the medical staff was an interpreter, Tenente Periconi. Prior to the war Periconi had been the night manager at the Park Lane Hotel in Piccadilly, London, and Nicky had met him then when he was staying there with the Wallabies. Periconi had been called to one of the players' rooms to reduce the noise level one night when they were partying. He also complained that the singing was atrocious. Now, he helped the prisoners whenever he could.

Among the doctors was Major Keith Moore, an Australian, who eventually operated on Nicky's foot and deftly removed the metal fragment. Nicky recuperated comfortably until a few nights later, at 2.30 in the morning, *La Sorella* was carrying out one of her unscheduled inspections. She bent over Nicky's bed and found it seeping with blood. Nicky was haemorrhaging seriously from the foot wound. He had obviously been bleeding for some time and had fallen into another coma—his third since being in the RAAF.

La Sorella felt for his pulse. It was too low! 'O mio Dio! Il suo polso é troppo passo.' She rang the alarm bells, quickly summoning medical assistance. Within a few minutes, the doctors arrived and arrested the blood flow. There were no blood transfusions available and Nicky's life hung in the balance for some time. He remained in a coma for the next few days and *La Sorella* rarely left his bedside, tending to his every need.

When he eventually revived, Major Moore confided, 'You know, Nicky, it has been a pretty close call. Clearly, you owe your life to this sister,' he said, smiling at *La Sorella*.

Indeed, her faithful attention, her unparalleled and unquestioned compassion, her devotion to her duties—all from the so-called enemy—touched Nicky deeply. And he told her so.

The friendships he developed with 'the enemy' during this time caused Nicky to change his philosophies concerning war, his ideologies of life and people. His new philosophy was that you can hate intensely what people stand for, in this case, Fascism and Nazism, but you don't necessarily have to hate individual people. At the same time, he was also realising all Italians weren't necessarily Fascists—most he encountered were good people who had been influenced by propaganda and force. In fact, he believed many of them weren't at all keen on being at war.

Just the same, while the Axis powers were winning during almost three years of war, there was strong, justifiable support from the German and Italian people for their leaders.

At this stage the prisoners started to receive their first food ration parcels from the Red Cross. This helped greatly towards a general improvement in Nicky's overall health. Eventually he could sit, then he carefully started to walk again. By late autumn, November 1942, he was beginning to feel very well. Well enough to be interested in escaping.

Nicky found that for most prisoners held in hospitals, the decision to escape is not easy. He had imagined that when captured, a man automatically longed to get away. He found this was not true and was surprised to find only a small percentage of prisoners made persistent attempts to escape; the majority generally accepted captivity and tried to endure it with as much cheerfulness and dignity as possible. For these men, the immediate difficulties of planning an escape and facing being hunted again often seemed insuperable.

To Nicky, there was absolutely no conflict here. He needed to get out as soon as possible, and then get home. He realised he was fortunate to have a strong incentive to survive and get home—his yearning for Dot had never been so powerful.

Dot would remain the prime motivation for Nicky's need to escape. During this time, he wrote two letters a week and sent them home through the Red Cross. A fair percentage reached their destination, although he didn't know that. Even though Dot still wrote almost daily and sent parcels, for whatever reason, he never received any mail or parcels from home himself. As well, he had heard no more of the progress of the war outside since he'd left Tobruk. He could not accept being held captive and restricted by anyone—he was not cut out to be a prisoner.

Nicky realised that because of his improved health, he would soon be sent to a prisoner-of-war camp, decreasing his opportunities to escape. Bergamo was in a good location to escape from: it was in the north, less than 75 kilometres from the Lake Country and the Swiss Alps. The obvious aim would be to cross the border into neutral Switzerland before winter set in. He could then either be interned there quietly until the end of the war, or go through an escape route which had been disclosed to Nicky and the other prisoners called the 'comet line', an underground system eventually leading to England. He decided that now was the best time to make his attempt.

Bergamo had an escape committee headed by the senior officer, a British Army major. Several long-term plans were in process, but aids for escaping—such as maps, local currency, rope, compass, suitable clothing and sustenance rations—were difficult to accumulate. A priority list controlled the sequence of these attempts to escape, so Nicky spent some time in solid planning before submitting his proposal.

The hospital was protected by a battalion of Italian soldiers lodged in an adjacent building. In the centre of the hospital was a garden with a lawn where the prisoners exercised. At one end of the garden was a building with a half window at ground level, which Nicky suspected could lead into the basement. There might be a way out through there.

Nicky knew that a key requirement for his escape plan was to set the position up thoroughly. He needed to inspect the area. He discussed his intentions with two Englishmen he had befriended. Then, over the next week, they met each day and planned the attempt. The building in question was protected with barbed wire but, on closer examination, the men found a weak point where the wire was plugged into the masonry around the window.

They acquired a fork and a broken-down penknife and while his two 'lookouts' sat in front of the window, checking backwards, Nicky worked at breaking and scraping the mould off the wall. He took care to twist the sharp ends of the wire away from the opening of the window, then, in a flash, when he was sure the guards were not watching, he squirmed through the opening.

He waited motionless for a few seconds on the other side; no noises from outside. Yes, he was safe. Holding his breath and moving quickly, he found another area that was full of offices. There was no one around. So far, so good. He moved down some steps and found he was among the sewerage system and water pipes and, to his repugnance, some large gulley traps filled with foul-smelling effluent. They were about a metre square and probably ran into an external system outside the prison.

Nicky quickly retraced his footsteps and finished up back in the garden with his friends. He breathlessly told them what he'd seen.

'I think we can do it. It's only a small opening and I don't know how deep or far it goes, but I'm willing to try it—I think it's worth the risk. Do either of you want to come with me when I go?'

The Englishmen were keen, but neither were well. One said, 'I really am too old, and,' smiling towards his friend, 'I think we'd slow you down.' His friend, Captain Brian Stone, laughed and agreed. He was a double amputee. 'But we'll assist,' he added.

Nicky's good friend, Roo Leu, had recovered from his injuries and had already been sent on to a prison camp, and most other friends he trusted were either too old or not well enough. He would go alone.

Now he needed a map.

This came from an English major who had been transferred from a senior officers' prison camp to Bergamo. This adventurous man had deliberately jammed some wire in and under his fingernail, damaging a nerve, with the explicit aim of being moved to Bergamo for treatment. He hoped to acquire some equipment here to inject life into the wireless set in his prison camp. He possessed a tattered map of Italy, which Nicky was required to memorise.

Nicky set about scrounging a small compass and some Italian lire. The doctors provided some waterproof sheeting for his damaged foot. Then, finally, by diligently trading the cigarettes supplied in his Red Cross ration parcels, he accumulated a small supply of energy food and chocolates.

He planned his escape for midnight as this way he estimated he would have four to five hours before the next rollcall or bed check. As well, at this time the sewerage system would not be in much use.

That night he wrote a final letter to Dot, finishing with an encouragement to remember the words of the popular song 'Mexicali Rose': 'Stop crying, I'll come back to you some sunny day.' He was ready now. This was the last note Dot would receive from Nicky while he was behind enemy lines.

Midnight. With the help of his two English friends, Nicky fabricated a body silhouette out of cardboard boxes retrieved from the Red Cross parcels, and camouflaged his bed. They also fashioned some 'hair' out of the ropes which had been used to wrap the parcels and placed it strategically on the pillow. Arranging for his friends to double for him at the rollcall next morning and then close over the wire in the window before the guards found the damage, Nicky melted into the night.

In the darkness, he crept down into the garden, hiding in deep shadows where possible. He found the window they had 'doctored', had a quick look around, then slipped through. Breathing deeply now and with his heart racing, he moved briskly down to the basement and sewerage area.

No noises from the dormitories outside; he was OK so far. Quickly he stripped off and knotted his clothing, shoes and a spare shirt on his head and around his neck. The night air was cold. He inserted his escape kit of compass and lire into his 'fundamental orifice', then crouched on all fours at the entrance of the tunnel. Bracing himself, he crawled into the ankle-depth sewage. The smell was overwhelming and the effluent was freezing. Within a few minutes, he was shivering, but he steadily pushed forward, taking great care to keep his injured foot out of the filthy muck. He was very conscious of infection and of the history of dysentery in the hospital.

The tunnel was pitch black and he found his left leg was not very useful for propulsion. He pushed on—making 20 to 30 metres. It was hard work. He was now losing considerable body heat. How much further? What would he find at the other end? He was having difficulty breathing as the air was stale and quite foul. He was also becoming tired—his elbows were weakening.

The pipes appeared to close in on him. No time for claustrophobia. The tunnel edged downwards. What if it dropped right down—into nowhere? The slime would make it difficult to crawl back uphill. As well, if there was a dead end ahead, or if it narrowed, he did not think it would be easy to turn around.

His emotions ran. If he collapsed or became trapped and died in here, nobody would ever know his fate.

An image of Dot appeared again. Keep going. This was no time to lose faith or courage. His adrenalin pumped. He checked his fears. His sense of hearing became acute and increased his consciousness of tunnel sounds and drafts. Some distance ahead, over the pounding of his heart and over his deep breathing, he became aware of the sound of air escaping from somewhere.

He was attracted by a faint, whistling sound which to Nicky reached the intensity and beauty of a homing siren. The sound stimulated energy from within him and he moved forward with renewed vigour. A few more metres ahead and he hit into what at first appeared to be a dead end. Damn. No, it couldn't be. There was wind coming from somewhere.

Frantically, on closer examination, his searching hands revealed he was actually at a T-junction and the cross-pipes widened a little here. The whistling sound, however, was coming from directly above him. His hands grappled further, probing along the slime-covered walls. He found a rung leading upwards. He then found two more rungs above that and he quickly climbed them.

He came to rest against a metal manhole cover. This was the way out. Where was he? Had he come far enough to be out of the hospital? Was he anywhere near the Italian Army barracks?

Luckily, the manhole cover wasn't a large heavy concrete one as he had seen on some Italian streets. Gathering his strength, he pushed upwards against the lid. The cover resisted, then creaked. Steadily, the stiffness eased and the cover slowly lifted. Nicky's heart leapt. He was immediately hit by a refreshing blast of clean, revitalising air. He sucked in large lung-fulls, relishing the life-giving oxygen. Hope filled his heart as his chest expanded and fell. He would be all right.

A quick look around. Yes, he was outside the compound! And in the clear! He hauled himself out of the tunnel and let his breathing settle. The feeling was indescribable. He was free!

SEVENTEEN

Lake Como

Nicky put his clothes on. Then, for a few moments, he sat on the edge of the road to gather his energy and thoughts. It was a strange type of freedom. He felt elated. The air even seemed better outside the prison. Everything about it was exhilarating. Yet underneath, his excitement was contained. Steadily the reality of the situation sifted through.

'OK, Barr, you clown. You've done it—you're outside. What next? You're not really free yet.' Sure, he had a plan, but nothing concrete. If he could get to the northern arm of Lake Como and if the water wasn't too cold, he could try and swim across to Switzerland. Alternatively, if he felt well enough—if his leg held out—he could continue on towards the foot of the Alps, beneath the snow line. For now, he was content to let this be his general scheme and he would consider each test as he came to it.

He walked briskly to the north-west of the town where he found a wooded area. Protected by the trees, he came upon a freezing stream which he lay down in, fully naked again. The water was, to say the least, invigorating, and the coldest he had ever experienced in his life. However, he needed to cleanse his foot and himself, so he immersed himself in the torrent until he was sure he had eliminated the risks of infection.

Shivering now, and fearing imminent hypothermia, he dried himself with his spare shirt, then dressed. Setting his compass, he started out in a westerly direction towards Lake Como. At first he attempted to run to try and regain his body heat but his leg only allowed a hard walk. Fortunately, there were special walking tracks parallel and adjacent to the road, so Nicky kept on these, allowing him to be reasonably anonymous. It took some hours to feel warm again.

The first day went by without incident and he was feeling hopeful that he had not been detected 'missing' as yet. In any case, he was not aware of any special search parties looking for him. After all, there was a battalion at Bergamo—by now, they would have sent dogs, trucks and men and any large-scale pursuit operations would have been obvious.

He continued the pace through the following day, then on the third day, 17 November, he crossed a main road going south to Como. From here he took a country track leading to what he hoped would be Poriezza on the western side of the Lake. His leg wounds had been holding up, although he'd removed some scabs that morning. There was still mucus oozing from them but they seemed all right.

Nicky walked all through that night, pushed on by the thought that the border and freedom were near. He scrambled over bush tracks and stony creek beds, past clumps of juniper berries and flowering Alpine meadows, every now and then aware of cowbells ringing. In the early hours, next day, in the morning twilight, he could see a reach of Lake Como emerging through the trees. He was almost there.

Then a dog barked, close. Nicky froze, tense.

'Hell, they've sent the dogs after me,' he grimaced. 'No, not now.' Switzerland was so close.

Emerging from the darkness, a thickset man wearing a long coat and looking to Nicky like a country landowner walked towards him, restraining his dog. The canine was large and black and was crouching menacingly in a stalking stance. A cross between a Doberman and a Rottweiler, it glared at Nicky with its teeth bared and ears pinned back. Reinforcing its threatening posture, it uttered a chilling deep-throated growl.

Nicky quickly considered his alternatives. He was not too sure who this man was, but he appeared to be alone. It would be a one-on-one situation and he decided to play it out.

As the man moved closer, Nicky became alarmed when he saw the man was wearing an army-type uniform under the coat.

'Damn,' Nicky murmured to himself. His mind raced, but he held his position. He would continue with the face-off.

'Buona sera,' the man called.

Calmly, Nicky returned the greeting. 'Buona sera.'

The man said, in Italian, 'I am a customs officer. You will come with me. We are here to stop people taking contraband into Switzerland.'

'Of all the luck,' Nicky cursed under his breath. A great deal of Italian art treasures were being smuggled out of Italy and he was about to be caught up in the net.

In the background Nicky glimpsed the first few tantalising reflections of daylight sparkle off the lake. Beckoning like a beacon, behind the lake, he could also see the first rays of the morning sun ignite the snow-covered alps a burning gold. How close he was.

The man walked towards him, and Nicky thought he was not carrying a weapon. He had to make his move—now. In an instant, Nicky's hand darted to the ground and picked up a heavy, round stone. The officer, sensing Nicky was about to do something, turned and called on his dog.

'Attack,' he yelled.

Then all hell broke loose.

Nicky took immediate aim and with the stone in hand, swung directly at the man's head. With a thud, it smashed into the side of his cranium. The officer dropped instantly to the ground and lay there, motionless, as if he had been hit by a train.

At the same time, the dog yelped, then, with a blood-curdling baying howl, catapulted towards Nicky like a coiled-up missile. Focusing through slitted eyes, the powerful animal landed on Nicky's chest. Nicky could feel its hot breath on his face as its snarling teeth snapped in the air, searching for his neck.

In the same instant, Nicky braced himself and reacted. From his own primitive depths, his hands flew to the dog's throat. His fingers squeezed against the hackled fur around the neck and with fear and adrenalin fuelling his strength, he hauled the dog off him and lifted it in the air. With a mighty effort, he flung the dog backwards while trying to avoid the slashing razor-sharp claws. Nicky was determined to be free.

The animal landed a couple of metres away, spun, recovered and prepared to attack Nicky again.

Suddenly, Nicky was aware of other barking dogs sprinting out of the shadows, then moving like black flashes to surround him. Other voices yelled out, accompanied by whistles, calling the dogs to heel. More customs officers raced up to the scene and restrained the dogs. The men were all carrying rifles.

Nicky knew it was over—for the moment. He relaxed his aggressive stance and caught his breath as one of the officers knelt and examined their fallen comrade. Another went to assist him while the third approached Nicky. His posture was tense. His nostrils flared as he snapped in Italian, 'Who are you?'

Nicky gave the required name, rank and file number. As the officer came closer, Nicky sensed unbridled menace and anger. The darkness hid the man's lethal punch as it shot out of nowhere, king-hitting Nicky on the temple. Nicky fell directly to the ground.

Instinctively, he covered up as he fell, but the man slammed his alpine-booted foot into his midriff. As Nicky lay there, gasping for breath, the officer followed up quickly with another aggressive kick to the head. Nicky started to black out as he tried to cope with the sudden blinding bursts of pain. Meanwhile, the two other men had left their downed companion, then raced towards Nicky and the third officer. They yelled something in Italian, concerning their compatriot.

The mood turned very ugly as the three men, seized by the need for violent retribution, together dealt Nicky a vicious beating. In turn, they rained sickening punches and bruising kicks to his body and hit his head with teeth-jarring cracks from their rifle butts—on and on. A dog raced in, barking and snapping.

Mercifully, Nicky passed into unconsciousness.

Nicky struggled to open his eyes. For a long time he stared mindlessly into space, his senses registering nothing. He had no idea where he was, or for that matter, who he was. His memory was a blank, no pain, lights or awareness of anything. After some hours, with effort, he could focus on the ceiling of his room. His complete existence and knowledge was limited to what he could experience through his eyes. Eventually, he became aware of the clanging of surgical dishes and movement. Thought pathways opened up. He must be in a medical clinic or hospital. There were voices somewhere.

His mind searched for evidence of an identity and the reason for him being here. Several more hours passed before he became aware of his limbs and the potential for movement.

Finally, and ever so slowly, his coma lifted enough for him to gain some inkling of who he was, of the fact that he was alive and that he was recovering from a beating.

A voice from the next bed helped him to focus on his reality.

'Well, young fellow, what have you been up to?'

It was a friendly voice. It came from a wounded lieutenant-colonel from the Royal Forresters Regiment—an Australian businessman from Adelaide. His name was Cooper and he came from the brewing family.

Nicky responded to the question and as the fog which was shrouded over his brain steadily cleared, he asked questions of his own. Nicky found out he was in a specialised prisoner-of-war hospital in Milan. It was a few hundred metres from the Central Railway Station and he noticed the wards were clean and airy. It was adequately stocked with medication for serious cases, and Nicky ascertained he had been well cared for.

A close examination revealed he had sustained bruises over most of his body and legs and even some canine teeth marks on his buttocks. The black discolouration from the bruises had been mainly absorbed and were now a muddy yellow colour, indicating he had probably been unconscious for as much as four or five days.

Staffing was also good and he learned that his doctor's main concern was whether he had developed cumulative cerebral problems as a result of successive concussions, going back to his plane crash in June.

His balance had been affected, but with graduated exercise and good food, both his proprioceptive deficiencies and his battered body steadily improved. Well enough for the doctors to admit a visitor, an Italian Army lieutenant-colonel. Nicky was rather shocked when the colonel abruptly charged him with homicide.

'Major, you are to be court-martialled in two days time. The customs officer you hit on the head has died and you are to be charged with his murder.' Nicky had only intended to knock the man unconscious while he made good his escape; he certainly had not intended to kill him. Regardless, he didn't feel unduly remorseful. This was war and he considered his actions justifiable within this context.

Nicky was disturbed at the turn of events, as he was very concerned he would not be granted a fair hearing. In fact, when he considered fully the ramifications of the accusation, particularly after placing himself in his enemy's shoes, he understood that if indeed he had killed the man, he was definitely in for it; he would be shot. This realisation dismayed him even further.

Meanwhile, he had befriended an Italian lieutenant who had been a regular visitor to the hospital for other matters and, later the same day, confided his dilemma to him. The Italian expressed his surprise and even consternation, 'I suggest you act promptly and seek the intervention of the Swiss protecting power—the International Red Cross. I have some influence with them. Let me contact them for you.'

Another act of kindness from the enemy.

The next day, Nicky received a visit from a Red Cross representative. He was a Swiss citizen—a colonel—and apparently well trained in such circumstances. Nicky found him to be charming and explained to him what had happened.

The colonel was concerned. 'Things don't look too good. You know what this means?'

Nicky nodded. They both knew that if he was found guilty, it could mean the death sentence in front of a firing squad.

'Well, I'll see what I can do. This sort of thing can be allowed for during war, as part of the Geneva Convention. I'll see you in court.'

Nicky sweated out a very uncomfortable two days as he considered his alternatives and the possible consequences.

The courtroom had been set up in an annex of the hospital. It was a shabby, low-key area about the size of an average boardroom and there were numerous clerks and legal men in attendance, mainly military. Nicky's was the only case to be heard and he noticed several of the customs officers standing and sitting around preparing their briefs. The Red Cross representative was nowhere to be seen.

'Damn. Where is he?' thought Nicky, feeling very alone and vulnerable. By himself he was decidedly disadvantaged.

There were three army officers presiding and Nicky was asked if he would like an interpreter. He accepted.

The hearing commenced and the customs officers produced their evidence. Two of the officers confirmed that the injured customs officer had in fact died. They confidently claimed that Nicky had been violent and pugilistic, and that the purpose of bringing Nicky to court was that he should be sentenced for murder.

The man who Nicky had allegedly killed, it transpired, had been a very important person. Besides being a high-ranking officer in the Border Guards, he was also a commander of a famous unit of the Italian Army, the Bersaglieri Regiment. Nicky knew of them—they wore felt hats with black feathers and ran at the double, a very mobile infantry unit. No wonder they were after his blood.

It was soon Nicky's turn to speak and there was still no sign of the Red Cross representative. Through the interpreter, Nicky presented his story. He firmly told it the way it had happened. He informed them that he was an escaped flier, and he had been trying to make it to Switzerland when he had been confronted by the customs officer within sight of the mountains and freedom.

He told them that, as he believed the officer was by himself, and the border was so close, he decided his only chance was to knock the man out. He stated that his intention was simply that—to render the man unconscious. He certainly had not intended to kill him.

After his delivery, even though he felt he had been forthright enough, Nicky sensed the situation looked generally unfavourable for him. He felt that the courtrooms' general attitude was one of disdain and cock-a-hoop. At this stage of the war, the confident Italians considered that they were winning and they did not need to be moderate. The presiding officers appeared unmoved. They called for a lunch break and asked everyone to reconvene later in the afternoon.

The next two hours were difficult for Nicky as he fully expected to be sentenced to death. His immediate thoughts were of yearning for home and of Dot. He hoped she would eventually receive a fair account of what his final fate had been. He wondered briefly how he could have done things differently, but realised such thinking was a worthless exercise. This was the way it was and he would do it again, given the chance. He was not made to be a prisoner. Dammit. This war had already taken a heavy price, and he cursed the fact that within a few hours, it would demand an even higher one. His life would be over before it had really begun.

Nicky was also annoyed as his defence counsel was still not to be seen. Nicky had expected that this man's legal experience would have assisted him in some way. He was also angry as he felt the hearing was strongly prejudiced against him.

The court reassembled and Nicky nervously awaited his sentencing. However, before the final summing up was called for, to Nicky's great relief, the Swiss colonel made a dramatic last-minute appearance. He had, in fact, been sitting in the back of the courtroom for most of the proceedings, but Nicky had not been aware of his presence.

As he moved towards the bench, he smiled at Nicky, which gave Nicky some small reassurance, then he took his place on the stand. With a degree of decorum, he addressed the court.

'Sirs. I have heard the evidence given by the customs officers. I have to tell you, they are all wrong.' He pointed with some flair to the officers. 'I have just returned from Turin. I have just returned from talking with the supposed "dead" man. He is, in fact, alive at Acqui, 60 kilometres outside of Turin. He is alive and well!'

The man paused as the court absorbed his news, then he continued. 'I ask that this case be dropped. In fact, I would go so far as to request that you should respect this man—that you should empathise with him. He was doing exactly as any of you in a similar situation with military background, ethics and training would do. He deserves understanding and leniency.'

The presiding officers looked at each other, triggering a cacophony of high-speed Italian to break out all round the room. Pandemonium. There was much gesturing and excited debate as this new development and Nicky's future were discussed. One section of the courtroom burst into acclamation and congratulated Nicky, shaking his hand as well as that of the Swiss colonel, who simply stood there silently and very calmly, allowing it all to happen around him.

Nicky asked, 'What's going on, colonel?'

'Well, that news has swung them. Instead of the death sentence, you are being sentenced to Gavi, Prison Camp No. 5. When you are there, before you are taken to your cell, you will have to serve 90 days solitary. That's outside the Geneva Convention—which only allows 30 days—but they'll put you in for 30 days, give you an hour's break then you'll be marched in front of the commandant in the courtyard, then put back inside. That will happen twice—you'll get 90 days.'

Nicky sat and stared in disbelief, stunned at this new development and the verdict. His life would be spared; he was not going to face a brick wall. The prison sentence was stiff, but he could endure that. Nicky warmly thanked the colonel and was then escorted back to his hospital bed. His relief was palpable.

For long moments, he sat and allowed things to sink in and to contemplate their significance. It had been a more trying experience than he had thought it would be. Acceptance of his unbelievable good fortune was restrained a little, mainly because he was concerned about what he might experience at Gavi. He realised he was not well enough yet to cope with this daunting prospect.

Then, suddenly his deepest instincts overcame him. He was exhausted from the day's proceedings and he could suppress his emotions no longer. He broke down and began to sob un-controllably—deep, gut-wrenching sobs, his body shaking with the effort. He allowed himself to cry openly and it felt good. He was surprised at the deep relief he gained from it.

Nicky thought he was alone in the ward, but after some time he was surprised to hear a compassionate voice ask him if there was anything he could do to help him. It belonged to a British Army captain from Wales.

The necessity to reply snapped Nicky out of his misery. Weeping was obviously a necessary coping mechanism but now he needed to get out of himself and to focus on other methods of survival. It was important for him to recuperate mentally, physically and spiritually. He needed time.

During an epiphanic moment, he concluded that this war business was tricky stuff and, in his self-deprecating state, he decided that he was not much good at it. He had experienced too many failures. In his foul mood, he considered that he had been missing and shot down too often, resulting in him being wounded twice and burnt, and now even his escape attempt had failed. He would have to change things.

EIGHTEEN

Gavi: The Metamorphosis

Nicky had heard of Gavi. It had been described as 'The Bad Boys' Camp'—only the most troublesome prisoners were sent there. Located north of Genoa in the foothills of the Alps, it had been built on and carved into the huge rock at its base, about 280 AD. It was well documented in British Government White Papers to be substandard and Nicky knew they had asked for it to be closed.

The ancient fort had been restored and redeveloped as a prison during the early period of the Fascist regime, but Mussolini had closed it down in 1936 due to the high mortality rate. It was reopened again when Italy attacked Ethiopia and named *Il Campo di Concentramento Numero Cinque per Ufficiale Pericoloso*—'Concentration Camp No. 5 for Dangerous Officers'.

On 12 December, Nicky was escorted by a heavy guard of six officers and transferred by train to Acqui. From there, a short drive by public motor bus took him to Gavi.

Nicky's first view of the aged stronghold was, literally, quite daunting. Dark, foreboding and bristling with fortifications, the menacing complex was dominated by a large stone tower and protected by high concrete walls. It stood perched atop a hill and commanded a strategic vantage position in all directions, being the converging point for three roads. It looked impregnable.

The inmates represented a cross-section of people from the

war who were classified as 'dangerous people'. Among them were religious and political radicals, criminals, murderers and a large assortment of military prisoners.

Nicky was conveyed by his guards through large wooden doors into a medieval courtyard in the lower compound of the stone tower. Here he was stripped naked and given a very thorough body search. He was commanded to remove his foot bandages.

'Why?' he asked.

'Because we believe there is a map hidden there.'

Nicky had indeed acquired another map, copied from another inmate while in Milan—the hospital must have tipped them off about it somehow. Nicky gave it over. His clothes and his small bundle of personal items (which were mainly of Red Cross origin) were also searched. He was then handed over to the prison commandant, Colonel Muscatelli.

The colonel was pleasant enough and told Nicky what was required of him. He was reminded that, 'No one has ever escaped from Gavi. Anyone caught trying will be shot!' Nicky was then blindfolded and led to his cell for solitary confinement.

There were three cells for this purpose, situated on the upper compound. Once inside, Nicky's blindfold was taken off. After adjusting to the light, he saw he was in a type of grotto about the size of an average prison cell, one wall being formed from the rock on which the fort was built. It was dark, with some small illumination struggling in through the bars of a grille.

The grille sat in an external wall built up from the floor and opened into a cobblestone area where prisoners exercised. It provided the only light and ventilation and was kept closed by structures pressing against it in the courtyard outside. The only furniture was a low-slung rudimentary stretcher about 10 centimetres off the ground, and an open can for a latrine. There was no heating of any kind and he was supplied with a basin, on the floor, for washing.

Nicky was not allowed to read, play cards or communicate with anyone, and he was permitted no contact with the guards. The place was cold and stank of mould.

At the bottom of the lower compound were additional cells occupied by non-commissioned British personnel—about 30 of them—whose tasks were the preparation of food and the general cleanliness of the prison. Twice each day, Nicky was brought food by one of them, a different person almost every time. They were always cheerful and optimistic, and he often grabbed a few minutes conversation with them.

For the first couple of days, he mainly slept and rested, then on the third day, to his surprise, there was a rattle from the grille. The prisoners outside in the courtyard had distracted the guards and moved the structure covering the grille, enough to allow one prisoner to briefly exchange a few words. The man was the Senior British Officer (SBO) Lieutenant Colonel Ken Fraser of the New Zealand Army. Ostensibly, he came to welcome him, but also to reassure themselves that Nicky was, in fact, from the Allied Forces. At least two German implants had been uncovered, so Nicky had to 'pass muster'. Rugby football helped his acceptance: even though he was still experiencing some memory losses, he fortunately remembered the names of some prewar All Black and Springbok players and their positions.

After these preliminaries, Fraser asked, 'How are you handling the solitary?'

'I'm doing OK.'

'You've only got one enemy.'

'Who's that?'

'Time. If you can learn to handle time, you'll come out all right. You can do it by strong recall. Remember everything you've done in your life. Activate your memory. Your school, studies, books, friends, relationships, then make a plan for when you get out.'

This was good advice. Nicky had plenty of absorbing memories to ponder over. He had always loved poetry and he began by reciting poems that he enjoyed. One in particular amused him from his school days. He had been given an exercise then to recite the words of Wordsworth's poem, 'I Wandered Lonely as a Cloud', and was then directed to comment upon it. The last verse ran:

For oft, when on my couch I lie
In vacant or in pensive mood,
They flash upon that inward eye
Which is the bliss of solitude;
And then my heart with pleasure fills,
And dances with the daffodils.

He remembered having written, 'How on earth could solitude be blissful? How could the memory—"that inward eye"—ever take the place of getting out and doing things?' He smiled wryly to himself as he remembered he was given low marks and was told he might do better when he was older.

Witnessing as he had, many months of concentrated warfare, then as a prisoner experiencing the uncertainties and hardships of prison life, the incessant interruption of one's life with rollcalls, searches and inspections, he considered that being on his own was peaceful indeed. Not truly blissful, but certainly peaceful.

He had ample time to take stock of his life and to review his situation. This solitude would be his therapy—his '40 days in the wilderness'. It would sustain him. He had been through violent and troubling times and nothing in his pre-war experience had prepared him for the degree of trauma he had undergone. This would be a reprieve. Life had been too fast and too ugly. This was not what he'd been promised. This was the 'dark woods' of the fairytale.

He needed answers to many questions. His mortality had

been confronted many times and, in the process, so too had his spirituality. He needed to review all the events and aspects which underpinned his inherited life values and to challenge many of his ordained belief systems.

With the advent of war, Nicky's Christian faith had taken a hammering. He had seen the dead, the dying and the wounded, both in the field and in various hospitals and he was having trouble rationalising and reconciling a loving God with the carnage, terror and suffering which surrounded him. Granted, men make wars, not God. Nonetheless, history had taught him that many conflicts had started 'in the name of God', somebody's God. He needed to work on this. As part of this process, he was critical of himself for only praying to God when he needed help. He disliked hypocrites. He was now having trouble convincing himself of the existence of a God, or of a promised heaven after life on earth.

Over the years, Nicky had studied many varying cultures, religions and philosophies of life. He tried to recall them and consider their relevance and, if necessary, to apply them to his life now.

In the next few months, Nicky struggled to develop a personal creed which, in essence, would ensure he lived this life to the fullest with integrity, fairness and dignity. He considered many hypotheses, ceaselessly testing one argument against another, debating possibilities as intellectually as he could. He reasoned if there was a God, he would start by searching deep inside himself. Over time, he steadily chipped away at the veneers and trappings of his old life, assessing each layer for relevance. With each examination, he revealed a clearer image of himself.

The mental exercise was stimulating, at times even liberating. How truly free it was to fly beyond the fortifications of ironbound dogmas. But there would be a price. The buck would have to stop with him—he needed to always accept clear responsibility for his own actions. His religious upbringing had already developed in him a fairly principled conscience, but he would have to test it even more. He would have to create his heaven here on earth. If there was a hereafter, it would be a wonderful bonus. In the meantime, he would extract as much good as was possible from life—even in a world at war—and hopefully be judged a virtuous man.

One of the philosophies which assisted his deliberations was the wisdom he gained from the words of a poem he remembered called *Such is Life*, written by a fourth-century AD Indian mystic, Kalidasa.

Yesterday has gone, it is no more than a memory,
Tomorrow is in the future, for which you plan and hope,
Today is Life.
Make the most of this day, for in it is all the truth
and reality of your existence,
The heartache and happiness of learning and experiencing new
things,
The joy and glory of action,
The splendour of beauty.
Today, well-lived, makes every yesterday a dream of happiness
and every tomorrow a vision of hope—

Nicky was moved to create words of his own, adding:
No matter the God you have,
or the beliefs you hold,
This outlook, coupled with 'Love ye one another'
Surely creates your heaven
Here on earth.

Despite how compelling his ongoing spiritual search was, Nicky was aware that isolation, stench and chill might eventually melt his resolve. Without a focus, he could easily capitulate—

seeking answers to life's big questions could only sustain his survival for a limited period.

During his time in hospitals and prison camps, Nicky had noticed that in captivity, certain men with less to live for than himself—no absorbing purpose and much less resolute—lost heart and died.

He turned his mind to Dot. He ran through memories of their meeting, their days at Power House. He recalled every detail of their Saturday evening dances, their trysts at the pictures and the theatre, the tenderness, love and infatuation of their brief honeymoon. He played mental games wondering where she might be at a certain moment and what she was doing.

From the time of his first confinement in the grotto, Nicky had a strong feeling of contact with Dot that gave him an indescribable inner comfort. The blackness around him only served to highlight the intensity with which he could reach into the ether and find her there. His ability to focus on her while in confinement would prove stronger than the intentions of the twisted men and the systems that put him there. She would give him the courage to live.

In many other respects, this period of isolation helped Nicky to learn a great deal about himself. It also helped him to plan his immediate life. He knew fully well that he could not tolerate being held a prisoner, certainly not after being wrongly labelled a criminal. Nicky resolved to plan another escape attempt. His 'singleness of purpose' was largely generated by the need to hold the girl he loved in his arms once more. To survive, therefore, was an essential part of his planning. He determined he would both escape and survive.

Automatically, this brought into focus other matters like tactics, strategies, the absolute importance of timing and clear planning. He would be more of a thinking man now, and that, by definition, required him to practise patience, much work, adaption and application. He would need to 'hasten slowly', something he wasn't known for. He would need also to get fitter. Now, with hindsight, he realised he had not been fit enough for his Bergamo escape. As well, even though Nicky knew he was already regarded as something of a loner, he would be even more so now.

NINETEEN

Bergamo Revisited

Despite being in solitary confinement, Nicky wasn't always alone. He did experience periods of as long as a fortnight where he would see or hear nobody. Generally, however, every few days somebody would approach his grille and ask, 'Are you all right? Anything you need?'

The strange aspect was that he felt safe in solitary. He experienced a tranquility in his cell. He felt comfortable as he could sense his peace of mind developing.

Using this 'grille tapping' as it was known, he was able to get a note to the senior camp doctor, Captain Bill Gray, a New Zealander, that he needed medications for his wound. His new friends smuggled supplies back to him. Most of the medications came from Red Cross parcels containing basic health items: toothbrush, toothpaste, soap, eye ointments and iodine swabs.

Nicky got to know several other prisoners using grille tapping, including a Yugoslav soldier who Nicky knew as 'Mac', shortened from Machalovitch.

Mac wished to improve his English and towards the end of Nicky's third term of 30 days, when Mac was sure there was a prisoner in all three solitary cells, he assaulted one of the guards in the courtyard. The guard was standing at attention with rifle and bayonet when Mac, a stockily-built character, came up behind him, measured off and kicked him up the backside.

Predictably, he was marched off to the commandant's office and sentenced to solitary confinement. As he knew the cells were full, he asked if he could share Nicky's cell. The commandant obliged, so the last two weeks of Nicky's sentence were completed with Mac as company. He was a definite character and arrived carrying a blanket and wearing a wound in his buttocks where he had been prodded with the bayonet.

The time with Mac was served profitably by Nicky. Mac happened to be a Croat and a professor of languages who, in return for Nicky's assistance with his English, helped improve Nicky's German and Italian. Nicky also learned some Croation. The two men became friends, but even though Nicky considered Mac to be basically a good man, he was wary of his dark side. He showed no fear and Nicky found him consumed with hatred for the enemy. Mac vowed he would kill any Italian or German man, woman or child—clear cut!

He also had a charming side. When Nicky and he were released from solitary, he prevailed on the guards to allow them to have a party. With some assistance from the medical fraternity, the prisoners created an alcoholic cocktail. It was extremely potent and resulted in most of the inmates becoming quite drunk. The Russians, particularly, enjoyed themselves. They sang with great gusto a traditional song, 'The Red Flag Song', to the tune of 'O Christmas Tree'.

On his release from solitary, Nicky found the prison was full, with about 160 inmates all up. Its military prisoners were a truly motley lot—all officers, from many nationalities and services—commandos, submariners, and bomber and fighter pilots. All had been deemed as dangerous by their captors, especially those recaptured after escaping.

Nicky was allocated a cell in the top compound which he shared with three other men, a squadron leader from the RAF who was a bomber pilot, a submariner lieutenant from the Royal

Navy and a flight lieutenant fighter pilot from the RAF. The cell was built of solid stone and masonry and seemed escape proof. In any case, for most of the first week, Nicky's attention was diverted as he spent time in the infirmary seeking treatment for his leg.

Nicky hoped he might be able to catch up on the latest war news, but as there was no radio, and no new prisoners for months, the prison camp was bereft of any up-to-date information. All Nicky had heard was that the Eighth Army had moved back to a line at El Alamein just a few days after he was shot down and they were regrouping there, preparing for a large confrontation with Rommel. That was July 1942—nothing since—just conjecture and rumours. Wishes and imaginations were running wild. It was now April 1943.

Nicky was glad to be reunited with his friend Roo Leu, who was transferred from another prison camp for being highly disruptive. He was a great poker player and Nicky often joined him in his daily challenges with the other inmates. Nicky, in fact, had been placed in charge of 'gambling activities' in the camp. Australians were supposed to know how to manage such things.

Gavi had a small council headed by the SBO, Colonel Fraser, which represented the prisoners to the prison commandant and also organised escape plans. Nicky learned there were at least four approved escape plans under way. These were complicated affairs requiring much preparation of escape material, and a great deal of co-ordination, as guards had to be distracted, men placed on shifts and debris from diggings smuggled out of tunnels. One tunnel that had been under construction for two years had actually broken through walls and rock and was now working through topsoil, but was hampered by matted grapevine roots. A botanist in the prison considered there were less than 2 metres to go before reaching the surface. For two months, Nicky and Roo Leu, as well as working in rotation on the other projects, formed a team with about six others and worked out their own escape scheme. This was in the upper compound and a higher level above it, where a fissure in the rock, which formed one of the communicating corridors, allowed some access for patient engineering work.

By June, the council decided that someone would have to be sent from the prison to obtain recent war information and somehow return this 'situation report' to the inmates. The only known way to get out was for an individual to obtain approval to be transferred to an outside hospital for specialised medical attention. The camp doctor, Dr Bill Gray, had informed the commandant that he had two men who needed such attention.

Because of his injured leg, Nicky was chosen. He thought that though the plan seemed straightforward it might turn out to be a real can of worms to implement. As his companion, the council selected a young Englishman, Lieutenant James Cook, from a Regiment of the Line, who had suffered an infection in a wound acquired during a tank attack. Nicky had hoped New Zealand Army Major Tom Straker would be his partner. Nicky told the commandant he would like to go to Bergamo because of the known medical services there and, surprisingly, the commandant was quite agreeable. They would go by train with six guards.

Meanwhile, the resourceful Dr Bill Gray had made a pleasant-tasting concoction that was laced with sleeping powder. He had tested it on several people and it worked perfectly. Within a few minutes, the victims fell fast asleep.

The plan was to escape while on the train trip. The two men were to gain the guards' confidence, then offer them a drink, render them unconscious, and escape. Flimsy and simple they all agreed, but worth trying.

Gray gave some rations and two flasks to James Cook, one 'laced' the other normal. Nicky was soon to find out this James Cook bore no resemblance to the famed explorer James Cook.

His James Cook was pleasant and courageous, but Nicky soon wondered how he ever got his commission; he found him to be dull and silly. Nevertheless, the joint venture had to succeed.

They boarded the train at Acqui and, after some hours, Cook whispered shamefacedly to Nicky, 'I don't know which flask is the laced one!'

'Didn't you put a mark on it?' Nicky asked incredulously.

'I forgot.'

'Cookey, you're a clown, an absolute congenital idiot! Well, let's bide our time.'

The train ride continued as the eight men shared a cabin, four on either side, facing each other, the six guards brandishing rifles with their unusually short bayonets.

Cook tried to communicate with the guards in broken Italian. It had looked simple in the films they'd seen, but not with these guards. It was hopeless, albeit humorous. There was no chance of them escaping this way. They tried going to the toilet, but they were too closely supervised. No chance that way either.

Night-time approached. There was one slim chance. Cocktail time. Nicky pulled rank. 'Okay Cookey. You got us into this. Drink from one of the flasks.'

Cook selected one flask and nervously held it to his lips. He took a blind swig. It was the wrong flask. Within seconds, he was out to it, snoring louder than anyone Nicky had ever heard. Nicky looked quizzically at the guards and smiled. By 11.00 p.m. Cook was still out to it, not having moved. By the time they'd reached Milan, the guards had decided to offload Cook.

This left Nicky in a no-win situation. There was no point in him trying to escape by himself. As well as blowing their cover, it would probably endanger Cook if they found he'd been drugged. Cook, with an irritating smirk on his face, was out in dreamland, oblivious to the world. Nicky could appreciate the humorous side, but nevertheless he was angry with him. Reliable news was urgently needed back at Gavi.

The train continued on to Bergamo.

When Nicky arrived at Bergamo, he was immediately recognised and taken straight to the infirmary. After treating his leg, the medical orderlies were then directed to encase his right leg in a full leg plaster with a 70 degree bend in it. They were not about to have him escape again. Once back in his ward, Nicky acquired a razor and cut the plaster down the inside, fashioning a hinge for the two halves. He wore pyjamas and kept the plaster off most of the time, only replacing it when the guards came round on inspections.

While at Bergamo he was able to fulfil his mission—to secure an update on the war—and it was all good news. He learned that the RAF were taking the war to Germany and delivering large air strikes over the Ruhr and other industrial areas and cities. The best news was that the Eighth Army had soundly defeated Rommel in a spectacular and bloody ten-day battle at El Alamein in November 1942. The Americans had also well and truly entered the war and the Allied forces had totally defeated the Axis forces in Africa in May. There was talk of an invasion imminent somewhere on the Italian peninsula, probably Sicily. Closer to home, in Australia, he also heard that the Japanese were being turned back, firstly on the Kokoda Trail and Milne Bay in New Guinea by the Australians, and then by the Americans at Guadalcanal in the Solomons.

Well, at least that would explain the softer attitude of the Italian guards back at Gavi. Many Italian soldiers had been taken prisoner during the African campaign and had been reported to have been well looked after. Further, the war might soon be over for the Italians. Better to be tolerant.

It was time for Nicky to get back and report. The doctor pronounced Nicky well enough to return to Gavi, so he prepared to leave—under heavy escort again. In the compound, in front of a crowd of prisoners and Italian guards, Nicky unhinged his leg plaster, swung it above his head and walked out to the clapping and cheering of his audience. It was a fun moment. The Italians appreciated the performance, but were not unhappy to see him go.

On his return, Nicky had a session with the SBO. While he was away, Ken Fraser had been displaced by a higher ranking officer, Brigadier George Clifton, a highly decorated New Zealand Army officer said to have been the right-hand man of Lieutenant General Bernard Freyberg, commander of the Second New Zealand Division. Among other citations, Clifton had been awarded four DSOs (Distinguished Service Orders).

'Four DSOs?' Nicky asked Clifton.

'Yes, I was too bloody silly to get a VC,' he laughed.

Nicky was invited to speak at dinner time. All the prisoners had every meal together, benches being located in the middle compound. There were 97 gathered that evening and Nicky delivered his morale-boosting information.

After he reported on the Allies' successes at each battleground, the prisoners responded wildly by rattling their cutlery. They were particularly excited about the revelations of the El Alamein victory and burst into spontaneous cheering. To them, after months of believing they might be losing the war, this news was life-giving.

In Nicky's absence, as well as becoming SBO, Clifton had assumed control of the escape committee and promptly announced he was going to escape himself. He had chosen the time and had appropriated from the communal stockpile a map, compass and money. He planned to leave via the window from a cell adjacent to Nicky's, which had easier access to the roof. There was no guttering or downpipe and it was at least 65 metres from the rocky outcrops on the ground, so he had practised pull-ups to hoist himself onto the roof. This required a high degree of strength and absolutely no fear of heights. Clifton was both strong and fearless, which along with other reasons caused Nicky to have some reservations about him.

There is a customary pecking order in prisons relating to escape attempts which gives priority of escape to prisoners who have been locked up the longest should they wish it, particularly if utilising community escape supplies. The 'Brig' made himself unpopular by 'pulling rank'—jumping the queue. Nevertheless, on the prescribed date, Nicky and two other temporary weight-lifters helped to push Clifton's legs up so he could clamber onto the roof. He had a long cord coiled around his waist (which had been plaited by other prisoners from the ties of Red Cross parcels), and his escape kit was wrapped in an oil-cloth cylinder which he inserted into his rear passage for security and ease of transport.

As he scuttled along the ridge of the roof, gunfire opened up. Guards above on the higher level blasted into the night. Bullets whined over the battlements. Some ricocheted off the tiles, shattering them and sending the bullets spinning off into the blackness. Nicky then heard Clifton race back across the rooftop in full retreat. Next he saw his legs dangling down in front of his window.

'Get me in,' he yelled, gasping. 'Quickly!'

Six strong hands pulled Clifton back into the cell, a tricky business.

By this time the courtyard below was bedlam. Guards raced around as bells clanged. They fired at anything, real or imaginary, that looked like an escaping prisoner. Within a few moments, there was banging at the cell door.

By now, the 'Brig' was desperately trying to get rid of the 'escape kit' from his 'fundamental orifice'. As he hurriedly bent over to drop his trousers, the valuable cylinder shot out and landed near Nicky. Nicky dropped to his knees to retrieve it simultaneously as the door burst open and the guards raced in.

Nicky's hand grasped around the wad as a bayonet flashed over his left shoulder, skimming past his eye. The bayonet attached to the rifle was a small, sharp pointed weapon and pinned Nicky's hand to the floor. It sliced straight through the flesh of the index finger of his left hand, pushed through the wad and onto the concrete floor. Nicky gasped in shock, then yelled in pain. He carefully extricated his finger which was wildly spurting blood. Angered, he delivered a broadside to the 'Brig'.

'When a man reaches the rank of Brigadier, George, I expect a bloody sight more brains and much less bravery.'

Clifton laughed, totally unperturbed. Quick as a flash, he shot back, 'I'll use that in the preface of a book I'll write after the war.'

He pulled his trousers up, then was marched out of the cell, directly to the commandant. Nicky was diverted to the infirmary where Bill Gray treated his injured hand. He was classified as 'walking wounded' and returned to his cell. The 'Brig' was given 30 days' solitary confinement, which he did not serve.

The attempt and its aftermath confirmed two points to Nicky. First, it reinforced his opinion that fearless men are, in many circumstances, a real risk. The ability to react to fear is a barometer of a man's sensitivity. Fearlessness reduces the respect for life and has the potential to compromise judgement, emotions and alertness.

It also confirmed to Nicky the change in attitude of their captors. Prior to the battle of El Alamein, there was a harshness about the treatment of prisoners and a severity in their enforcement of discipline. Now, as the tide of battle was conspicuously turning, the guards had started talking pleasantly to them, rations had improved, rollcalls and inspections were less frequent, letters were being posted, clothing had been distributed and punishments were clearly lenient. In themselves, these incidents were not monumental events, but for the prisoners it raised their spirits unbelievably.

Meanwhile, other external happenings were unfolding which would change things again. In early July 1943, the Allies invaded Sicily with the largest amphibious landing ever. By mid-July, it was clear that nothing could prevent the British and American armies from over-running the island. The Italian mainland would be next. By the end of July, Nicky had some personal satisfaction in hearing that Mussolini had been dismissed from power by the King of Italy, Victor Emmanuel III, and was on the run. Italians had grown weary of the war and of two decades of Fascist rule and promises.

In mid-August, the Prisoners' Council in Gavi asked for a conference with the commandant. The 'Brig' led the deputation, supported by Ken Fraser and Tom Straker.

'Sir, it would appear the Italians will soon surrender. We insist now that you hand over the prison to us, before the Germans get here.'

'I'm sorry I can't do that,' the commandant apologised with a degree of understanding. 'I already have Germans here. It would be risking my own men. I'm afraid that notionally we will have to retain you here as normal. The full German contingent will soon arrive to take over. We will need to appear to be giving them all assistance.'

That very evening SS troops arrived for the changeover. These troops were surly, trigger-happy, angry men who had served on the Eastern Front against Russia. They had no wish to be here. They had just commenced their first rest period since the war started and were called back for this duty. The prisoners were informed they would be sent by train to special concentration camps and stalags in Germany.

Germany Bound

As a result of the news of the incoming Germans, the Prisoners' Council had given approval for those prisoners who wished to attempt to escape during the changeover to remain in the prison if they wished, before the final Italian rollcall. There were five groups at this time working on escape, including Nicky's. Some members of other groups opted to hide out in their escape areas and take a chance of getting away after the other prisoners had departed, believing there would then be no resistance from the Italians. Nicky had decided against this.

After the changeover and a German rollcall, the Germans realised their numbers did not match up with the Italian roll. The rest of the prisoners were moved out and waited in a field at the bottom of the prison for trucks to take them to the train station at Acqui.

One by one, loud explosions were heard echoing back from the ancient fort. The SS had sent in a special squad who found old passageways and many tunnels. They then grenaded them. No one survived. The carnage could be sensed from the field as the remaining prisoners soberly boarded the trucks.

At Acqui, the prisoners lined up on the platform and waited for the special train. Suddenly, two of them made a break from the line. They managed to reach a nearby hillside before they were sighted. Immediately the guards opened fire, pouring round after round into the wooded area.

Some of the prisoners attempted to create a diversion, with a view to disrupting the guards' aim. They chanted in German, 'You're firing at a woman': '*Das is ein Frau*'.

Still angry, the guards turned their fire on the massed prisoners, aiming in the direction where the heckling came from. Nicky flattened on the ground as bullets whined over his head. Others were not so fast and three were hit.

Then a German SS officer stepped forward. He ordered the prisoners into a tighter line and addressed them in perfect English,

'We now have an accurate rollcall. It will be more accurate as we know who is going into each wagon. I want you to know that if the same number is not there for the morning rollcall, all remaining people in the wagon will be shot. Does anybody want me to repeat it?'

No one spoke. Nicky was learning about the Nazi method of intimidation. Control by fear.

Nicky gathered up the men from his escape group and moved them into the same freight wagon as himself. There were about 40 men to a wagon and, after they clambered in, the heavy timber doors were rolled shut. They were locked by two large, clamp-like devices, rotated by a short lever on each one, one high on the outside of the door, the other nearer the floor.

The freight wagons were clean enough, with reasonable ventilation. However, there wasn't enough room for all to sit down on the floor comfortably.

The senior officer in the wagon was an Australian, Colonel Spike Marlin. He was from Melbourne and a veteran of World War One. During the early Middle East campaign, he had been in command of a Sixth Division Battalion and had been captured in the Western Desert. He had been SBO of the predominantly Australian prisoner-of-war camp at Sulmona, east of Rome, and had a reputation for standing up to the Italian commanders so was sent to Gavi. On initial physical assessment, he was a weak-looking character, with no chin and a wobbly 'Adam's apple', tempting Nicky to wonder how he gained rank. He was about to find out.

Nicky had a sense the train journey was going to be their best chance to escape. Around them, Italy was in turmoil. Ahead, in about two days' time, there was Germany, an unknown situation, although they had heard of prisoners being sent to extermination camps. By now, Nicky's 'reformation' had been complete. He was fit, his batteries were recharged and he was ready to go.

Nicky's team had smuggled on board some basic hacking tools—knives, forks, buckles and various sharp metals. Nicky formed his men into three groups of two with four in reserve. He, with Roo Leu, made up the first team and began scraping on the door in the area where the door lever could be reached. Another two, including another Australian, Pete Peterson, went to work on the floor and another two at the rear wall, grinding away between the buffers. They all hacked, chipped, rasped and cut furiously.

As the train rattled on into the night, with the German's death threat hanging over them, some of the other prisoners started to hassle and remonstrate. Before long, the floor group were being restrained physically, causing Nicky to look to Colonel Marlin.

'Sir, we have to do something about this.'

'I have to agree.'

Above the noise of the wagon and in the darkness, Marlin called for silence. 'I know what some of you are thinking here. That when this train stops tomorrow morning, there will be a rollcall. If we are not all here, the remainder will be shot.'

Agitated murmurs of 'Yes … yes' were heard. The mood was bordering on mutiny.

'There are others who want to get out and feel it is their duty, and believe this is their best opportunity. You can go with them if you like. The door won't be closed. It's your choice. But whatever happens, you are *not* to interfere with them.'

Then, with some scorn in his voice, he continued, 'I want all the *non*-combatants up the front end of the carriage. If the escape is successful, *I* will accept full responsibility at the morning rollcall!'

He appeared laid back, yet this was heroic stuff. Nicky admired his excellent example of leadership.

Reticently, but respecting the man and his rank, the men settled back and allowed the teams to continue working. As Nicky and Leu scratched away at the panel, Nicky noticed Leu's hands were bleeding freely. He had been severely burnt when he was shot down and even though his hands had healed, the skin was parchment thin. Nicky admired his friend's controlled audacity. What a mate!

Eventually, victory. He and Leu were the first through. They had scratched a hole wide enough to place a hand outside the wagon and then manipulate the lever, and yes, it was connected by a steel rod to the lever-locking device. They functioned as a pair.

Nicky lifted the lever upwards, unfastening the door, and rolled the heavy door slightly open. Nobody in the carriage knew the rail line or the train's expected stops. The train had stopped once already. The guards, who were stationed on the roof and in the rear guard and locomotive sections, would frequently fire their machine-guns along the side of the train and onto the tracks, instilling terror into the already nervous prisoners. Nicky squatted, then lowered his legs over the edge of the carriage and prepared to jump.

Briefly, in the semi-darkness he peered up the tracks, checking for any signals which might be in his trajectory path, while listening intently to the trains 'clacking' sound which would change tone noticeably should the wheels roll over a bridge. There was no merit in jumping into a bridge or a river.

Some deep instinct held him back; it prevented him from springing into space. Almost imperceptibly, he must have sensed the train was slowing down. He hesitated. An impatient English Captain blustered forward, 'Go on, jump. If you are not going to jump, I will.'

'No don't. You aren't going to jump. You will imperil us all. I think the train is stopping. I am closing the door and just hope we aren't detected.'

The Englishman, who had worked hard that night, barged to the door, but was held back by another Englishman, Leu and an Australian AIF officer, Captain Ray Conway. Colonel Marlin interceded and calmed them down, 'I told you not to do that, you silly buggers'.

Even though it was dark and Marlin could not rely on body language to assist his leadership, such was the esteem with which he was regarded that very quickly the scuffle settled.

Within a few seconds, the train screeched to a halt. At the same time, Nicky just managed to roll the door shut. It was obvious the train was waiting for 'all clear' signals in order to proceed. Nicky could hear the guards and officers running up and down outside and, to his horror, they congregated right outside their wagon.

Everyone in the carriage waited nervously and ever so quietly. Nicky breathed to himself, 'Please don't look up at this door, pretty bloody please.'

There was much talking and shouting outside. What was going on?

One of the prisoners could understand their German conversation. He translated, 'We are going east. We have just been through Piacenza, and are on our way to Bologna. From there, we go north to Germany through the Brenner Pass.' This confirmed to everyone what they suspected. They would need to make their move very soon.

The signals changed. The guards returned to their posts and the train started chuffing again, gradually building up speed.

Roo Leu breathed an audible sigh of relief.

'You and your sixth sense, Nicky. I don't know how you knew we were going to stop—you've saved this attempt.'

Nicky was never sure either. However, he suspected that somehow after experiencing many life-threatening situations, he had stimulated and developed an acute instinctual awareness of danger. His danger senses were always on full alert, supported by huge helpings of luck.

Fortunately, the few minutes' break gave the men a chance to reorganise.

As the train settled into a steady rhythm again, the men determined the best technique and strategy to make a successful jump. They planned to face the direction in which the train was heading, then leap far enough out to miss the sleepers. While in the air, they would maintain their feet in the running position, so that they might hit the ground running. In his mind's eye, Nicky vividly practised rolling techniques for when he hit the ground.

Earlier, every man had been given a small bundle of rations at Gavi, consisting mainly of food and clothing from the Red Cross issue.

The plan was for the 11 men who opted to jump to line up around the door. Nicky was to jump first, but before he launched himself, he would hand his bundle to the second jumper, Roo Leu. This would enable Nicky to keep his hands free while landing. Leu would then throw Nicky's bundle after him, then pass his own bundle to the third jumper, Ray Conway. Leu would then spring himself and so on down the line.

Nicky rolled the door open again. A brief look up the track. His eyes strained through the darkness. It was clear. He was ready. In this instant, Nicky felt so proud to be an Australian. Without them in the wagon—Leu, Conway, Pete Peterson and Marlin—there was no way he would have had his chance to jump. He took a deep breath and gave a quick wink to Roo Leu. Then, in a sublime moment of inspired madness, he hurled himself into black space, his legs working furiously in running mode.

TWENTY-ONE
Pontremoli

Earlier, through the shades of darkness, Nicky had aimed to land on a downward slope of the railway line embankment. He sensed that the ground would fall away steeply here. Now, with a tremendous rush, the earth raced up to meet him. He landed heavily down the slope and, with a flailing of arms and legs, rolled helplessly for some metres and came to rest at the bottom of the incline. He lay there for a few moments, motionless, thinking, listening.

In the stillness of the pre-dawn light, echoing back through the trees surrounding him, he was aware of the sounds of the train rattling off into the distance—without him. His earlier adrenalin rush now fuelled his excitement. A feeling of great exhilaration came over him. His heart thumped in his chest and in rhythm with his neck pulse, as the full realisation of his situation hit him. He was free again; no more would he be confined to a space, no more endless rollcalls, no more searches and no one telling him what to do.

Nicky steadily rose to his feet and checked himself for injuries. His left foot was bleeding again, nothing unusual about that, and he had sustained a few bruises, but nothing serious. He was all right.

He raised his eyes to the new dawn that was just breaking through the trees. Embracing the moment, he lifted his head and squared his shoulders. He then commenced searching for Roo Leu and his other friends.

Suddenly, ringing through the quiet, he heard the muffled report of a machine-gun as it resonated around the embankment enclosure. He steeled himself, but eased when he realised the sound was coming from the receding train. Had they been discovered? Would they stop and search?

The gunshots hastened Nicky. He recovered the little bundle of meagre possessions which Leu had almost lobbed on him, then moved off in the direction where his friends would have landed. He could find none.

In fact, Nicky later learned that during the course of the night, some men from all the wagons escaped, one way or another. Leu jumped 100 metres further down from Nicky and Conway further along again. All ten of Nicky's friends jumped without being hit, but unfortunately one of his team, a British major, Wally Wadeson hurled himself into a bridge and was killed. Nicky's friend, Mac, the Yugoslav, had entered the wagon behind the engine and, tragically, also died as he launched himself into a torrent. When the train arrived in Germany next morning, and the discrepancy in numbers was found, nobody was shot. The train guards had changed at 3.45 a.m. and the death threat had not been communicated to the new squad. Good old Spike did not have to sacrifice himself.

Nicky decided on a plan. He made a decision not to move north to Switzerland. It did not appeal to him to spend the rest of the war, an unknown period, in internment. He considered trying to connect with the 'Comet Line', controlled by the French 'Maquis'—the underground—where escapees were spirited through southern France into Spain then Portugal and out of Lisbon to England. However, because of the success of the Allied landings in Sicily, and the strong prediction of an imminent landing of Allied Forces on the Italian mainland, he decided to move south through Italy and attempt to join up with the Allies once they landed.

For the first few days, Nicky walked by himself, carefully trying to gauge the political mood of the locals as he met with them. There was much going on in Italy and Nicky found it was difficult to know who to trust. 'Survival' dominated every conversation.

There was a great deal of infighting between the Royalists—people loyal to the King, Victor Emmanuel III—and the Fascists, Mussolini's 'Blackshirts', the villains. The Fascists themselves had split, with much factional and regional infighting.

Over all this, the Italian people were beginning to realise they were being used and controlled by the Germans. The Nazis employed techniques to instil abject fear and intimidation among the populace. Specialised SS troops would seize, at random, small groups of Italian people from the village square and imprison and torture them. Other citizens were abducted and would simply disappear. A few were allowed to return and duly advertise the atrocities they had experienced and witnessed, setting up a state of fear. It was a most effective way for a small but well-trained unit to control many people spread over large areas.

With all this happening, at first Nicky was very wary on entering villages. However, he soon found if he walked in openly, even brazenly, he was less likely to arouse suspicion. Physically, he also learned to cope with his new lifestyle.

For the first few days, he found he could survive comfortably without food, but he needed water. So, no matter where he travelled, the dominating thought was: 'Is there going to be any water?' It meant frequently moving into the hill areas where water was caught in catchment creeks. When moving through villages, he would go straight to the fountains and wells. Eventually, he gained courage to buy some gelati from a vendor (with his lire acquired in prison).

Occasionally, as he grew more comfortable with his situation, he would present at a house and ask for food. He was generally accommodated, and was often warned of any potential problems in the local town—Blackshirts or Nazis. He rarely stayed overnight, preferring to sleep either in the open or in farmers' stone caves at the back of a farm. Once, he tried to catch a hen, but it squawked too loudly, so he stole the eggs instead. Sometimes, he pilfered fruit or vegetables from the farmyards.

After some days, he teamed up with Ray Conway, the Australian AIF captain who had jumped third. They began travelling together at dusk or early dawn, then holing up for the day. At night, they would go their separate ways, meeting at a predetermined point the next morning. By the third day, Conway didn't turn up. Nicky retraced his steps, but could not find him.

Conway had, in fact, become lost, and was recaptured.

Nicky made a conscious decision. From then on, he would definitely remain a loner. He would help anyone he could and then work with them, but he would resist setting up a permanent basis of operation in company. He felt he would achieve more if he did not have to rely on or be influenced by anybody.

Two weeks later, he wandered into Pontremoli, a village 100 kilometres south of Piacenza. Here, he was introduced to an Italian colonel who was an avid anti-Fascist and was determined to harass both the Blackshirts and the Germans. He had organised a group of Royalists and partisans and invited Nicky to assist. This idea appealed to Nicky as it appeared to be a way he could physically help to 'do his bit' to shorten the war. News had come through that the Italians had capitulated on 8 September, and the day after that a massive Allied force had landed at Salerno, south of Naples. In reaction, the German Army was streaming down from the north in a bid to bolster the main force at Salerno, which was commanded by Field Marshal Albert Kesselring.

There were several other guerrilla-type groups working in the area and the intentions focused on clandestine activity designed to harass German convoys travelling south.

There were at least two divisions of Axis troops in the area between Pontremoli and Pistoia, and much of the work involved the cutting of communications, roads and railway links between these units and the north. This often resulted in close encounters with the enemy, many culminating in open confrontation and hand-to-hand fighting. To succeed, pre-planned and very fast withdrawals were essential, virtually 'hit and run'.

For most of this time, Nicky slept in mountain caves or bushland, sharing the guard duty with two other members of the group, an Irishman and a South African. For some time, he was placed in the basement of a house, a rather civilised change.

Nicky got to like what he was doing and found that even in the toughest life-threatening situations, he could handle the stress and live with himself. He slept comfortably at night, secure in his belief in himself and that he was helping the war effort.

However, after two months of this adrenalin-burning existence, as the Germans intensified their terror tactics on the locals, the risk of betrayal was also increased. One day, working in the mountains north of Pistoia, Nicky and a handful of the group had carefully wired a bridge and set the detonator so that it would be triggered by the wheels of the train as it passed over it. There was often some pantomime in these operations and the team leader asked, 'Now, all we need are the explosives.'

It turned out they had been forgotten. A member was sent back to address the problem and Nicky and four other men waited. After almost a day, they decided to adjourn home and meet later at a nearby park.

At the predetermined time, Nicky and the other men set out towards the park, but never reached it. They were apprehended by German soldiers waiting in a side street.

Nicky uttered an inaudible groan. 'We've been betrayed.'

A few hours later, the five men, including two Italians, an Englishman and an American, were brutally manhandled as they were herded into a rail wagon, similar to the one Nicky had earlier jumped from. Even with their hands up (prisoners never put their hands behind their back—they always had to have them on view), the men were hit with rifle butts and boots and succumbed to heavy scuffling. Nicky was bruised, but not seriously hurt. Two guards with guns were placed inside the wagon and the heavy doors rolled shut. The train whistled, chuffed and, with a jerk, commenced its journey. The men could see nothing outside and were not told of their destination.

Nicky's mind raced. He was angry and disappointed at being caught again. Never again would he work for anybody. He would work with them, but never for them. He would become even more the embodiment of a loner. But first, he had to escape again.

Within a few hours, the train screeched to a halt. The prisoners were blindfolded and led from the train, then they walked for some distance. Nicky was nervous as he considered they might be shot. Under his top coat he wore a RAAF uniform which he had been given by the Red Cross at Bergamo. Hopefully, this would prevent him being mistaken for a spy. If they considered him to be a spy he would definitely be executed.

Eventually they were led to a large room and, with some relief, were allowed to take off their blindfolds. They were in a type of portable 'demountable' building and the SS officer in charge told the prisoners they were in an 'Interim Transit Prison' where they would be held until their final destination was established.

The next morning, in daylight, they could see that the building was surrounded by two rows of barbed wire fencing with an open area of ground in between. In one corner stood a raised sentry box which was manned by guards carrying machine-guns. Over the next few days, Nicky met other prisoners who informed him he was now in Austria. They had come up through the Brenner Pass and were now near Obsteig, just over the Italian border and not too far from Innsbruck.

That night, Nicky found one of the other prisoners had appropriated a large set of pliers capable of cutting barbed wire. During the night, in turn, the men would slither up to the wire, cut a few strands, then retire for a breather. It was tense, close work. Just one sound and the guards would be alerted. Within a few hours, a pathway had been opened through the field and, very quickly, 15 men including Nicky crept through and were on their way.

Once outside, most of the escapees had already determined they would try and make for Switzerland. Once again, Nicky considered this, but felt strongly it would serve his interests better to get back into Italy and connect with the invading Allied troops. He had to get back to Dot. Switzerland, to him, did not represent freedom. Besides, there was a strong rumour now that the Allies were to create a second beachhead at Livorno on the Ligurian coast. Nicky reconfirmed he would go south.

It was a decision he would live to be grateful for. Over the next few weeks, the 14 other men did not enter Switzerland. They were all rounded up and executed.

Nicky started travelling parallel to the densely active Brenner Pass, but found the roads were very busy. He elected to follow one of the side tracks, just below the snow line. Some hours after setting out, on sunset, after rounding a corner, he was astonished to suddenly encounter a most glorious alpine vista. On all sides spread a breathtaking panorama of green and blue mountains with yet more white-capped mountains unfolding behind. Snow streaked the ground with brushstrokes and the wind buffeted wildflowers in the valley below.

Then, on a knoll, sitting on a rock a few metres ahead, Nicky noticed a young man immersed in the scene. Nicky approached cautiously, looking for gestures and body language that might show aggression. In poor German, Nicky ventured, 'Guten morgen.'

The young man turned. He wore thick glasses and appeared to be friendly. He explained he was a school teacher near Obsteig and he was an Austrian. Nicky divulged he was an Australian, to which the young man responded, 'Would you like a drink?'

Nicky accepted gratefully and the young man walked, with a bad limp, to a hut, which was just around the corner of the knoll. The limp had rendered him ineligible for military service, he explained.

He returned with a delicious drink that tasted like malted milk. He also gave Nicky some 'dark blood' German bread, which was very sustaining. Then surprisingly, he produced a small hand gun. It was a beautifully made revolver with the maker's name on the barrel—Sauer and Sohn. Before Nicky could react, the Austrian pressed the gun into the palm of Nicky's hand. 'Please, take it,' he said. 'It's loaded. Never point it unless you are going to use it.'

Nicky was amazed at this—a gun from the enemy. He accepted it and placed it behind the buckle at the front of his belt and down his trousers. He was very lean. Bemused, Nicky farewelled his new-found friend and continued south through the Wipp Valley towards the Brenner Pass.

Near the Austrian border, the snow line was many metres above the pass, heralding a cruel winter. This was early November 1943. At the gatehouse ahead, Nicky could see border guards set up across the road. He took a detour, walking and scrambling along a ridge far east of the road, eventually skirting around the border margins, then moving down alongside the Pass.

Since the fourteenth century, the Brenner Pass had been one of Europe's great trade routes linking Austria to Italy. The

100 kilometre route has been in use since Roman times and, as well as a road, a railway now ran through 22 tunnels and over 60 major bridges. There was a great deal of traffic moving both ways through the Pass, and Nicky would regularly walk past German trucks stopped at the small lakes in the catchment area to refill with water. Many times soldiers were singing heartily as if they were going to a picnic. Most people he met and talked to were Italians moving back to Italy.

An unsparing wind energised him. It was cold, but not desperate. He was still feeling exhilarated after his recent escape and his leg was the best it had been. The wound seemed to have gummed up, maybe with the cooler climate. He wasn't in a hurry and was enjoying both the walk and the freedom. Once he was cheeky enough to steal from a German canteen. Another time, he took some biscuits from an alpine hut and ski lodge he'd located while circumnavigating a major bottleneck on the Pass.

In that confused corridor, no one appeared suspicious of anyone, no one expected to encounter the enemy, and not once was he asked to show papers.

It took almost five days to exit the Pass, and once through, Nicky continued alongside the principal road south which connects to the Po Valley system. He then moved through the Isarco and Adige Valleys, just south of the Dolomites, finishing further south near Piacenza, the area where he had earlier jumped off the train.

Italy was clearly in deep turmoil, everyone preoccupied with their own affairs. No one showed interest in this limping figure, slowly winding his way south.

After walking and climbing close to 300 kilometres, his leg was starting to become painful again, so he decided to chance a train ride. Confidently, he moved into one of the packed carriages of a train, rubbing shoulders with German soldiers and Italian civilians. The train was heavily stocked with the products of war—SS troops, weapons and military supplies, all heading to the front. No one was interested in him; he wasn't challenged by a conductor or anybody else. He found a spot to sit down, rested back unconcernedly and watched the pretty Italian countryside pass by.

A few hours later, towards mid-morning, as the train was approaching Rimini, a large railway junction town on the Adriatic coast, Nicky was a little disturbed when the train came abruptly to an unscheduled stop. There appeared to be some congestion ahead. A train officer investigated and indeed, he reported that there was some interference on the line leading into the railway junction. Rimini was in the process of being bombed and strafed, and he suggested everyone should get out of the train as it would be an easy target. Nicky could hear the buzzing of fighter bombers screaming into the attack and he could clearly hear the crash and crump and feel the slight earth tremor as the bombs exploded not too far from where the train was stopped. Following the sound, he quickly moved through a cluster of trees and emerged on a hillside overlooking the town, and the Adriatic Sea.

Twelve Kittyhawks peeled in from the Adriatic, flying low. Nicky watched with some pleasure as they screamed across the sky, then unloaded their bombs directly over the Rimini train yard. At the same time, with guns blazing, they strafed the area. Within a few moments, the yards were littered with splintered railway carriages and buildings as the bombs exploded on impact and bullets shattered and razed the installations. Smoke and dust rose from the area echoing the sound back up to him.

The planes then accelerated back into the sky in preparation for another run. Immediately in front of him, one Kittyhawk streaked in low passed Nicky and released its 500-pound bomb while strafing at the same time, something which is rarely done. Nicky read the sign on its fuselage—CV-N. They were No. 3

Squadron's planes. He was suddenly excited and cried under his breath, 'Go, go, go, boys'. Nicky's emotions soared with pride. 'My CV.' How wonderful to see them and someone was flying 'N', the letter he had used.

Then there was an enormous explosion. A bomb had ignited a wagon full of ammunition destined for the front. Carriages were upended, timber and metal sprayed everywhere and flames roared to the sky. Then tragedy. As Nicky watched, the plane speared into the exploding debris as it rocketed skywards directly into the Kittyhawk's flight path.

The plane immediately caught fire, giving the pilot no chance to escape. It crashed in an inferno, emitting a blinding ball of flame and shooting black and red tinged clouds of smoke high into the sky.

Nicky was stunned at the violence and the tragic outcome, but he quickly forced himself to recover. He couldn't give himself away. Encouraged by the obvious sign of Allied aggression so deep in enemy territory, Nicky left the scene. This was a great morale-booster for him. He walked back alongside the railway line and headed south again. He felt like whistling.

Before long, he was able to jump onto the side of a slow-moving passenger train. War traffic was thickening up and many itinerant and displaced persons were also clinging to the carriages. He settled in for a journey that would take him almost to the frontier. There were pleasant periods during the trip where he was satisfied to simply enjoy looking out at the ocean and to watch sleepy seaside fishing villages race by.

Now he would relax. His next challenge, he knew, would not be easy. Somehow, he would have to infiltrate the dense German lines, then cross over to the Allies and—finally—freedom.

Abruzzi

The Winter Line was forming along a boundary centred on Cassino, on the western side of the range, across the rugged mountainous interior to the headwaters of the Sangro River, following it eastwards to the Adriatic Sea. This Eastern Front had been the scene of some heavy fighting and was suitably called the Sangro, meaning blood, taking its name from the river coursing its terrain. Right now, the line was static, as the coldest winter for decades was closing over Italy.

Nicky prudently left the train some 50 kilometres north of the front at the coastal town of Pescara, then carefully began moving inland. In view of the strong German presence gathering in the region to bolster the front-line, he decided he should mainly walk at night.

The countryside was mountainous and quite beautiful and, even in the moonlight, held some interest to Nicky. He regularly passed stalwart old farmhouses, solidly built from a multitude of different bricks, appreciating their characteristic arches and curved tiles.

Adding an Arcadian touch, silhouettes of cypress trees, fruit orchards and ancient vineyards that were clipped back for the winter, completed the rustic landscape.

Some days into his walk, as Nicky approached the village of Popoli, he reacted with some caution as a group of four men came towards him. One was wearing army camouflage gear and was fully armed, complete with grenades hanging around his neck.

This was not unusual. Because of the general political turmoil, the area was often crowded with soldiers. There were elements from many factions, the Royalists, the Blackshirts and several of their Fascist splinter groups, the Germans, arriving in large numbers, as well as many prisoners of war who had either been released or escaped. This was further complicated as there were also many Italians who, since the surrender, were now trying to get back to their own settlements.

Nicky had passed many other soldiers and not been challenged, but this one focused on him. Nicky saw that the soldier's uniform was a little darker than others he had seen, a little like the British Army issue. He also realised he'd been spotted. He would have to acknowledge them.

Nicky ventured, 'Buon giorno, come sta?' 'Come off it!', the soldier replied, the 'off' coming out as 'orf'.

Nicky smiled, caught off guard at the unexpected cockney accent. Then they both laughed. The soldier explained he was a member of a Special Airborne Operations (SAO) group, which had been trained in England and had been parachuted in behind the lines. They were basically a commando group and some of the taskforce were Italian-speaking Americans. Their main activity had been to set up a local network and report on enemy movement in this vicinity, then to relay the information via transmitters back to Allied Military Intelligence Headquarters in southern Italy. Their central focus was on L'Aquila where they believed the German commander, Field Marshal Albert Kesselring, had set up his headquarters.

Kesselring's jurisdiction extended south from the Pisa–Rimini line. He had at least eight German divisions already at his disposal (a division comprises about 14 000 men) and more were expected. By early December 1943, the Allied Forces of the

US Lieutenant General Mark Clark's Fifth Army in the west and General Bernard Montgomery's British Eighth Army in the east, now bivouacked south of the Sangro River, were brought up to their operational strength of 14 divisions.

The group also had a mission to gather up any escaped prisoners of war they could find and pass them back to a group south of Sulmona who would then spirit them over the Apennines in what was known as the Alpine Route. Upon the surrender of Italy, a few prisoner-of-war camps had set free their prisoners. The experiences of the former prisoners of war were very mixed. Many were recaptured by the Germans and sent off to unknown destinations, some were shot, while others attempted to infiltrate the front-line. Others adopted the safer option of remaining hidden in a quiet area until such time as the Allies advanced to liberate them. As such, there were always groups of prisoners of war wandering around or hiding in the countryside.

Another task, which appealed to Nicky, involved forms of sabotage and destruction, designed to harass the enemy— clandestine operations.

Their final function was to give assistance to Italians who were seeking liberation. The commando explained they were operating in the broader area of Pescara, Chieti, through to L'Aquila, down to Popoli and Sulmona and across to Rome.

'Look,' the soldier continued, 'there was 60 plus of us originally, but we're being whittled down. Maybe you'd like to join us. We need an interpreter. Can you speak Italian?'

'Well, yes I can, a little.' Nicky was slow to commit initially, even though he admired the scheme and the group appeared well-disciplined. The commando insisted he return with them and meet the major. 'We have a policy of not knowing or using names or rank—except the major. That way, if we get caught and tortured, we honestly know nothing.

'In fact, we try not to know much about anybody. Where they live or even how they live. Obscurity of individuals is important. The Germans are good at getting information from people. We do have two central meeting places, at Pontremoli, up north, and one locally here at Chieti, although our central stronghold is at Pescara.'

Nicky followed the soldier into a laneway, where they entered a nondescript house. After introductions, the major, who exuded confidence and was clearly very competent, confided to Nicky, 'We're in a desperate spot here. We've been ambushed several times and our numbers are now down to 30. We need someone we can trust to be an interpreter.'

Nicky considered the request. Reinforcing the obvious advantages of helping the war effort, his decision was influenced by the difficulties at this stage in actually climbing over the precipitous Apennines. From here, the Apennines were a formidable barrier, even in good weather. With a freezing winter closing in, it would be even more dangerous. As well, he had been informed that there were only two reliable tracks over the ranges, and there was a regiment of crack German Alpine troops based at Campo di Giove, a small village on the mountain plateau, covering these tracks. He had been told that some groups who'd tried to escape recently were apprehended by them. Better to stay here, consolidate a little, and plan his escape carefully—for the right time. In the meantime, he might be able to do his bit here.

He told the major, 'All right. I'll give it a go. I guess I can see it as a way of helping the overall effort. But I want you to give me an undertaking that you will, at your first opportunity, when you are sending a broadcast back to Intelligence Headquarters, alert them that I am with you and that I am well and to make sure my wife knows.'

The major replied that he would do that. This was important to Nicky as he held deep concerns that Dot, his twin brother and family might not have received news from or about him for at least a year. Even though Nicky was under a mild delusion that Dot might have knowledge of where he had been up until Gavi, he really could not be sure.

Nicky started his work by venturing into villages and meeting people. Sometimes he would be given a name by a member of the group, other times a name would be passed to him by someone loyal to his cause. Mostly he would use instinct, and target certain individuals. At this stage, most Italians were becoming aware they had been conned by Mussolini and the Germans. Even though he followed no real pattern, it was always safer to make advances at night.

This, of course, involved a certain amount of risk, but if he wanted to gain the locals' trust and acceptance, it was a gamble he had to take. He told the villagers that he worked with a friendly Allied group and he tried to reassure them that if they confided and co-operated with him, it would help secure a safer area for them after liberation.

He found he had most success with the farmers, or peasants. He made many useful contacts and, over some weeks, he received much valuable information, mainly concerning German troop movements, transports, their numbers and size and names of units. The group would then either act on this themselves or transmit the information through to Intelligence Headquarters.

The group increased their guerrilla activities, causing a great deal of damage to the Germans—cutting off communication and telephone lines, interfering with sections of railroad tracks, particularly in the area leading to Sulmona and the front-line and, in the mountain areas, setting off avalanches which blocked and damaged military traffic. Basically, they committed any type of skullduggery that would harass the Germans. (Their activities enjoyed the elevated title of 'clandestine operations'! Cloak and dagger from *The Boys' Own Annual*.)

These activities were satisfying to Nicky. One successful episode occurred when he and two other group members were to count the numbers of military traffic moving from the Adriatic to the east coast. They found a strategic position high on an outcrop of a winding and steep road, but the darkness made it difficult to identify and count the vehicles.

Huge boulders were balanced precariously up the slopes of the road, to the extent that the drivers were warned of their lethal potential by large danger signs. The three men dislodged these rocks, setting off an avalanche, boulders careering onto the road and crashing onto the convoy below and down into the valley.

Besides damaging many vehicles, it caused a bank-up of trucks for kilometres. More importantly, it created a clear target for Allied bombers the next day, who succeeded in exacting a heavy toll on the static enemy. Another time, Nicky requisitioned some explosives. (Most of their supplies, including food, ammunition, guns and money were parachuted in at night.) He had the intention of blowing up a key bridge that allowed mainline rail traffic through to the front. Unfortunately, there wasn't enough gunpowder to complete the job, so he and his men burned the sleepers and supports, successfully crashing the bridge into the ravine.

Regretfully, the consequences of these activities were often borne by the villagers. In retaliation, the Germans would impose their reign of fear upon the residents in any area where sabotage had taken place. Every time the group pulled a job, some locals would have their houses burnt or their property destroyed, or worse, some would be randomly abducted or even killed. Eventually these retributions created a terrible effect on the villagers' lives and minds.

It became increasingly difficult for the group to measure the balance between what they had achieved and the cost of it—both to the locals and to themselves, as they also regularly lost men during open confrontation. They needed the information the community could give them, but they had to carefully consider the consequences.

While the major was wrestling with this problem, pressure was building from Allied Headquarters to find out more of Kesselring's plans. This was late December 1943, and there was talk of another Allied landing, possibly on the coast around the Anzio region. The plan would be for this invading force to move inland and link up with the Allied US Fifth Army, which was now stalled on the Winter Line. Allied Intelligence needed to know more about German troop replenishments, feeding in from the north.

TWENTY-THREE

Goriano Valli

Nicky was asked by the major if he would make the first visit into L'Aquila. He asked him also to make contact with locals along the way and, as before, explain to them the purpose of the group. He offered Nicky a revolver for himself, and some cash to give anybody who would assist them. Nicky opted to stay with the gun he already had.

Nicky approached several houses and informed the occupants that if they could help he would issue them with a *biglietto* (certificate) acknowledging that the bearer had assisted the Allied effort. Such generosities as supplying food or harbouring escaped prisoners of war, as well as informing the group of enemy activity, would be properly rewarded after liberation.

As Nicky was moving through Acciano, a quaint little spot perched on the side of the Popoli Road not far south of L'Aquila, a huge military convoy snaking its way towards Rome virtually cut off his intended route.

He edged downhill off the main road and, to his delight, wandered into a secluded valley. After some distance, he crossed a railway line and then a small bridge spanning a stream. Just to the left was a village complete with a small church near its centre. Behind it, looming into the sky, was a most impressive mountain ridge dominated by Mount Sirente, unique with a plume of snow flying off its peak.

He decided this might be a safe haven for himself to spend the night. And indeed, in this sylvan valley he could see the potential to shelter some of the escaped prisoners of war while they were waiting their turn to filter through the lines. This was Goriano Valli.

Nicky followed the cobblestones past the ancient church. Once through the village, he noticed some small stone cave-like huts on outlying farms, which appeared uninhabited. It was approaching evening and becoming cold. He would sleep in one of these that night.

Just around the corner, an agile, middle-aged and shortish man bounded towards him. In his very best Italian, Nicky greeted him, 'Buona sera. Come sta?'

The man, wearing a raincoat, didn't immediately reply. He stopped, looked Nicky up and down, then, in clear English, he asked, 'Where are you heading?'

Nicky, in turn, sized him up. Then, after speaking for some time, he considered the man was onside, particularly when he found out he was a Jew, a German Jew.

The man introduced himself as Franz Koblitz. Nicky continued, 'I'm hoping to sleep here tonight, but I'm also trying to establish a type of "safe house" area for groups of escaped prisoners. Most of them are in pretty poor shape and they'll need to be strengthened before we can walk them through the lines. I'm just about to move on to the next town, Secinaro, where I was told I could contact a solicitor, Mr Vacca, who could help me to buy a safe house. I have plenty of lire.'

'Well, you'd better not go at the moment. It's alive with SS troops and Gestapo. They're "cleansing" the area. It's a bit late. I think you had better come to my place.'

Nicky was reticent. He had not had time to survey an effective escape route. However, he trusted Koblitz, who led him to a small peasant stone house. Here he was introduced to an attractive young woman.

'I'd like you to meet my wife, Greta.'

There was also an Italian peasant woman there who was introduced as 'Aunty', although she was not related to them. Her name was Zia Colomba and she owned the cottage. Zia lit the open fire on the stones in the centre of the floor and they shared a sustaining lentil soup—a memorable meal.

Nicky confided in them of their SAO group and of their mission and activities. The couple indicated they would be willing to help. It was a very satisfying meeting. The Koblitzs appeared to have connections with people who could assist all the way to Rome, and they seemed to know a fair amount concerning Kesselring's movements. Nicky offered them some money, but they refused as they had no need of it. They had funds. Nicky was intrigued and listened to their story.

Koblitz in fact, had once been incredibly wealthy. He had also been one of the most highly decorated German officers during World War One on the Eastern Front, and had been personally decorated by Hitler in 1934. He had owned and managed large corporate activities in Berlin and throughout Germany, however the Nazis, with their anti-Jewish policy, imprisoned and killed his first wife in an extermination camp. They then confiscated most of Koblitz's property, although he did manage to spirit some money and possessions out of the country.

Because of his impeccable military and public record, Koblitz was permitted to leave Germany—under duress. He was given an airline ticket to Rome but was interned by the Italian Fascists on his arrival. Here he met Greta, an Austrian who was also an internee. They married and eventually came to Goriano Valli where they had been co-ordinating their own covert operations. They were multi-lingual and locally known as 'the Swiss people'.

Nicky considered this valley would be an ideal place for

him to stay. The track dropped sharply down into the valley below, leading to an old water mill. In the fields lining this pathway, Nicky had earlier noticed a series of caves dotting the landscape. Some had been built long ago from local stones and some were carved into the side of the nearby hill bordering the fields. Nicky chose one such cavern and slept in it for the night.

The next morning, he continued with his original task and took the main road north to L'Aquila. L'Aquila was well known as a ski resort, and possessed a Grand Hotel—*Albergo Grande*. This was where Kesselring had set up his headquarters.

On the outskirts of the town Nicky located another couple, both Royalists, one an academic from Florence University. Both were keen to help him. Nicky reinforced that he particularly needed information concerning Kesselring's movements.

As part of the information-gathering process, the major dispatched a young Scotsman called Geordi on a mission to transport a message to this particular academic a little further north of L'Aquila. The soldier was tough, an ex-Gorbal Diehard from a Scottish Regiment of the Line from Glasgow. He had worked on an Italian farm as a prisoner of war, and could speak the local Italian dialect quite fluently.

After some days, when the man had not returned, the major and Nicky became concerned for his safety. On the fourth day, he turned up at Goriano Valli, apologetic and with a story to tell.

'What the hell were you doing?' Nicky asked.

'Well, I'd walked into L'Aquila just on dark, and the *osteria* [pub] was open, so I had a few drinks with the locals, trying to pick up information. I had quite a few, and by then it was dark, and a picture show was just starting. It was in English and at the end when they played their national anthem, I stood up and sang "God Save the King".'

'You clown,' Nicky admonished, controlling his mirth.

'The Germans picked me up and put me in a holding prison on the outskirts of L'Aquila. They brought in an SS officer to interview me just as he was retiring. He was only partly dress-ed and was taking off his *stevali* [long boots]. So I picked one up and hit him over the head with it—knocked him out. I then got dressed in the officer's uniform and as I walked through the gate, I got a smart salute from the prison guard. Around the corner I changed back into my own gear and delivered the message. Sorry I'm a bit late.'

Nicky liked the young man. He was a memorable character, but he had been irresponsible.

'You know about torture. It's not good enough. You could have dobbed us all in.'

'Oh, come off it. It was my twenty-first birthday!'

Over the next few days, Nicky gathered up any escaped prisoners he could find and, with some of his own commando group, placed them in the little caves around Goriano Valli. With the Koblitzs' aid, he arranged for the villagers to assist with food and clothing. Some of the residents were quite terrified at this prospect and were indeed poor themselves, yet they were rich in human spirit. The men rarely went without.

Even though Nicky still had other groups of prisoners hidden around the Abruzzi region, housed mainly in disused religious buildings, old ruins, large caverns, several outhouses and even disused ski accommodation quarters, he desperately needed more locations.

He therefore continued with his plans to buy his own house so that the group could establish some control. With the assistance of Signore Vacca, the solicitor from Secinaro, Nicky said, 'It's freezing now. I want a place where our fellows can stay warm and sleep in some peace. Somewhere that if someone knocks on the door, it will be a friend. They will be safe. They need time and we need to feed them up a bit. They must have a great deal of endurance to climb the Apennines. Can you find a place for us?'

Signore Vacca found a suitable property in a little village called Roccapretura perched on a hilltop in the middle of an almond growing district, a little further north of Goriano Valli.

Nicky spent much time there himself although, for security reasons, he alternated between there and Goriano Valli. During this period, Nicky mixed socially and happily with the locals, increasing their mutual respect for each other. As well, he continued to gain their confidence by helping with the local industry—cracking almonds—which were used for making cosmetics. He even played some tunes on a little bellows organ in the local church and learned some of the regional folksongs. The Italians had changed the rollicking 'Roll out the Barrel' into a dreamy love song.

It wasn't only Allied prisoners looking for a chance to escape. One day, in early January 1943, Nicky received a message to meet some German and Austrian deserters in a little village called Roccardi Caramanico, about halfway between Popoli and Sulmona. Nicky walked over to meet them.

'Sir,' the Austrian leader of the group said, 'we wish to escape from here. We know you help to arrange for escaped POWs to get over the mountains. Can you please assist us?' To convince Nicky of their good faith, he added, 'One of the things we do as part of the cause is to alter clothes and give them to deserters.'

Nicky was suspicious, but said he'd offer them a chance. 'We have a group going over the mountains very soon. I'll contact you.'

Over the next few days, Nicky gathered up some other escaped Allied prisoners, then collected the deserters and led all ten men to a little isolated Alpine house, not too far from Sulmona. They were to wait here for a signal from the guides, who would take them around the outskirts of Sulmona, and then escort them over the Apennines.

Nicky knew the guides well. They were Renato and Dominico, both brave civilians and experienced athletic mountaineers, and they came from Campo di Giove. About 11.00 a.m. the next morning, the sun was just warming the day, taking the chill out of the air. Nicky heard a noise from the gully outside and thought it might be the guides. He was feeling a little uneasy and eager to get going.

Nicky froze as he saw, moving out of the ravines and emerging from the dark shadows, some sinister-looking figures dressed in snow gear, armed and at the ready. They were German soldiers and had completely surrounded the hut and were closing in fast. Two of them had SS badges on their lapels which flashed as they moved into the morning sunlight.

Nicky and his group had no chance. They were caught cold. In shock, Nicky's first thought was, 'Damn. We've been betrayed.' Then his anger abruptly turned to abject fear since he knew that if anybody was caught with a weapon on them, the rules allowed the enemy to summarily execute that person. He still had the little revolver given to him by the Austrian schoolteacher back in Obsteig—stuffed down the front of his trousers behind his belt! It was too late to get rid of it.

Nicky and his group were aggressively forced outside and ordered to line up. Were they going to shoot them all—now? The two SS officers began interrogating each man in turn, then carried out a very thorough body-search. The third man down the line was a New Zealand sergeant, a most reliable type, and he had previously told Nicky that if he was discovered he would take some of the enemy with him. He had a hand grenade on him, and didn't throw it away.

The grenade was very quickly discovered by one of the officers, who coolly lifted his revolver, pointed it at the head of the sergeant and pulled the trigger. The man's head snapped back sharply, blood pouring from his temple, then his body dropped. Nicky looked on in dismay. He was three men further down the line and broke into a cold sweat.

By the time the officer had reached him, Nicky was close to a state of panic, but he could do nothing. He would have to bluff it through. The Nazi's search was very thorough. He frisked Nicky inside and outside both legs, crutch, back and armpits and repeated the procedure in the bent-over position. All the while, Nicky tried to control his fear; if the officer found the gun, he would only have seconds left to live. He worked desperately not to give anything away. In his favour, Nicky was very lean from being underfed and the flat bulge under his belt lying in the centre of his stomach above the pubic area was not conspicuous.

To his great relief, the soldier did not check there. Nicky could not believe his luck. The German passed on to the next man, leaving Nicky gasping quietly in great shock.

The men were then marched down to a utility-type army vehicle. The soldiers filled the truck with eight of the group and threw the New Zealander's limp body unceremoniously onto the back tray, then drove off north towards Popoli. Nicky was left with another chap, a Scotsman who co-incidentally was also named Geordi and was from the same Scottish regiment as the young adventurer at L'Aquila. They were bundled into the back seat of a large Mercedes car with one armed soldier either side of them and one driving. The car drove south on a winding road towards Sulmona. Just outside of a small village, they were placed in an Italian watch-house, off the side of the road.

Once inside, Nicky and Geordi looked at each other, grateful to be alive, but not too sure of their future. They heard the car drive off, giving them some time to assess their situation. The gaol was a very old building with an extremely heavy wooden door. The Germans had locked the door from the outside by turning the ancient key, and it was still in the lock. It had a long shaft and the end extended into the cell by about 2 centimetres. The men tried to turn the protruding end of the key by hand, but it was very resistant, and they needed more leverage. Geordi smiled and said to Nicky, 'I can get us out of here, but we should wait till the wee hours.'

There was not much light in the cell, and the men were fairly tired. Nicky, particularly, was still recovering from the shock of his near escape. In a quiet moment, he thought about how, during a body search, rarely does one examine the abdominal region. What a stroke of luck.

They had not been given any food, but were left with some water. As the afternoon moved on and darkness began to fall they could feel the evening chill come down. Towards dusk, Geordi winked at Nicky and said, in his best Scottish brogue, 'We should undo the wee lock now.'

Nicky, still a little dazed, looked quizzically at Geordi. With some small ceremony, Geordi placed his foot on a chair and showed Nicky that it had some wire tied around it. He undid the wire, deftly shaped it into two half hitches and placed these around the protruding shaft of the key. Nicky was impressed with the man's initiative as he tightened the extensions of the hitches to form handles, allowing them to act as a lever. Geordi started working the key and eventually it turned and fell into its correct patterned position.

Nicky was watching intently. After some more manipulation, Geordi moved the key to a quadrant area. He smiled once again, patting Nicky on the back, 'Won't be long.'

He applied more pressure to the wire and, an instant later, the lock clunked open. Victory. However, they decided it would be prudent to wait and escape under cover of darkness. In the early hours of the next morning, they pushed the creaky old door open, briefly checked for the enemy, then walked out, free.

Once again, Nicky was exhilarated. He joyously congratulated Geordi and his ingenuity, then assisted him forward to Sulmona. He advised him how to continue on the way over the mountains, then he carefully and lightheartedly walked back to Goriano Valli.

Nicky later learned that Geordi did make it through the lines, but there was no record of what happened to the other men— their names were not known to Nicky.

The whole of Nicky's existence while behind the lines had an air of unreality, with its constant instability and transience. Italy was in the throes of great change. For months, hundreds of people moved in and out of his life like ships in the night. Often no names were given but both the escaping prisoners and the locals helped each other to defeat a sinister enemy.

Around this time, the Germans learned of Nicky's role in the group's activities through a Blackshirt and they put a price on his head. It wasn't a great deal of money and Nicky pretended he was a little insulted. However, as the villagers were so terribly poor, he was always impressed with their extraordinary loyalty to him, particularly as they had full knowledge they could be shot if they were found assisting escaped prisoners of war.

They consistently went to great lengths to protect him. Frequently, there was discussion about his colouring. With his blond hair and eyebrows, and pink complexion, he was a ready target. As the German presence intensified, Nicky was given some treatment by Zia Colomba—the 'Aunt' who owned Koblitz's cottage—by coating him with some dark oily substance that Nicky believed was mainly walnut oil. After two treatments, his features were considerably darkened and stayed that way for weeks.

The villagers would also warn him of any German presence in the area. Whenever he returned from a raid or a mission, somebody—usually some of the children—would always be waiting. Then he would detour up a track to the high plateau beyond the houses and camp overnight in an isolated stone hut.

During the next morning, it was customary for someone to arrive with food and information about the latest situation. One particular morning, no one turned up, so Nicky moved to another hide-out in the next valley for a few days. On his return he was told that two of the children had had a frightening experience and a narrow escape from the Germans.

At this stage, Nicky had been sleeping most nights in the home of a woman called Marietta Iannucci. She had three children and, at great personal risk, they kept Nicky fed and informed. One morning Domenico, 15, and Julia, 14, set out with their donkey to gather firewood and to take some food up to Nicky. They were accosted by three German soldiers and asked, 'Where is the major?' (This was Nicky's title in the area.)

They looked at each other quizzically, and said, barefaced, 'We don't know what you are talking about.'

They were roughed up and thoroughly searched, as was their donkey. To the children's dismay, under the firewood the soldiers found the package of food prepared for Nicky. Recovering quickly, the children brightly told them they had planned a 'gita specale per un picnic'—a special occasion, a picnic! To their great relief, the story was accepted. The children's quick-wittedness and courage saved Nicky.

However, one time, the Germans did find their way to the stone cave-houses in the field where Nicky and some of the other prisoners and commandos were hidden. He could hear them coming. Someone, wishing to ingratiate themselves with the enemy, had told them exactly where they were! They were probing into one of the huts nearby where a French captain, Pierre, was hiding. Nicky heard the Nazi officer rasp in English, in a gruff guttural tone, 'Are there any German friends in there?'

There was no reply. Then a hand grenade was thrown in. Nicky heard a muffled explosion and a few moments later they carried the dead Frenchman's body out.

Nicky's hideway was next. Once again, there was no time for Nicky to escape. He considered his hut might have a small advantage. The access was via a tunnel about a metre high. Inside, about 3 metres along, a small wall had been built, perhaps to deter the wind, the cold or field vermin, then the tunnel opened into a small niche, which was Nicky's cramped sleeping and living quarters.

He heard the soldiers stop in front of the opening to his cave and listened with some trepidation to their question, 'Are there any of our German friends in here?'

Nicky remained silent, not moving and scarcely breathing. It was quite dark, but there was enough light for him to suddenly see a gleaming black grenade fly into the tunnel, crashing into the side of the wall. Nicky instinctively ducked. The noise was deafening in the confines of his cell and the shock, smoke and dust almost caused him to scream. He bit his lip and crouched desperately against the intervening wall.

A second grenade came spinning in. This time it bounced over the rim of the wall and landed next to Nicky. Briefly, he stared at it in horror. Then, on reflex, he picked it up and quickly lobbed it back over the wall. Like the first grenade, it also exploded with a deafening roar. In the process it shattered the roof of his cave, causing part of the ceiling to collapse on top of him. To add to the terror, murderous splinters of rock and shrapnel screamed around the small quarters, some lodging in Nicky's body. Once again, he contained his desire to scream, to rush out of the claustrophobic, dust-filled hellhole.

After some moments, the fragments settled and quiet came from outside. When he was sure the soldiers were gone, Nicky shakily crawled out of his would-be coffin and embraced the air, once again grateful to be alive. It seemed he was not meant to die this way.

In the meantime, the group continued with its harassing and reporting activities. By far the largest amount of information concerning the enemy came from the Koblitzs. They had many Italian friends who were intelligent, high-powered and loyal to the Italian King and who, no matter the risk, were more than happy to pass reliable information on to the Allied Forces.

For instance, in mid-January, they received news that a full German division was coming down to support Kesselring's army. This was the Hermann Göring Division, an armoured unit and officially part of the Luftwaffe. They also found out that the 15th Panzer Grenadier, a mechanised infantry formation, was already well on the way, stiffening Germany's ground troops by more than 30 000.

Nicky and some of his commandos tracked the Hermann Göring Division down the coast over some three or four nights monitoring them as they passed from the east coast over to the Anzio area, the suspected invasion site on the west coast. The division had large amounts of weapons and anti-aircraft cannons but, as it was dark Nicky's men experienced difficulty establishing the exact identity of all the vehicles and weaponry.

They needed to get closer to make a more definite inspection. Nicky and some of the men scrambled up to a precipice at a particular site overlooking the road. As a section of the convoy passed underneath, the men dislodged and rolled some nearby rocks towards them. As the boulders picked up speed and tumbled out of control, they created a minor avalanche that crashed into one of the trucks, isolating it from the convoy.

The vehicle swerved then smashed into the soft shoulder of the winding mountain road and rolled onto its side. The screeching of metal against rock drowned out most of the screams from the men caught and crushed inside the back of the truck. There wasn't much time. After a few minutes, when no one emerged from the wrecked transport, Nicky raced down the hillside with the intention of examining the signage on the vehicles or on the badges of the dead soldiers to determine the identity of their unit.

Unfortunately, by the time he had clambered down over the rocky terrain, some of the German soldiers were still alive and had crawled out of the truck. Nicky ran into their midst and was immediately taken prisoner again. Angrily, he thrust his hands high in surrender. However, several of the soldiers were bent on revenge. They proceeded to deliver a lethal beating to Nicky, landing heavy punches on him and hitting him with their rifle butts. Nicky dropped to the ground, winded and in pain. He expected he would be shot within a few seconds.

However, in the next instant, some rifle shots echoed from behind the crashed vehicle. Two of the German soldiers fell, mortally wounded. Nicky looked up. His commandos had followed him down and opened up a fierce fusillade, spraying the confined space with bullets.

The Germans took up the fight, exploding the mountain quietness with the crash of wild gunfire. A strong smell of cordite filled the air as men cursed, shouted and screamed.

Combatants on both sides were hit as bullets whizzed around in the dark. Nicky, regaining his breath, used every ounce of strength and dragged himself out of the immediate killing ground, but not before he noticed the Germans were wearing a badge with a Luftwaffe motif on it—the Hermann Göring unit.

Within seconds, the fierce battle was over. Seven German soldiers lay dead, crumpled among the wreckage of the truck and the corrugated Italian mountainside. The commandos searched for Nicky and, not finding him, moved off into the darkness.

Nicky had in fact crawled out of the area and, slowly but painfully, over the next few hours found his way back through the mountain passes to safety.

After five days of this concentrated clandestine activity, Nicky was recovering with Franz and Greta Koblitz in the mountain hut hideaway near Mount Sirente. By this stage, Nicky's morale was low. He had recently lost some good friends from various missions, including this last one, and he was beginning to seriously question the value of the group's harassing activities. He was not well himself, both from his recent beating and also because his subsistence diet and the tense and dangerous lifestyle were leading to exhaustion and general malaise.

Nicky and the Koblitzs were sharing some lentil soup which Greta had prepared. There was no audience, no publicity; there was no need to say anything, but Franz turned to Greta and said, 'I think the major is the most extraordinary man I have ever met.'

Coming as it did from a distinguished former German officer whom Nicky respected greatly, the accolade was well timed. The words, uttered with full sincerity in the quiet of the hut, gave Nicky a much needed boost.

Meanwhile, as a result of the group's intelligence report, the major in charge sent a strong message to Allied Headquarters. He told them he considered there would be a better place for a beachhead than at Anzio as he felt the coastal area would be extremely well fortified and defended.

TWENTY-FOUR

The Alpine Route

The advice was not heeded. On 22 January 1944, the Allies proceeded with Operation Shingle, landing at Anzio. As it was, the Germans were caught by complete surprise and, by midday, the British component of the invasion force had advanced 3 kilometres towards their objective and the Americans 5 kilometres.

However, instead of pressing his advantage, the Allied commander of the combined force, General John Lucas, an American, resisted any spirited action and elected to consolidate his ground. By the fourth day, he had moved ahead only 18 kilometres. Enough time had passed for Kesselring to bring in elements of five more divisions (including the Hermann Göring) to bolster the eight divisions already deployed around the beachhead.

The Germans prepared a counterattack and, that night, Nicky, from his hideaway in Goriano Valli, could see the flashes reflect and race across the sky as the battle raged. While the confrontation was at its height, Nicky received a visit at Goriano Valli from one of his group members who was based at Pescara, their stronghold. The man was driving an Italian ambulance and was transporting a very sick escaped soldier to a priest in Rome. The priest was a member of the underground and had devised a system to hide escaped prisoners of war all around the Seven Hills of Rome. The man had a message for Nicky.

'Nicky, the group would like you to take over. We've just lost the major. He went on a contact mission with a courier from the northern group around Ancona and, I regret to say, was captured and shot. We've had a fairly high attrition rate recently. Besides the raids on the Göring column, we lost a couple more men— signallers—along with their transmitters. Even though they moved on as soon as they sent their messages, as often happens, they left tracks in the snow and were easily followed. We only have six signallers left. On top of that, there's no one left with a commission except you. The group would like you to come to Pescara to lead them.'

Nicky walked over to Pescara, where he called a meeting of the group. He detected a drop in morale, as the major had been an effective leader and had been held in high regard. Nicky addressed them and called for an open debate concerning their role and their future. He told them he was concerned about what they were doing.

'We're not much good to anyone if we don't survive. Besides that, the Germans are taking a fairly heavy toll on the locals in retaliation for our harassing activities. The point is, we probably aren't doing enough damage to be really making a difference. The Germans are very efficient. They soon repair telephone lines, railway lines and bridges. Maybe it's time to cut back on our guerrilla tactics.'

Then Nicky asked the group, 'Should we focus our attention more on the escaped prisoners? Should we not involve ourselves in anything that would harm the local people? And also activities which potentially alienate their support? Should we in turn give them more support?'

To assist their deliberations, they sent a radio transmission to headquarters informing them of their situation and of their discussion, and asked them how important the intelligence and information they were relaying back to them was.

The answer came back: 'Nothing is as important as the information concerning German strength and troop and head-quarter movements.'

So, from these discussions, the role of the group changed. From now on, there would be no more clandestine terrorist-style missions. Most emphasis would be placed on gathering information, and they would give more support to the locals. Finally, they would continue to assist escaped prisoners. There would now be more money to spend on food and to build up the prisoners' resistance before they attempted to cross the mountains.

For the next two weeks, this new system worked well. The locals were asked to keep their sources of information open. They were obviously encouraged in this direction by the visible lack of German retribution. As well, Nicky and his group continued their rounds looking after the prisoners who were stacked away in various hideaways.

By now, however, Nicky's general health was beginning to deteriorate noticeably. He had been undernourished for a long time, but had subsisted on adrenalin and the need to perform. Finally, he succumbed to a severe attack of 'Roman Sickness'—malaria. Nicky was surprised mosquitoes could survive in such frostbitten areas, but he learned that malaria had been a problem in the Pontine marshes around the far reaches of Rome long before Nero's time.

He radioed headquarters for advice. Should they send in a new commander, disband or come back through the lines? They advised him to try and return over the mountains.

Nicky called his remaining men together. 'I've been in touch with headquarters. My health is failing and I've been advised to try and go over the Apennines while I have the energy. They don't want the group to disband. I've installed a warrant officer from our Pescara group to take over. While I've been leader, we've continued with an established pattern of discipline set up by the previous major and I think our new policies are working well.'

Nicky never really felt that the group needed him as a leader as they were already a well-disciplined group. He considered his main worth was as an interpreter, and he didn't imagine himself to be a genuine leader. However, he was satisfied with the group's accomplishments while under his command.

He said goodbye to each of them in turn, then asked if there were any sick or exhausted members who needed to walk out with him. Nicky told his men, 'We'll gather up a large group, including some prisoners of war, and move out. We'll go through the lines with Dominico on the full moon.'

A few days later, as the full moon silvered the landscape, Nicky and 12 other men marshalled at a special point south-east of Sulmona. The temperature was close to freezing and fog shrouded parts of the mountain. The plan was to climb up towards Campo di Giove through the snow on the high ridge, then trek down towards the coastal plains on the Adriatic. This would put them just a little north of the Sangro River. To avoid crossing here, where it would be fast flowing, they would travel higher into the ranges and cross around its source, then move towards Vasto on the Adriatic coast.

A real worry was that the area was crawling with Germans. In recent weeks, two groups attempting to cross the lines had not made it. They had been picked up by Alpine Patrols. Nicky believed the groups had been betrayed. He told his group they would need to remain focused, to have stamina and a certain amount of luck.

Nicky had a raging temperature himself and was not well. The terrain was steep and difficult to negotiate. As well, elements of the path were quite dangerous, being slippery from ice and snow. The men climbed all night, carefully choosing their footing by the pale moonlight; one mistake had the potential to be fatal. As the walk continued, Nicky noticed other men appear out of the wilderness and join his entourage.

Within an hour of leaving Sulmona, his party had grown to 18, and by the time the early morning sun had filtered the first few shafts of light through to the staggering column of men, Nicky counted well over 20 had joined them. They were now clambering down the Campo di Giove side of the mountain, and were beginning to feel excited.

Then, suddenly, machine-gun fire echoed around the mountain ridges. Nicky crouched and searched for the source of the gun fire. They had been spotted by a German Alpine Patrol, possibly from the unit based at Campo di Giove. We are so close, he thought. They can't stop us now. Luckily, they were out of range and their shots were falling short. With some relief, Nicky noticed there was also a large ravine between his escaping soldiers and the German troops.

Nicky borrowed Dominico's powerful rifle and fired several shots. They landed quite near to the Germans and, hopefully, it was just enough warning to the Alpine Patrol that this superior weapon might give Nicky's group an advantage. Luckily, the Germans did not follow.

Dominico pushed the pace. There wasn't far to go. Then, coming towards them, the men encountered a scouting party of British troops. They were part of Monty's Eighth Army—the same army Nicky had flown with back in the desert.

The captain, playing it cautiously, extended a greeting in German. Nicky wasn't waiting for a debate. He knew they were English. 'Hello,' he called back in English.

The captain smiled and lowered his rifle.

After 21 months behind enemy lines, Nicky had finally made it back. It was early March 1944.

The feeling was overpowering. His triumph was complete.

TWENTY-FIVE
Cutello

Nicky was driven directly through the lines and escorted to an old stone building. The antiquated dwelling had been seconded to serve as a debriefing room for Advanced Allied Military Intelligence Headquarters, and here Nicky was interviewed by a British colonel and two junior officers. He was elated finally to be in safe territory, and even though he was exhausted from his overnight escapade, and the snow-capped mountains were now far in the distance, Nicky enthusiastically spoke of his adventures through most of the morning.

After lunch, the colonel, in a soft yet deliberate voice, told Nicky matter-of-factly that they had all the knowledge concerning the situation north of the Sangro that they needed. It became obvious to Nicky that any information gained by a junior officer was seen to be of little value to the commanding echelon. The colonel thanked Nicky and emphasised the importance of security, stressing the need for Nicky to forget all about the events of this period.

Nicky was astounded at this suggestion, which was more of a command than a request. After all, Nicky considered he probably had some important first-hand information that, if delivered to the right strategic minds, might assist the Allied effort. On the other hand, he realised he would have little difficulty fulfilling the Colonel's directive as he had experienced many incidents which he would rather forget anyway.

'Say nothing to anybody,' he was reminded.

Nicky couldn't resist a play on words. 'Do you mean I'm not to speak at all?' he smiled.

The colonel laughed in turn and replied, 'No, you need only say, "Nothing happened." However,' the colonel continued, 'we're going to ask you to pinpoint a target, and if you can fly, we'll ask you to act as a marker for us to take it out.'

The colonel conveyed to Nicky that they knew the Germans had a large stockpile of ammunition and fuel at a place called San Demetrio, and they would like Nicky to help blow it up.

'Certainly,' Nicky said. He knew the area well. San Demetrio was about halfway between Popoli and L'Aquila.

'Excellent. We'll talk later,' the Colonel replied.

The session was over and Nicky moved outside. The doors closed behind him and he immediately felt the blood drain from his head, as if he was flying against multiple G-forces.

Nicky sagged to the ground and collapsed. He lay unconscious, falling into a deep coma.

When he regained consciousness some time later, he found he had been transferred to the Advanced Indian Army Hospital at Vasto, on the Adriatic Coast. The superintendent of the hospital was a charming Indian, educated in Britain, with a fellowship in surgery from Edinburgh. He sat at the end of the bed.

'I know what you want to know: How soon will you fly again?' he said.

Nicky laughed. He agreed, but knew he wasn't well. The doctor, directly but compassionately, informed Nicky of his situation.

'You are a total mess,' he smiled, 'mentally and physically. We are going to have to work on you and you are going to have to look after yourself.

'You are very run down,' he continued, 'besides malaria and malnutrition, you have a type of systemic blood poisoning from where your burns and leg wounds have become infected. Your weight is down to eight-and-a-half stone (55 kilograms) and you are suffering from chronic stress and exhaustion.'

Worse, Nicky realised he had no libido whatsoever. Nicky wondered how he could have degenerated like this? He imagined that, realistically, he had probably become so involved in surviving and spent so much time living 'on the edge', burning adrenalin, he just wasn't aware of his deteriorating condition.

Added to the obvious physical factors had been the ever-present concern of being betrayed and recaptured. Invariably, he had also worried about his responsibility for others in his care. He had just simply burnt out.

He could not face Dot like this. He would have to get well. An image appeared of Dot. Their few weeks together had been enough to infatuate Nicky to the extent that she had become the central focus of his thoughts, the one for whom he was able to endure so much. He needed time to recuperate; he needed to be a whole man again. The potential to be reunited with her would be his healing therapy.

But first, he needed to find out if Dot had received the message he had requested be forwarded some months earlier. He found out from Intelligence that the message had, indeed, never been sent. The previous intelligence commander had considered that it might constitute a security risk. This angered Nicky a great deal. The promise given to him on his undertaking to assist the group had not been fulfilled: his loved ones still did not know where he was.

The only letter which reached him here, at this stage, was from Group Captain Bill Duncan. Duncan, who was still the RAAF liaison officer in Cairo, warmly welcomed Nicky back, telling him Dot's letters were stacked up in Cairo and London.

Nicky lapsed in and out of consciousness over some days. Eventually, as he drifted out of his coma, he found three faces peering down at him. He recognised Ted Tunbridge, the transport officer and a good friend of his from No. 3 Squadron which was now based at Cutello, fortunately not too distant from the hospital. One of the other men was Ken Watts, a young, successful flight commander from No. 3 Squadron, and the third man was the Reverend Dr Fred McKay, an air force chaplain.

The three men passed on messages of goodwill from the squadron and invited him back when he was ready. In the meantime, Fred McKay undertook personally to send a telegram to Dot informing her and Nicky's family of his situation. This settled Nicky a great deal. He could now concentrate on getting well.

And indeed, McKay's cable did reach Dot, who was extremely relieved, having known nothing of Nicky's whereabouts since Gavi. If Nicky was worried about patience, hope and courage, he needn't have been. Dot had enough for the two of them.

Even though the hospital superintendent had warned Nicky not to expect a miracle with his recovery, initially Nicky responded reasonably quickly to treatment. Physically, good food, peaceful and uninterrupted sleep, fluids, a helpful and caring nursing staff and the realisation that he was in a safe environment and without fear for the first time in 21 months greatly assisted his return to health.

Mentally, however, the process was a little tougher. Recurring incidents replayed in his mind and certain thoughts began to haunt him. He developed trouble sleeping, as ghastly and frightening memories jumped out at him. He was diagnosed as suffering from a temporary form of reactive depression. It was difficult to handle, but Nicky found that by a combination of rest and deliberately exercising his brain, the symptoms steadily receded.

There was a large library at the hospital and the doctor recommended he should try reading. This helped tremendously. He started writing letters and he began to be more physically active as well. He also received many letters as, by now, news of his adventures had spread.

Within a few weeks, the synergistic effect of adequate rest and appropriate exercise, of both his mind and body, started to show a positive effect. This, coupled with the pleasure of knowing that he had 'beaten the odds' raised Nicky to a level of health and contentment where he was soon ready to try flying again.

For another reason he was keen to have a break from the hospital. Some members of the English press had found him and he considered most of them fairly thoughtless. Some were obstinate and rude, questioning every thing he said, while others were invasive and generally insensitive. Nicky wasn't keen to tell them about his private life. He didn't need them. He informed the British colonel who'd interrogated him earlier that he was ready to fly.

The fact was, Nicky was still quite frail. He realised he would not have the stamina to get involved in any bombing or strafing raids, but he was keen to fly as a target marker as had been requested.

On 21 March, he was driven to Cutello where he was warmly welcomed back to No. 3 Squadron. The reception gave Nicky great satisfaction as, privately, he appreciated the symbolism of returning to his squadron after so long away. Here he was introduced to Major Fricker, the instructor for his new plane, an American Mustang, the P-51.

The Mustang was built by the North American Aviation Company, and No. 3 Squadron had begun flying them in November 1943. The plane had a reputation as fast, manoeuvrable and rugged and it had shown it was a match for the latest Me-109s.

Even though it had been almost two years since Nicky last sat in a plane, as he approached the Mustang, then climbed into the cockpit, he had the strange sensation of having flown only the previous day. The feel of the controls returned to him immediately, as Fricker ran through the cockpit drill and standard familiarisation exercises.

Nothing was missing from Nicky's skills as he took her aloft. The same thrill was there as the glorious roar of the engine reminded him of voices from the past. The experience was one of liberation. He allowed himself one mock run over the drome, then took his place at the head of the waiting Martin B-26 Marauder bombers already circling in formation above.

The Mustang was a beautiful plane. Nicky found it so easy to trim and he marvelled at its power. He felt as if he was being reborn, and couldn't help but judge it against his beloved Kittyhawk, as one would compare a greyhound to a reliable warhorse.

Within a few minutes, the Sangro river and the Apennines appeared ahead. Nicky pulled back on the joystick. Instantly, the powerful bird responded and raised its nose, dragging the squadron above the jagged mountains. For a moment, as the plane passed over the crevices and eroded uneven surfaces, Nicky mused on the contrast to his all-night odyssey over the same topography less than a month ago. He could see himself struggling over the windswept and craggy peaks and he marvelled again at his fortune, both in finishing the journey and also in evading the dreaded Alpine Patrols.

He was also relieved that right now there was very little ground fire shooting towards his formation, and so far there had been no air activity. He had been concerned because the day before, four of the newer and heavily armed German Focke-Wulf FW 190 fighter planes with their powerful long BMW radial engines had flown over the hospital and he suspected they might show again today. So far, they had been lucky; the air was theirs alone.

After a few more minutes, Sulmona appeared, framed in the cockpit window. About 15 kilometres further in the distance,

Nicky could make out the familiar village of Popoli, and the Aterno River at the opening of the lush green valley which he knew lead to L'Aquila.

Nicky guided the squadron above the valley, and then San Demetrio rushed into view. Nicky noticed that the fuel stores had grown since he had last visited the area, indicating an increased enemy presence, obviously building for the coming spring offensive.

From his position a little forward and somewhat lower than the squadron, Nicky slid back his cockpit hatch. The slipstream was cold yet embracing. He had been given two Verey pistols, one loaded with a green smoke cartridge, the other with a red. In turn he fired the green one vertical to the horizon, indicating his position to the squadron, and the red one downwards aimed at the target.

Like great hawks loosing long vertical lines of cigar-shaped canisters, the Marauders dropped hundreds of bombs towards the depot down below. Nicky watched as explosions of dust, flame and smoke pocked the earth, then zipped in crazy patterns through the surrounding countryside, racing towards the supply and fuel dump. An incandescent roar of orange flame signalled a direct hit as fire and black smoke mushroomed then spiralled into the sky.

With some regret, Nicky noticed a few bombs had sprayed into the village, but the mission had been an otherwise unqualified success.

In early April, Nicky was advised that he should try and return home to Australia. This was tremendous news. However, there were no Australia-bound troop ships leaving from Italy. He was told he would have a better chance of getting home from Cairo, so No. 3 Squadron command arranged for him to return to Egypt.

Nicky was transferred by an RAF Dakota DC-3 to Cairo, where he was warmly welcomed by Group Captain Bill Duncan, the RAAF liaison officer. Duncan arranged a monumental party for him at 'The Snake Pit', a lower ground room in the RAAF Headquarters building.

There were about 40 men and women (mainly RAAF and WAAF) at the reunion, all keen to welcome him back. He knew a great number of them, including many who had escaped, like himself, and were also waiting to get back home. Some, like Charles McWilliam, from No. 112 Squadron, had been waiting as long as six months.

Duncan had spared no expense on grog, and the party was soon high with singing and dancing. Nicky's friends were delighted to see him again, and after some glorious imbibing and outright frivolity, the OC called for quiet. Solemnly, he reached up onto a shelf and pulled down a squeeze-box—it was Freddy Eggleston's, and had been there since Eggleston had been shot down two years previous.

'I've been saving this for you,' he said. 'Play us a tune, Nicky.'

Nicky was overwhelmed. He wiped the dust off the keys and shook the accordion. Half of the desert seemed to fall out. It hadn't been touched. Nicky was rusty and the squeeze-box took some limbering up to get it to work.

After some moments, he successfully rendered some air force ditties, then he concentrated fully on his instrument, and sang an emotional version of 'Lily Marlene'. He was so involved in his performance and enjoying the moment, he was not aware of what was transpiring in the crowded room. When he raised his eyes from his squeeze-box, he saw that nobody was talking. The whole room had their eyes on him, and most of them had tears streaming from them. McWilliam was openly bawling and Duncan was sobbing, lost in his memories. There was no need to say anything; Squadron Leader Nicky Barr was back, and he had been missed.

Finally, it was all too much, Nicky put the squeeze-box down and freely wept.

TWENTY-SIX

Normandy

There was a legacy to the party. Bill Duncan became so riotous he sang and drank until he collapsed and had to be driven to a hospital to recover. Nicky visited him next morning, where he was informed by Duncan that he wanted him to take over his job temporarily.

As Nicky had already established that there was no chance of him directly returning to Australia from Cairo, and the only realistic opportunity was to wait for a flight to England and arrange a home berth from there, he accepted the position. He brought important mail into Duncan daily, then he carried out the everyday working activities himself.

His new position gave Nicky an opportunity to chase up and confirm the whereabouts of the five fliers who had attended Khartoum but not turned up at No. 3 Squadron. To his annoyance, he found they had all wangled their way back to Australia, most receiving a promotion without combat experience. The revelation angered Nicky. He could have used them at that critical time.

The challenge and responsibility of his Cairo position suited Nicky; he enjoyed the work. The daily visits he had to make to the Sixth Scottish General Hospital (the same one he had attended with his earlier flying injuries), allowed him to continue with his own treatment. With time, exercise and medication his body was steadily recovering.

He had a couple of sessions with a psychiatrist who explained to him that the symptoms he exhibited confirmed the extent to which he had exhausted himself. The doctor attributed his condition to a combination of poor nutrition, fatigue and chronic anxiety. He advised Nicky to try and change his ways of thinking. He had, after all, undertaken some pretty scary, crazy things. What was bothering the doctor was that, to him, there appeared to be an aspect of recklessness about Nicky's behaviour.

Nicky reassured himself that he had purposely decided to be aggressive and that nothing he had done was blatantly foolhardy. He had tried to balance any risks against benefits, and even when he had unavoidably managed to get himself into life-threatening situations, he had never let himself believe that 'this was it'. He would try and save himself. It was a matter of perspective. He looked at tight spots as being a different experience and accepted the challenge to beat the odds. This attitude helped to prevent negative worrying thoughts from dominating and it allowed him to seek opportunities to change things. He did not believe that the intensity of his war experience was self-inflicted.

At this stage of his recovery, which was painfully slow, the results of his stress breakdown often resulted in Nicky suffering mood swings and a form of mild reactive depression. Sometimes he began to believe his pack of cards was starting to crumble. It concerned him greatly that here he was, a newly married man with his young wife back in Australia, and he was 'washed-out'. He had reservations about returning to Australia while still half a man.

He had to take stock of the situation. He realised he needed to get away from Cairo and change things. Three weeks after arriving in Cairo, Nicky was able to arrange a flight for himself to London. On the night before he left, he and Charles McWilliam drove out to the pyramids. There was a full moon and they joined a rather wild party taking place deep in the temple under the Great Pyramid, attended mainly by air force personnel. Nicky and McWilliam attempted to climb the pyramid, but the darkness and their inebriated state only allowed them to climb halfway. They rejoined the party, and Nicky celebrated his final night in Africa until the early hours.

The next morning, somewhat worse for wear, Nicky was picked up by a taxi from the pyramids. He asked the driver to stop off at the Scottish Hospital on the way to Heliopolis Airodrome. Here, he said goodbye to Duncan, who was now well on the way to recovery.

'Well, I'll look forward to seeing you back home in Australia, Bill, when this thing's over,' Nicky said.

'Thanks, Nicky. You look after yourself. You've really livened up Cairo.'

Nicky arrived in London in late April 1944. He was keen to rest, but he was also keen to fly, as he considered both would be good therapies. At the same time, he wanted to play down the degree of his exhaustion as he did not want to be medically downgraded. That would have been an anathema to a fighter pilot.

Nicky reported to Air Vice-Marshal Wrigley who was the RAAF's head officer in London. Wrigley had read Nicky's files from Cairo, and Nicky's desire to both fly again and to recuperate was reinforced. He welcomed Nicky and asked him what he wanted to do.

'Sir, I want to get to Australia. I'd like to get back to my wife, but while I am here I would also like to do what I can to help finish this war.'

'Well, unfortunately, there aren't any ships or flights to Australia,' Wrigley replied. 'I will, of course, keep you posted, but everybody is involved in a major effort with the coming invasion of Europe.'

It was no secret that the Allies were planning a major offensive against the Axis. Every available resource was being utilised towards this project. The only secret was where and when. The invasion threat was excellent propaganda in the meantime.

'We'll arrange a medical for you and after that there are a couple of options you can consider. Alan Rawlinson, one of your friends from No. 3 Squadron, has command of a parachute training school at Richmond, back home in New South Wales. You could do a parachute course here and possibly take over from him. On the other hand, in England we have a wonderful family with a long association with the Rhodes Scholarship Council and, since the thirties, they've been taking in Australian Rhodes Scholars and caring for them. They still help us. They are Sir Robert and Lady Burrows, and they live in a beautiful residence up near Manchester called Bonis Hall—one of the stately homes of England.

'Sir Robert is head of British Rail Transport and is seconded to the Invasion Planning Committee. He represents the British contribution to the Eisenhower plan. They will welcome you.'

'Now,' he continued, eyeing Nicky's khaki drill from the desert. 'You'll need some new clothes. We'll get you measured up straight away, then I'll take you out to a good dinner, just round the corner in The Strand.'

Nicky was duly sized up for a new outfit by Wing Commander John Gully, who was in charge of stores and an old friend from Power House. Then Wrigley took him to Simpson's On The Strand, a restaurant noted for its roast beef and top cuisine. This was marvellous. In many ways, Nicky was still celebrating his freedom, and such was his state of exhilaration that simple treats as clean clothes, showers and good food gave him great pleasure.

Even though the beef was tempting, Nicky had a fancy for fish. When the plate was served, Nicky was disappointed to discover the fish was quite cold. He complained to Wrigley.

'My fish is cold, sir.'

'Tell the waitress, old chap,' Wrigley admonished him.

Almost apologetically, Nicky informed the young waitress that his meal was cold.

'Really, sir,' she snapped, 'don't you know there's a war going on?'

Nicky smiled resignedly, although he couldn't quite see the connection as to why his fish should be cold because there was a war on. Wrigley took command. Firmly but gently he informed the waitress, 'Young lady, if anyone in the world knows there is a war going on, you are talking to him.' He then related some of Nicky's adventures to her, and was unfortunately—to Nicky's mind—overheard by two journalists at the table next to theirs.

The journalists introduced themselves. They were from the Manchester *Guardian*, and proceeded to gain some finer details of Nicky's exploits behind the lines. The next day, Nicky's story was widely publicised in London. So much for 'nothing happened'. The story was picked up by Dot's grandmother and family, who lived in Manchester, and then forwarded to Dot.

A few days later, Nicky's new uniform was ready. It did look smart—a distinctive blue twill outfit. He placed the ribbons of his DFC and bar and his Eighth Army African star on his chest, and was pleased at the effect. He was looking healthier now, and he was beginning to feel like a squadron leader.

While in London, Nicky was put up in good accommodation in Harrington Gardens, a relatively safe area, out of the main flight path of German bombers. He was then obliged to undergo a medical check up to consider his status for flying. With some relief, he passed the test, and a few days later, began his parachute course at Prestbury.

He introduced himself to the commander, who welcomed him.

'You know,' Nicky joked, 'I can understand jumping out of a plane under duress, a situation with which I have had some experience, but I can't really see the point in jumping out of a perfectly good plane otherwise. Seems a bit odd to me.'

Nicky did undertake two jumps, but his injured leg reacted badly to the landing. He opted out medically, and then decided to have a recuperative period, as had been suggested by Wrigley.

He caught the train to Manchester, where he was met by Gai Crossley, one of Sir Robert and Lady Burrows' daughters. Bonis Hall was the centrepiece of a beautiful English country estate, set amidst a great deal of rolling green land, complete with thoroughbred horses in residence. The mansion also boasted a swimming pool and a diving board, which Nicky was keen to take advantage of.

The family had received a brief on Nicky's history and they welcomed him unconditionally, exuding warmth and understanding. He mused on the good fortune of himself and any Rhodes Scholar who was lucky enough to reside there.

The nanny and kitchen staff personally undertook the responsibility of 'fattening him up', while the peaceful surroundings and the regular exercise he took helped to settle and calm his spirits. He would often walk around the farm and he regularly swam and dived in the pool. The two high-spirited Burrows daughters—Gai, married to an army major, and Sheila, engaged to a military officer—regularly teased him and helped to lift his now more infrequent periods of silence and depression.

While at Bonis Hall, an interesting highlight occurred for Nicky when he met some of the key designers of the Invasion Planning Committee. As Sir Robert was seconded to this plan, members of the committee would often be invited for relaxed evenings at Bonis Hall. One evening, he was introduced to three of the pivotal leaders, Generals 'Ike' Eisenhower, George Patton and Mark Clark, commander of the United States Fifth Army in Italy. He became known to them as 'the boy from Alamein'.

He protested jokingly, 'Not exactly true, sir. I lacked stamina. Didn't last till then.'

The generals made him feel very comfortable. He found Clark to be a delightful man, charming and amusing. 'Ike' Eisenhower had great charisma and was a brilliant communicator and conversationalist. Nicky especially enjoyed his company, as he gave the impression that while he was talking to him, the general was genuinely interested in what he was saying. He was surprised to find that Patton presented as softly spoken and measured, not the get-up-and-go, staccato-talking image the press portrayed him as.

Nicky met them several times over the few weeks of his stay. Bonis Hall had a ballroom where there were often parties and lots of singing and dancing. He was pleased to be regularly asked to join the generals in the drawing room and they often asked about his adventures, particularly his numerous escapes.

Nicky told them just how much effort goes into escaping. First, he said, there was a mental decision to admit that you intended to escape. You then have to develop an awareness of what you needed to do to adequately prepare yourself. Then you had to provide an opportunity to escape. The entire enterprise generally meant enlisting many other people to support and assist you. He made the observation that there was a vast difference between undertaking something that is foolhardy and doing something that was planned and based on accepted risks.

At which Eisenhower turned to Patton and said, 'You see what I mean?'

Patton had the justifiable reputation of doing things which were knee-jerk reactions. At this stage he was still sheepish after being carpeted for this type of behaviour. During the Sicilian Campaign, in highly publicised incidences, he had impatiently and emotionally attacked two traumatised soldiers. Patton took the reprimand in good humour. Everyone laughed.

After several weeks of this level of relaxation, Nicky was making steady improvement. At this stage, he received a letter from Air Vice-Marshal Wrigley's aide, Flight-Lieutenant Harris (a recent No. 3 Squadron member), suggesting Nicky might be interested in doing a special course. Headquarters had received a request from Australia to train somebody to fill in certain vacancies in command in Australia. This would entail working with Spitfires, Typhoons and Tempests.

He was also invited to join one of the teams called Air Support Control. Its purpose was to assist the Allied Forces landing in France during the imminent invasion, and to provide air support to any ground area that was needed. Nicky was feeling well but he needed more time. He was torn as he desperately wanted to get home, but there were long waiting lists. He accepted the offer to join.

The course was very concentrated, with lectures lasting over eight hours a day. It was held in rooms near Whitehall and was under RAF control, although apart from Nicky, there was a mixture of French, English and Americans involved. Four groups in all were being trained, and their prime mission would be to land after the invasion force, then to liaise with units who were already in forward positions. They were then to relay requests for assistance to squadrons held in reserve back in England.

The graduation was particularly riotous and memorable. The venue was an old manor which had been vacated to act as the Officers' Mess. The commander, who had carried out many assignments in Lysander aircraft to assist the French Underground, was fairly boozed to the eyeballs.

After dinner, he picked up a plate and spoke into it as a microphone, and in a quasi-official voice, requested the men clear an area on the floor. He organised for them to place candles on plates in such a manner as to create a 'landing strip'.

'Righto, gentlemen. You may now land your aeroplanes.'

The floors were highly polished and waxed, presenting a beautifully slippery surface. The men proceeded to run at full speed around the circuit area then dive headlong onto their chest and bellies, sliding the length of the 'strip'. The path was found to be too short, so they placed the candles further back against the wall. The more inebriated and more adventurous pilots poured oil over the 'runway' and onto their chests, then resumed their glorious landings. Eventually, one 'flyer' knocked a candle onto the wall curtains, instantly setting them on fire. Within minutes, a roaring blaze had developed, causing a frantic panic as the men went searching for a pail. However, the problem was quickly solved as one enterprising fellow grabbed the burning curtains and simply pulled them down. Very few 'planes' were in their hangars that night.

Then came the news that the free world had been waiting for. The assault phase of Operation Overlord—the code name for the European invasion—began shortly after midnight on 6 June. Three Allied airborne divisions landed near predetermined drop zones in Normandy. At 6.30 a.m., leading elements of five United States, British and Canadian divisions hit invasion beaches codenamed Utah, Omaha, Gold, Juno and Sword on the Normandy Coast.

After establishing beachheads and sustaining some of the most bitter and bloody fighting of the war, by the second day, the main body of the army had pushed the Germans a few kilometres inland.

On the evening of 8 June, Nicky was assembled with about 50 men at a landing jetty east of Southampton as part of Air Support Control. They boarded a landing craft and travelled towards Normandy through the night. Nicky and his team were destined for one of the American sector beachheads, Omaha, the site of some of the most intense fighting during the first 24 hours of the invasion.

Omaha Beach washed up to the village of Saint-Laurent-sur-Mer and, as Nicky's craft made its way towards the beach, the relics and carnage of the earlier fighting was still very much evident. Burnt-out landing crafts and vessels, tanks and armoured vehicles lay crumpled in the water and sprawled on the adjacent beach, their black hulks now a silent testimony to the bitter confrontation.

Strewn around the beach were the sinister remains of many thickly planted mined obstacles, including a series of upright iron frames called Belgian gates, as well as a 3-metre deep line of heavy wooden stakes angled towards the sea. At the water's edge, steel hedgehogs, positioned to stave in the bottom of landing craft, bared their obnoxious teeth, still pointing towards the ocean.

The beach, about 300 metres across, and dominated at each end by cliffs 30 metres high, appeared to Nicky not to be the best place for an amphibious landing. He winced as a small artillery bombardment crashed onto the beach nearby. He quickly scrambled up the steep bank of coarse pebbles and sand dunes, then crawled over the sea wall. Within a few minutes he was quickly led to a barn some 300 metres inland. The front-line was a few kilometres forward at the River Aure and, after setting up with his team, Nicky soon began to receive messages requesting air force assistance, bombing, strafing and missiles.

Nicky co-ordinated the incoming requests and other members of his sector relayed the messages back to England. Invasion headquarters implemented the requests.

Nicky worked in this situation over the next two days. Outside, the war was fairly chaotic, as ambulances and clean-up patrols coped with casualties and damage caused by the incoming artillery.

At this stage, the American major in charge of Nicky's station became aware that Nicky was an escaped prisoner of war. He became concerned that if Nicky was recaptured he would be shot, or, Nicky suspected, perhaps he just wanted somebody better! Nicky admitted that indeed he was an escaped prisoner of war, but he protested, 'Sir, their cross-referencing system is good, but it's not that good. They could never identify me with another fellow they picked up in Italy.'

At the same time, Nicky had been disillusioned with the communication and support system he had been involved in and decided that he should be forthright with an opinion.

'Sir, I think what we're doing here is probably an exercise in futility. I think England is just such a short distance away, we're bogging the process down when every minute may be important. The message should go direct. There should be no need for an interposer.'

The major nodded and thanked him for his observation.

Nicky considered that his suggestions were going to be accepted, so next morning at 2.00 a.m., he was on a routine return landing craft headed for England. The following day, he boarded a train at Victoria Railway Station and overnighted to Petersham. Here he enrolled for the course previously offered by Harris at the Central Gunnery School at Sutton Bridge.

This was interesting to Nicky as it gave him the opportunity to upgrade his shooting skills and to meet some of the celebrated fighter pilots who had survived the Battle of Britain, including Johnny Johnson and Colin Gray from New Zealand. Over the next few weeks, he was trained to fly several of the new breed of fighter planes, including the latest Spitfire, the Tempest and the latest Typhoon.

While here, he was also given an opportunity to undertake some operational flights over France, flying out in Typhoon Mk IBs, affectionately known as 'Tiffies', with No. 258 Squadron. Nicky developed an affinity for the Typhoon, a pugnacious-looking single-engine fighter produced by the Hawker Aeroplane Company. It had a large air scoop squatting under the propeller spinner and gave the appearance of an English Bulldog—it oozed threat. It was designed as a low-level attack plane and Nicky flew several missions over Pas-de-Calais, the site of the launching pads of the new German 'secret weapon', the long-range V1 unmanned aircraft.

This 'flying bomb', as it became known, was going to win the war for Hitler. When Hitler first received news of the D-Day landings, he issued orders to start the bombardment of London with them immediately. Some launching sites were being built, most of them in the Pas-de-Calais area, and nearly 12 000 of the huge flying bombs had been stockpiled in northern France, Belgium and Germany.

However, by the time the V1 campaign actually began on the night of 12 June, only seven launching sites were operative: the rest had been damaged by Allied bombing raids.

The bombs had a distinctive noise, being propelled by a pulse-jet motor. They were quickly dubbed the 'buzz bomb' or the 'doodle-bug'. To the British citizens, the characteristic putt-putt sound had the effect of creating extreme terror as, when the motor cut out, they knew the 2000-pound bomb warhead had the potential to create immense devastation—immediately. Thus the urgency for the RAF to neutralise these 'vengeance weapons'—'Vergeltungswaffe', as Hitler called them.

As Nicky's squadron approached Pas-de-Calais, the air became thick with black and red smoke. Bursts of flak fired from German anti-aircraft guns exploded around him—much more than Nicky had experienced in the desert. It was nerve-wracking as several planes were damaged during this peppering and one burst into flames. Nicky soon worked out that the front planes afforded the least opportunity of being hit, so he endeavoured to be up there with the leaders.

The launch ramps of the V1s were massive pieces of engineering. On one raid, the camouflaged hoods had been rolled back and the squadron caught them during launching. Nicky fired his rocket missiles—four under each wing—directly at the site, and was pleased to see that it added measurably to the damage accounted for by the squadron. Over the weeks, the squadron was also credited with a few V1 kills, although Nicky didn't encounter any himself. He was pleased later to hear that, officially, the result of their bombings significantly delayed the V1 program.

On 19 July 1944, Nicky graduated as an above average instructor and marksman from the Central Gunnery School.

Soon after this, he received an opportunity to return to Australia via America. As his health was really starting to improve, he jumped at the chance. Before embarkation, he attended a low-key affair in his honour at Brandesburton officers mess. Here he was presented with his third 'Flying Boot', the air force's unofficial recognition that he had been shot down, had returned from being behind enemy lines and had resumed operational flying again.

'Thanks for a priceless piece of metal,' he smiled in grateful acceptance.

Home sounded good. Really good.

TWENTY-SEVEN

Australia

Nicky, along with three other RAAF aircrew, had been able to obtain a berth in a Liberty ship which left from the Manchester docks area. The Liberty ships were specially produced, being turned out in 38 days by the Americans to a brilliant new design. They were completely welded together, with not a rivet in sight. They were not particularly comfortable ships, but Nicky was pleased they offered good food and were serviced by good crews.

There was no real danger from submarines at this stage, and there was some interest to Nicky as the ship followed a course over the next two days around the 'rum line', moving close to the arctic circle (the route of the old rum and slave traders). As the ship was full of American servicemen, there was great excitement as they sighted the Statue of Liberty on approaching New York. To Nicky, 'the Lady' was a symbol not only of the freedom he had been fighting for, but a positive sign he was temporarily out of the firing range and well on his way home.

In Manhattan, he reported to the Australian Group Captain at RAAF Headquarters, the centre of responsibility for the Empire Air Training Scheme in the United States. The commanding officer had already received advance notice from General Mark Clark that Nicky would be arriving.

As there would be some delay obtaining rail tickets to San

Francisco, the commander asked if Nicky was willing to speak at one or two American military bases on economic warfare and being behind the lines. In return they provided Nicky with VIP treatment, including a chauffeured pick-up car and a single-engine Beechcraft.

With a navigator, he flew himself out of New York's La Guardia Airport 2000 kilometres down to the large Naval Academy at Pensacola in Florida. Here he spoke to a large assembly where his experiences and ideas were well received. On his return to New York, he also presented an informal talk to local military personnel and was generally feted around the city, picking up on shows, Carnegie Hall and a round of parties. The war was a long way off.

But so was home. Within a few more days, he boarded a train and travelled across the States from New York to San Francisco. The three-day journey was chock full of interest as he contemplated the vastness of the Great Western Plains and the grandeur of the Rockies. He then embarked on the *Lurline*, one of the Matson Line ships, which was bound for 'somewhere in New Guinea' in the Pacific theatre of war.

The ship was crammed full of troops and war materials and it was generally an uncomfortable voyage. After two weeks, Nicky disembarked at Lae. From here, he picked up a ride on a Mitchell Bomber flying to Townsville, where he was hopeful there might be a flight waiting for him. After all, he had been away three years.

There was to be no such luck. He caught a train to Brisbane, then continued in an overnight sleeper to Sydney. He stayed in Sydney with his cousin for the day, where he eventually spoke to Dot by phone, the first time he had heard her voice in three years. The sound of her brief words over a crackly line fired him and filled him with anticipation.

'How are you?' she called down the line.

'I'm well,' he enthused.

'Are you sure?'

Nicky had a twinge of concern that Dot didn't think he was being truthful about his wellbeing.

'Yes, I am,' he said positively. 'I can't wait to see you.'

'When are you coming down to Melbourne?'

'As soon as I can. Unfortunately there aren't any flights available. I'm leaving by train—tonight.'

There was no need for either to reconfirm their commitment of love to each other.

'I'll see you tomorrow morning.'

He was so close; one more day.

He caught the overnight train to Melbourne and, the next morning, as the familiar landscape and buildings which preceded Spencer Street Railway Station rushed passed his window, he began to feel very tired. Suddenly, and ironically, the scene triggered in him strong feelings of apprehension.

His feelings of apprehension were not towards the woman he had married so long ago, the image of whom he had focused his yearnings on so completely and had fuelled his desire to survive. No, he simply had a sickening thought that he might have changed so much that Dot might not accept him as the man she had married; might not even recognise him.

The rugged, muscular athletic body Dot would have last seen was still unfit and wasted. Nicky knew his drawn face would reflect his ordeals from both his desert crusades and the deprivations he had experienced while behind enemy lines. Doctors had told him it would take some time to make a full recovery.

The tension for the next few moments was almost un-endurable for Nicky. He had prepared in his mind a few things to say to Dot concerning his wellbeing, including the 'missing' categories, but now, as the train came tortuously nearer, his courage almost failed him.

Finally, with a venting of steam and the grinding of metal on metal, the train screeched to a halt. When Nicky alighted, he immediately caught sight of Dot standing on the platform. With her was her mother and father, and Nicky's twin brother. An instant twinge of sadness crossed Nicky's heart at the absence of his late mother. Other friends stood in a group waiting to welcome him, some from Power House, as well as some representatives from the press.

Dot appeared relaxed and composed. She looked marvellous, wearing an elegant blue coat and dress with a wide fox fur collar, in deference to the cool Melbourne weather. Her fashionable hat, a darker shade of blue, was turned back, allowing Nicky a full view of her face.

At the same time, Dot caught a glimpse of Nicky alighting from the train. The hair was as blond as ever, and his eyes looked bluer than she remembered. She flashed a joyous smile towards him and his heart leapt. Nicky caught the lovelight in her eye. For a tender numbing instant, they looked at each other without speaking. There were no words to say, no need to say anything.

They took each other's hands, looked into each other's eyes, then embraced. In that second, Nicky knew absolutely that everything would be all right—their faith and trust *was* unconditional. The great challenge had been met and conquered. For both of them, it was an unforgettable moment as they clung together in a mutual outpouring of joy that took away their breath and words.

All too quickly, a procession of well-wishers, friends and relatives began pumping Nicky's hand, offering him congratulations and welcoming him home. The press managed to grab a few words with him and captured the moment with photographs. Eventually the couple were whisked off to Dot's family home.

After a brief chance to relax and the luxury of a hot bath,

Nicky prepared for the welcome home party which had been arranged for that night. It was to be at the Alexander Hotel in Spencer Street, where he and Dot had stayed after their wedding.

It was a tremendous celebration and reunion. Friends from all facets of Nicky's life congregated to wish him well—Power House, rugby, his prewar workdays and representatives from the Defence Forces, particularly members of the RAAF, including many of his No. 3 Squadron colleagues. There were messages from many other well-wishers including Bobby Gibbes, who was now chief instructor of Fighter Operations at Mildura.

The Jackson brothers led a formidable group of fliers who noisily and excitedly pushed the limits. Ed had flown with Nicky in No. 3 Squadron, and now worked with Gibbes at Mildura. Les had been commander of No. 75 Squadron during the Battle of Milne Bay, taking over from his brother John who was killed during the Battle for Port Moresby. There was a parapet running around the hotel about 15 metres above the ground, tempting Les Jackson to crawl out onto it. Once outside, he stood up and ran around it, joyously brandishing and firing a revolver into the night air. He called for Nicky and others to join him. Nicky responded that he hadn't travelled halfway around the world to be that foolhardy—not tonight, anyway.

Eventually, everyone left, leaving the two lovers alone. The fears and anguish of the previous three years were momentarily forgotten. For Nicky, the long, testing months of anxiety for Dot, and coping with the various 'missing categories' were now over. For Dot her strong faith in the belief that Nicky would come back was now fully vindicated.

One of the messages which had greeted Nicky on his return was a request for him to report to RAAF Headquarters at St Kilda Road 'in his own time'. Nicky interpreted that as expecting three or four days would be fair.

Over the next two days Nicky began to recover from the immediate exhaustion caused by his long trip from England, and the emotional excitement of reunion with his loved ones. However, on the second morning he received another message from headquarters urging him to report—now!

In the meantime, he had contacted Bobby Gibbes at RAAF Fighter Operations at Mildura, as a result of his earlier telegram.

'Got a job for you,' Gibbes said. 'I want to get up to the fighting area. I'm a bit restrained here. I've been posted to Darwin as wing leader of 80 Wing, with Mark VIII Spitfires. I want you to take over here from me as chief instructor.'

When Nicky reported later to RAAF Headquarters, they confirmed Gibbes' request. 'We want you to go up to Mildura immediately. We'd want you to do a medical, then if everything is all right, you'll be promoted to wing commander and take over from Bobby Gibbes. We want you to update them on all that you've learned from the Middle East and the European Theatres of War.'

After passing his medical, Nicky caught the overnight train to Mildura where he inspected the station. He was impressed and returned to convince Dot and her parents. 'This is the thing I need to do. It'll get me out of Melbourne, I can fly again and have you there with me all the time. It's what I've been after. It'll be great.'

And that's what happened.

Fighter operations at Mildura had been set up by Nicky's original commanding officer of No. 3 Squadron, Peter Jeffrey. Another contemporary of Nicky's from No. 3 Squadron was now the commanding officer, Wilf 'Woof' Arthur. Nicky had only been settled in for a few days when Arthur was sent to command a squadron at Noemfoor Island, off Dutch New Guinea, leaving Nicky as acting CO. After reading the training syllabus, doing the 'crash' operational flying course, and discussions with instructors who had completed operational tours in the Pacific campaigns, he realised the course was not related to the way the war was being fought in the Pacific.

He phoned RAAF Headquarters in Melbourne, saying he didn't think that people only experienced in desert and European air warfare were qualified to train fighter pilots for jungle and island fighting. He considered he was not suitable for the job.

The order came back: 'If you feel that way, get up there yourself; get qualified!'

At that stage, Group Captain Pete Jeffrey was directed to Mildura to take over as CO again. Nicky discussed his observations with him and, even though Jeffrey had originally set up the syllabus, he agreed it was now antiquated for the Pacific war zone. He also agreed Nicky should fly to the islands for first-hand experience.

Nicky was given a completely armed and operational Kittyhawk and took off for New Guinea. He broke the marathon trip at Sydney and Horn Island, eventually landing at Merauke, many kilometres west of Port Moresby in Dutch Hollandia.

From here he flew onto Moratai and undertook a few operational flights to the Celebes with Squadron Leader Dick Cresswell, including one where he strafed the jungle in the vicinity of where the Japanese were allegedly bunked in—'an exercise in futility', he recorded in his logbook. These bypassed island strongholds were the last outposts of remaining Japanese who had been left to 'wither on the vine', while the virile American war machine pushed on towards Japan.

Very quickly it was becoming obvious to Nicky—and many other people—that Australia and its war effort was also being bypassed. The Americans were forging ahead and not including Australia in any of its advances. It appeared that the Supreme Allied Commander, South-West Pacific Area, General Douglas

MacArthur, along with some Australian politicians, had relegated the RAAF to mopping-up status.

On his return to Mildura, Nicky marshalled all of his instructors and together they rewrote the syllabus. The new program centred on changing from aerial combat philosophy to strafing operations, and other ground-support roles.

The metamorphosis was implemented within two weeks, impressing Pete Jeffrey. 'I can't believe it,' he commented. 'However, I can see this is right. If we are being forced into a cleaning-up role, this is the way to train—strafing barges in the Murray River with camera guns is spot on.'

In April 1945, the feeling that Australia was playing a minor back-up role finally resulted in a confrontation with RAAF command. It led to eight leading air force officers resigning their commission, and being brought before a court-martial. The group included at least three of Nicky's friends—Bobby Gibbes, 'Killer' Clive Caldwell and Wilf Arthur—and among their grievances was that they were dissatisfied with the operational and administrative policy of the RAAF. In particular, they objected to carrying out work which had no bearing on the prosecution of the war. This incident became known as the Moratai Mutiny.

However, at this stage, in November 1944, there was still no official observation or recognition that Australia did not need to train specialised pilots for front-line fighting and certainly no communications of this nature filtered down to the enthusiastic and dedicated group of men at Mildura keen to help finish the war.

Nicky settled in to life at Mildura and, with great will, proceeded to train pilots for their role in the Pacific Theatre of war.

In early December 1944, Nicky was working in his office when Pete Jeffrey came in, smiling, 'What have you been up to Nicky?'

Nicky looked quizzically at him as he contemplated the loaded question.

'It's all right,' Jeffrey laughed. 'I've just been told you've been awarded a Military Cross. Congratulations!'

'Come off it. You're pulling my leg. They don't give those to pilots—only the army. What for?' Nicky asked, completely surprised.

'There's no citation. It is being withheld, but I think it's got something to do with your time behind the lines in Europe.'

Later, Nicky found out that the medal was awarded for his work in assisting prisoners of war, arranging for them to escape and, in particular, bringing out at least ten men himself. It had been recommended by the debriefing officer who had interviewed him on the day of his escape over the Apennines— the one who recommended that Nicky assert that 'nothing happened'.

Nicky stayed in Mildura until the war's end. He was actually in Melbourne on 15 August when news of the Japanese surrender was announced. There was tremendous elation, and Pete Jeffrey rang Nicky from Mildura.

'Have you heard the news? It's great, isn't it? Fly back safely and no beat-ups, promise?'

'No problems, Pete.'

On the way, he flew through a fierce storm which was a little troublesome but as he got closer to Mildura Airfield, he could see everybody out to greet the chief instructor.

What can I do that's a little special? he mused. It is, after all, an important occasion. Almost all aerobatics were passé.

He was flying a P-51 Mustang and planned on a different landing manoeuvre—one that was not normally recommended. It was called a 'side-slip' landing. By incorporating the use of a great amount of top rudder and side-stick, the plane lost height rapidly and approached the strip sideways, nose up. As the pilot kicked out of that, the plane needed to be in exactly the right position to land. Tiger Moths do the manoeuvre flawlessly.

Nicky brought the P-51 lower, and executed the side-slip manoeuvre. Just as he was lining up to land, he caught sight of Jeffrey walking out to meet him. Nicky pulled his plane up and circled around again. He then side-slipped his Mustang for the second time, then pulled into a perfect landing.

Jeffrey smiled at him.

'You're impossible to the end, Barr. I've just witnessed the best landing I've ever seen—and coming after a forbidden side-slip.'

Nicky left Mildura for good a fortnight later. Upon transferring from an RAAF station, the commanding officer is required to assess the person on a form which is pasted into the flier's log-book. On 30 August 1945, Group Captain Peter Jeffrey, DSO, DFC graded Nicky as 'exceptional'.

There was some pride mixed with humility at Nicky's acceptance of the accolade. He remembered back to their first unsteady meeting in the desert when Jeffrey was commanding officer of No. 3 Squadron. Since then, they and the world had changed irrevocably.

Any signs of perceived youthful brashness which Nicky may have exhibited at that time had long been replaced by a hard-earned respect, forged from years of character-building challenges. Now firm friends, he shook hands with his commanding officer and they saluted each other simultaneously, a gesture ratifying their mutual deep respect. The act formally completed five-and-a-half years of active service.

In the previous few weeks, even though Nicky's mental and physical health were now fine, he had been experiencing periodic lapses of fever and his damaged leg had been troubling him. Before his final discharge from the RAAF, the Mildura doctor, Squadron Leader John Deakin, booked Nicky into Heidelburg Repatriation Hospital in Melbourne to undergo a thorough medical checkup.

He underwent two exploratory operations, one on his knee and another on his wounded ankle, while a tropical medicine specialist treated his malaria symptoms.

While he was in recovery from his surgery, the hospital superintendent received a telegram from Rear Admiral Bracegirdle, the official secretary to the Governor-General of Australia, Sir Winston Dugan. The admiral advised the superintendent that Nicky was due to be decorated at a Government House investiture that week, however, Nicky had declined to attend because of his hospital commitment.

Bracegirdle requested that the presentation be made while Nicky was in hospital, as 'His Excellency feels that any Officer who was awarded the Military Cross and the DFC and Bar should have those decorations personally presented to him.'

The investiture was a memorable occasion. Someone had smuggled some drinks along and Nicky's ward was turned into a party venue. While Dot, now pregnant, looked on, Nicky proudly accepted the decorations. His words moved everyone in attendance, 'I know where these medals should go,' he smiled proudly towards Dot. 'To the girl who has waited so long and loved so much.'

Nicky retired from the RAAF in November 1945.

The Years After

No. 3 Squadron became the highest scoring fighter squadron of the Desert Air Force, destroying 217 enemy aircraft and producing no less than 14 aces. Nicky Barr was the highest scoring ace of No. 3 Squadron.

Here is a brief summary of what became of some of the men Nicky flew with—and against.

BRAUNE, Erhard

Before the war, Erhard Braune had an Australian connection, sailing in wheat Windjammers from Adelaide, going twice around Cape Horn. He joined the Luftwaffe and fought in the Spanish Civil War, then became leader of 1/JG27 fighting in the Desert War. In his squadron, he had five aces, four of whom had over 100 kills each, including Captain Hans Marseille, the top German ace on the Western (including Mediterranean) Front— 158 victories.

After the war, Braune joined NATO and was based in Spade in Germany. In 1986, he arrived in Australia for a meeting of 'Cape Horners' and sought out Nicky. They compared logbooks and found they were often fighting in the same battles on the same day, and both filled in many gaps in the other's experience.

CAMERON, Alan Cecil ('Tiny')

'Tiny' was taken prisoner on 11 January 1942 after being shot down for the third time. He escaped after being taken to Tripoli but was betrayed by local Arabs. He was then transferred to a prisoner-of-war camp in Italy. He escaped after Italy capitulated, but was caught again and was moved to Germany where he remained until the end of the war. After the war, he began charter flying at Tenterfield for 18 months. He then settled at 'Rockwood', east of Condamine, on a grazing and farming station. He was married three times and died in 1983 at Goondiwindi.

CHINCHEN, Geoff

When he was shot down and captured, Geoff was imprisoned at Sulmona in Italy, along with Freddy Eggleston and Bobby Jones (the pilot who was forced down when Nicky began his Senussi Adventure). When Italy capitulated in 1943, he escaped and was interned in Switzerland, but Geoff made his way to England before the war ended.

After the war, Geoff became CEO of Ford Motor Company at Eagle Farm in Brisbane. He then moved to a farm at Rochedale where he became a State Parliamentarian for many years. He is now retired and lives with his wife at Rochedale.

EGGLESTON, Freddy

After being imprisoned in Sulmona in Italy (with Geoff Chinchen and Bobby Jones), Freddy Eggleston escaped from a Germany-bound train and was interned in Switzerland. He met Heidi, whose parents owned a chalet in Arosa in Switzerland, and married her. Geoff Chinchen acted as the best man. After the war, he eventually became CEO of Comalco in Sydney. He died in May 1995.

GIBBES, *Bobby*

Bobby left the RAAF in 1946, after a most distinguished career. With his new wife Jean, an Arts Graduate whom he'd married in Darwin the year before, he moved to New Guinea. He worked for an internal Airline Company until 1948, when he started his own air freighter service, Gibbes Sepik Airways.

He established a coffee plantation at Tremearne in the Western Highlands as well as diversifying his business interests with hotels.

In 1973, he bought a yacht in England and sailed it back to Australia. He and Jean are retired and now live in Sydney.

JEFFREY, *Peter*

Peter married Colleen in 1943 and, after the war, owned a farm on the Murray River. In 1951, he rejoined the RAAF and helped the Korean War effort as commanding officer of Base Edinburgh in South Australia.

He then moved to Queensland where he opened a stock-broking operation on the Gold Coast and bought a cattle and sheep property at Emerald. He returned to Surfers Paradise in 1972, where he died in 1997.

JACKSON *Brothers*

John: When John left No. 3 Squadron, he became squadron leader of No. 75 Squadron at Port Moresby, in New Guinea. He was killed during a desperate battle for Moresby in April 1942. Jackson Airfield at Moresby is named after him.

Les: Les became commanding officer of No. 75 Squadron when

John was killed. He stayed in the RAAF for some time and had business interests in Roma and St George. He retired to Southport where he died in 1980.

Ed: After leaving No. 3 Squadron, Ed was an instructor at Mildura (with Nicky). After the war, he moved to a grazing property at St George until 1964, then a cattle farm at Laidley until 1974. He retired to the Isle of Capri on the Gold Coast where he died in 1993.

LEU, Rudolph ('Roo')

After leaping from the train with Nicky on the way through to Germany, Roo was eventually captured and served the rest of the war in a German Stalag. After the war, he returned to Queensland, where he married Gwenyth Youngman from Kingaroy. They bought a cattle grazing property and peanut farm at Taabinga, where he died in 1984.

His friend from No. 112 Squadron, *Charles McWilliam*—who Nicky spent some pleasurable time with in Cairo after his escape —married Gwenyth's sister. He became a pastoralist on the Darling Downs and died in 2000.

SPENCE, Lou

After the war, Lou stayed in the RAAF and became commandant of Point Cook Academy. When the Korean War broke out in 1950, Wing Commander Spence, flying out of Japan in a P-51 Squadron, was killed during a bombing mission.

RAWLINSON, Alan

After the war, Alan stayed in the RAAF, then transferred to the RAF, spending the rest of his working life in England. He retired a few years ago and is now living in South Australia.

And what of NICKY BARR?

After leaving the RAAF, Nicky stayed in Mildura. He became organising secretary of the Mildura Development League, a committee set up to develop the unification of the Murray Valley basin. Among other initiatives, in this capacity he was mainly instrumental in securing the establishment of a section of the Melbourne University in the old Mildura RAAF Station. He also secured three new industries for the town, and affected the decentralisation of departmental functions.

He resigned from the Developmental League to become managing director of AW Barr and Company Pty Limited, which was a subsidiary of Felt and Textiles (Australia) Pty Ltd. In this, he air-freighted about 60 per cent of the shoe production to all capital cities.

After about two years, in a dramatic confrontation, he resigned over certain ethical issues concerning the company's policies. He then responded to an offer to assist Bobby Gibbes, who was expanding his Gibbes Sepik Airway at Wewak in New Guinea.

As time went on in New Guinea, Dot became sick with malaria. The Barrs were unwilling to send their two boys, Robert (born 1945) and Brian (1947) to boarding school, so they left New Guinea.

Nicky accepted a position in Brisbane as general manager of the rapidly expanding civil engineering firm Thiess Brothers. There were 180 staff Australia-wide then and Nicky's main responsiblity was to manage them and the contracts. Often adjudication was required among the ten Thiess brothers and one sister, five of the brothers being fully operational within the business. Open-cut coalmining provided growth and operational stability.

The firm won the contract to collect war-scrap in the Pacific zone, which they restored and then used for mining and contracting. These were heady days and often exciting times as they built offices, made roads, carparks, bought and worked coal mines and shipped the coal to Japan and Pakistan.

In 1952, Nicky bought a farm, 'Glencoe', near Grantham, in Queensland, but his war injuries prevented him from working it efficiently, so he accepted an invitation to return as general manager/director with Thiess Brothers. This was just as the ambitious Snowy Mountains project got underway and Nicky became involved in the challenges of the contracts won by Thiess.

In 1956, he joined William Cooper and Nephews as marketing director. This was a large international firm that specialised in sheep dips, and sold a huge range of pharmaceutical goods and arsenic products. It was the beginning of the widespread use of organic phosphates. This position allowed Nicky and Dot the opportunity to travel overseas and especially back to Italy, as William Cooper was taken over globally by Burroughs.

Then, in 1961, he became general manager of Meggitt Limited. This was a company that operated mainly in the oilseed crushing industry, particularly linseed oil and vegetable oils, owning land and mills all around Australia. Meggitt Ltd was 40 per cent owned by Allied Mills Ltd and Nicky concluded his corporate life as executive chairman of Meggitt Ltd.

Nicky enjoyed his time there immensely and he stayed for more than 23 years. He was instrumental in bringing in soya beans, rape and safflower seeds, as well as setting up a scheme for future trading for growers, processors and users to allow them to hedge the value of their crops and products against market fluctuations. He was also chairman of a number of industry organisations.

In 1983, he was awarded the OBE (Order of the British Empire) for services to the oilseed industry, and in 1983–84 he represented Australia as Chairman at the International Oilseeds Group.

———

When Nicky walked over the Apennines to freedom, he considered it to be the most euphoric feeling that anyone could ever have. It wasn't just a short-term sensation; it has lasted and lasted. Anything of value that has happened to him since then has simply been a bonus.

As the text of the preceding story has highlighted, nobody just 'escapes'; there were many selfless and courageous people who contributed to Nicky's freedom.

Beginning in the late 1950s, Nicky, with Dot, returned to Italy many times. This allowed Nicky to search for and repay kindnesses to individuals who had befriended and assisted him during his time either in hospitals, prison or behind the lines.

He had already become an ardent member of the RAF Escaping Society which conceded full recognition of the work and courage of the people who gave assistance to escapers and evaders. This organisation generously supported the orphans and families of these helpers throughout Europe. The benefits were mainly to assist their children with education, travel and health. This legacy continued up until 1996 when the society deemed their work was complete.

However, Nicky found that the trail of many individuals was lost to him. For example, he could find no trace of the young German field doctor, or of Bruno, an Italian wardsman who had showed him kindness at Tobruk. At Sulmona, Nicky particularly wanted to show his gratitude and to offer recompense to Dominico and Renato, the two mountain guides. However, like Bruno, their trail was also completely cold. AMGOT (Allied Military Government of Occupied Territories) researched long and hard but to no avail.

He was luckier at Bergamo, again now a retirement centre for the old. He had a marvellous reunion with *La Sorella*, the nun who saved his life. Over the years, Nicky travelled to Italy as many as 18 times, and for the first few years, to the amusement of onlookers, he and *La Sorella* would greet each other with large hugs. However *La Sorella* gradually became quite frail and died in 1965.

In Milan, he searched in vain for the Swiss colonel who represented him so skilfully and with such dedication in the courtroom. He then tried to contact him through the Red Cross International Headquarters in Geneva, also to no avail.

In Goriano Valli, he sought out many individuals who had assisted him and the Allied war effort, and he made certain that all who deserved so were adequately compensated. Earlier in 1955, he had been influential in seeking the emigration of Franz and Greta Koblitz to Australia, and he assisted them to settle at Box Hill in Melbourne. He saw a great deal of them over the years until Franz died in the early 1970s. Greta went back to Europe, and Nicky kept in close contact with her until a few years ago.

Perhaps because of the harsh lifestyle of the villagers in Goriano Valli, when Nicky returned in the late 1970s there was no one left from the war years of his generation; they had all died.

When he visited Gavi, he was bemused to find that it had been turned into a museum, the Forte Di Gavi. Ironically, he had to pay 100 lire to get in.

Following a nomination by Clive Caldwell and Bobby Gibbes, in June 1987 Nicky received an invitation to take part in a seminar at the USAF Air Command and Staff College at Maxwell Air Force Base, at Montgomery, Alabama. It was to be an assembly of 18 elite pilots who were judged to have contributed to aviation in some special manner. Their ages ranged from a 92-year-old veteran of World War One, to astronauts of the space age. The occasion was called the 'Gathering of Eagles' and a program of events and seminars was carried out over four days.

When Nicky and Dot arrived in Montgomery, the city had prepared banners saying 'Welcome to the Eagles', and the traffic was brought to a halt for their coach. It was as good as a ticker-tape welcome. Over the course of the celebration, for the 'Eagles' themselves, the highlight was that each had a 'This is your Life' experience as their story was revealed with slides and accompanying music and commentary.

Nicky enjoyed the opportunity to meet many celebrated international pilots, among them Ken Walsh. He was awarded the Congressional Medal of Honour, America's top military decoration, for exceptional heroism in the Pacific War, in particular at the Battle of Midway.

Representing postwar aviation was one of the world's most famous pilots, USAF General Charles 'Chuck' Yeager, who on 14 October 1947, became the first human to crash through the sound barrier—'the right stuff'.

Nicky also met Wolfgang Spate, a Luftwaffe pilot from JG/54 Fighter Wing on the Eastern Front battlefield, as well as meeting one of 'the few', Group Captain Dennis 'Hurricane' David, who was a five time ace and a Hurricane pilot, gaining his honours predominately during the Battles of France and Britain.

There were also pilots from the Korean and Vietnam Wars, as well as the illustrious John Glenn, from National Aeronautics and Space Administration, the first American to orbit the earth in February 1962.

Also from NASA, and especially fascinating, was Joe Engle who in 1985 flew the space shuttle *Columbia* back from the moon manually after all the computers had failed, making a perfect touchdown.

The gathering of 'Eagles' left a strong impression on Nicky. These were comrades whom he would keep for life.

On the way home, he allowed himself to muse a little. Yes, there was no doubt he detested war, intensely and vehemently.

However, now, somehow, the sacrifice and hardships of those long arduous years seemed strangely acceptable.

Nicky is eternally grateful that in his time, his children and grandchildren have not had to fight a war—perhaps the best legacy of all.

Maybe he had a mandate to believe, on behalf of his mates who were lost, that it was all worthwhile for that reason alone.

AUSTRALIAN FIGHTER ACES OF WORLD WAR TWO

Australians with ten or more air combat victories in
World War Two are:

Rank	Name	Decorations	Aircraft destroyed
Gp Capt	C. Caldwell	DSO, DFC & BAR, Polish Cross of Valour	28.5
Flt Lt	A. P. Goldsmith	DFC, DFM	16.25
Sqn Ldr	K. W. Truscott	DFC & BAR	16
Gp Capt	J. L. Waddy	OBE, DFC, US Air Medal	15.5
Flt Lt	P. C. Hughes	DFC	15
Sqn ldr	C. C. Scherf	DSO, DFC & BAR	14.5
Flg Off	L. R. Clisby	DFC	14
Flt Lt	M. C. Shipard	DFC & BAR	14
Flt Lt	R. N. Cullen	DFC	13
Wg Cdr	A. W. Barr	OBE, MC, DFC & BAR	12.5
Flg off	B. A. Bretherton	DFC	12
Flt Lt	C. A. Crombie	DSO, DFC	12
Flt Lt	G. W. Yarra	DFM	12
Sqn Ldr	P. St. B. Turnbull	DFC	12
Sqn Ldr	H. T. Armstrong	DFC & BAR	11
Wg Cdr	H. C. Mayers	DSO, DFC & BAR MID	11
Sqd Ldr	R. J. C. Whittle	DFM	11
Wg Cdr	R. H. Gibbes	DSO, DFC & BAR	10.25
Flt Lt	V. P. Brennan	DFC, DFM, Malta Cross	10
Sqn Ldr	J. R. Cock	DFC	10
Gp Capt	W. S. Arthur	DSO, DFC, 2 MIDS	10

Flt Lt	C. H. Parkinson	DFC	10
Flg Off	I. B. N. Russell	DFC	10
Wg Cdr	J. R. Perrin	DFC	10
Gp Capt	A. C. Rawlinson	DFC & BAR	10

Source: Air Force Historical Section, Department of Defence.

Further Reading

Australian War Memorial, *These Eagles: Story of the RAAF at War*, AWM, Canberra, 1942

Badman, P., *North Africa 1940–42: The Desert War*, Time-Life Books, Sydney, 1988

Barton, L., *The Desert Harassers*, Australian Military History Publications, Loftus, NSW, [no date]

Botting, D., *The Second Front: World War II*, Time-Life Books, Chicago, 1978

Collier, R., *The War in the Desert: World War II*, Time-Life Books, Chicago, 1977

David, D., *Dennis 'Hurricane' David*, Grub St, London, 2000

E. G. O., *Libyan Log*, Thoth Bookshop, Cairo, 1942

Firkins, P., *Heroes Have Wings*, Hesperian Press, Carlisle, WA, 1993

Gibbes, B., *You Live But Once*, self-published, 1994

McAuley, L., *Four Aces*, Banner Books, Maryborough, Qld, 1998

Maughan, B., *Tobruk and El Alamein*, Collins with the Australian War Memorial, Canberra, 1987

Odgers, G., *The Royal Australian Air Force*, Ure & Smith, Sydney, 1963

Sakai, S., *Samurai*, Nelson Doubleday Inc., Garden City, New York, 1957

Toliver, R. J., *The Blond Knight of Germany*, Aero, Blue Ridge, Summitt, PA, 1985

Wallace, R., *The Italian Campaign: World War II*, Time-Life Books, Chicago, 1978

Warner, D., *Written in Sand*, Angus & Robertson, Sydney, 1944

Waters, J. C., *Valiant Youth*, FH Johnston, Sydney, [no date]

Watson, J. & Jones, L., *3 Squadron at War*, Halstead Press, Sydney, 1954

Watts, W. K., *One Airman's War*, self-published, 1988

Wilson, S., *The Spitfire, Mustang and Kittyhawk*, Aerospace Publications, Sydney, 1988